Ecology and Archaeology of Kosal Region

Ecology and Archaeology of Kosal Region

PUSHP LATA SINGH

AGAM KALA PRAKASHAN
DELHI

First Published 2011

ISBN : 978-81-7320-107-3

Published by:
Dr. Agam Prasad, M.A., Ph.D., Diploma in Museology
For Agam Kala Prakashan
34, Central Market, Ashok Vihar
Delhi - 110 052
Tel.: 27212195, 65688806-7
Fax: 91-11-27212195
Email: agambooks@gmail.com, info@agamkala.com
www.agamkala.com

Composed by:
Aman Printographics
Delhi - 110 052

Printed by:
Chawla Offsets
Delhi-110 052

Printed in India

"Dedicated in the loving memory of my parents whose demise caused irreparable loss to me"

Preface

The authoress hails from the Kosal region hence she has selected to pen the "Ecology and Archaeology of Kosal Region". Myriad Reports and books on history, culture & archaeology and socio-economic conditions of Kosal saw the light of the day. Mention may be made of Bishop R. Heber's *Narrative of a Journey through the Upper Provinces of Hindustan*, 1824, London; Sir William H. Sleeman's *Journey through the Kingdom of Avadh* in the years 1949-50, 11 Vols., London; Martin M., *The History, Antiquities, Topography and Statistics of Eastern India*, Vol. II, London, 1838; V.S. Pathak, *History of* Kosal, Varanasi, 1963; Hans Bakker's *Ayodhya*, Groningen, 1986.

Archaeolgical investigation in the Kosal region were carried out for the first time by A. Cunningham around the mid of the nineteenth century and explored Sahet Mahet along with other sites. He explored Sahet Mahet in 1863 and excavated it in 1876. A.C.L. Carlleyle explored some sites of Archaeological importance in 1874-75 and 1875-76.

In 1890, A. Fuhrer has mentioned the sites explored by Cunningham in his monumental book published in 1891. In 1897 V.A. Smith reported Piprahwa as an ancient stupa. In the subsequent years W.C.Peppe excavated it and found the famous Piprahwa vase. After Cunningham in the time of J.H. Marshall, A.J. Wilson and Dayaram Sahni excavated Sahet Mahet in 1907-08. In 1908,1910-11 John H. Marshall also excavated it. It may be noted that all these explorations and excavations were mainly carried out with a view to identify the Buddhist sites in this region.

All these reports and books shed lurid light on the archaeology of Kosal Region. Accordingly, need was felt to detail the comprehensive archaeology of the region. Numerous explorations and excavations carried out under the auspices of Archaeological Survey of India, New Delhi; Directorate of U.P. State Archaeology, Lucknow; Banaras Hindu University, Varanasi; University of Lucknow, Lucknow; University of Allahabad, Allahabad; D.D.U. Gorakhpur University, Gorakhpur; Deccan College Post-Graduate Research Institute, Pune. The archaeological excavation at Sravasti was carried out by the Japanese team which gave a U-turn to the archaeology of Kosal region.

The desideratum that how ecology of the area affected the archaeological personality is the central point of this study.

I express my acknowledgement to all the authors of the books and papers which have contributed is bringing out this monograph.

I am also thankful to my publisher Dr Agam Prasad of Agam Kala Prakashan, Delhi for publishing the book.

20 November, 2010

Pushp Lata Singh
Department of A.I.H.C. &
Archaeology
Banaras Hindu University
Varanasi

Abbreviations

AI	Ancient India
AMS	Accelerator Mass Spectroscopy
A.V.	Atharvaveda
BC	Before Christ
BP	Before Present
BRW	Black-and-Red Ware
BSW	Black Slipped Ware
CW	Corded Ware
GW	Grey Ware
Geog Dict	Geographical Dictionary of Ancient and Medieval India
IAR	Indian Archaeology: A Review, New Delhi
IHQ	Indian Historical Quarterly, Calcutta
I.A.A.R.	Indian Archaeology: Annual Report

I.H.R.	The Indian Historical Review, New Delhi
J.B.R.S.	Journal of Bihar Research Society, Patna
JNSI	Journal of Numismatic Society of India
NBPW	Northern Black Polished Ware
NK	Nayadhamma Kahad
PGW	Painted Grey Ware
PN	Pannavana
PTS	Pali Text Society, London
RW	Red Ware
R.V.	Rigveda
TL	Thermoluminescence
V.R.	*Valmiki Ramayanav*

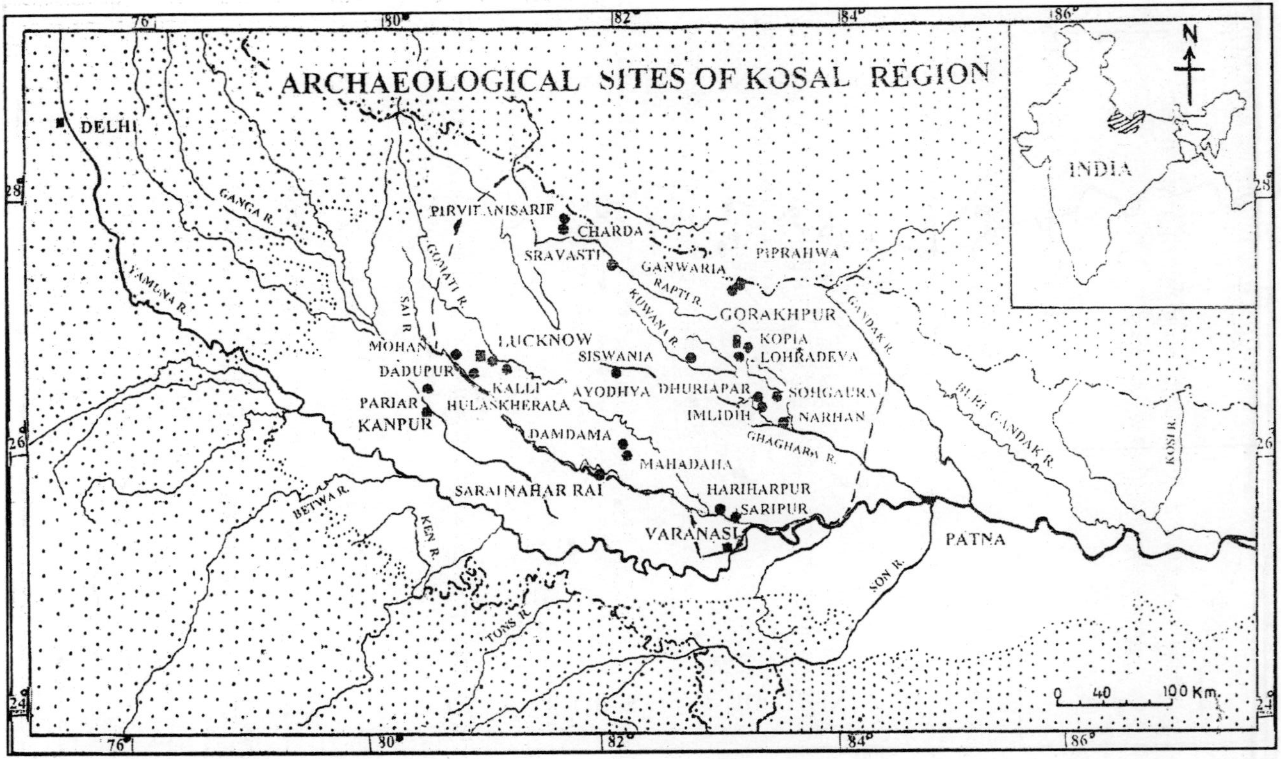
ARCHAEOLOGICAL SITES OF KOSAL REGION
INDIA
N
DELHI
GANGA R.
YAMUNA R.
GOMATI R.
SAI R.
PIRVITANISARIF
CHARDA
SRAVASTI
GANWARIA
PIPRAHWA
RAPTI R.
KUWANA R.
GORAKHPUR
GANDAK R.
KOPIA
LOHRADEVA
LUCKNOW
MOHAN
DADUPUR
KALLI
SISWANIA
AYODHYA
DHURIAPAR
SOHGAURA
IMLIDIH
NARHAN
PARIAR
HULASKHERA
KANPUR
DAMDAMA
GHAGHARA R.
MAHADAHA
SARAI NAHAR RAI
HARIHARPUR
SARIPUR
VARANASI
PATNA
BURI GANDAK R.
KOSI R.
BETWA R.
KEN R.
TONS R.
SON R.
0 40 100 Km.
76°
80°
82°
84°
86°
28°
26°
24°

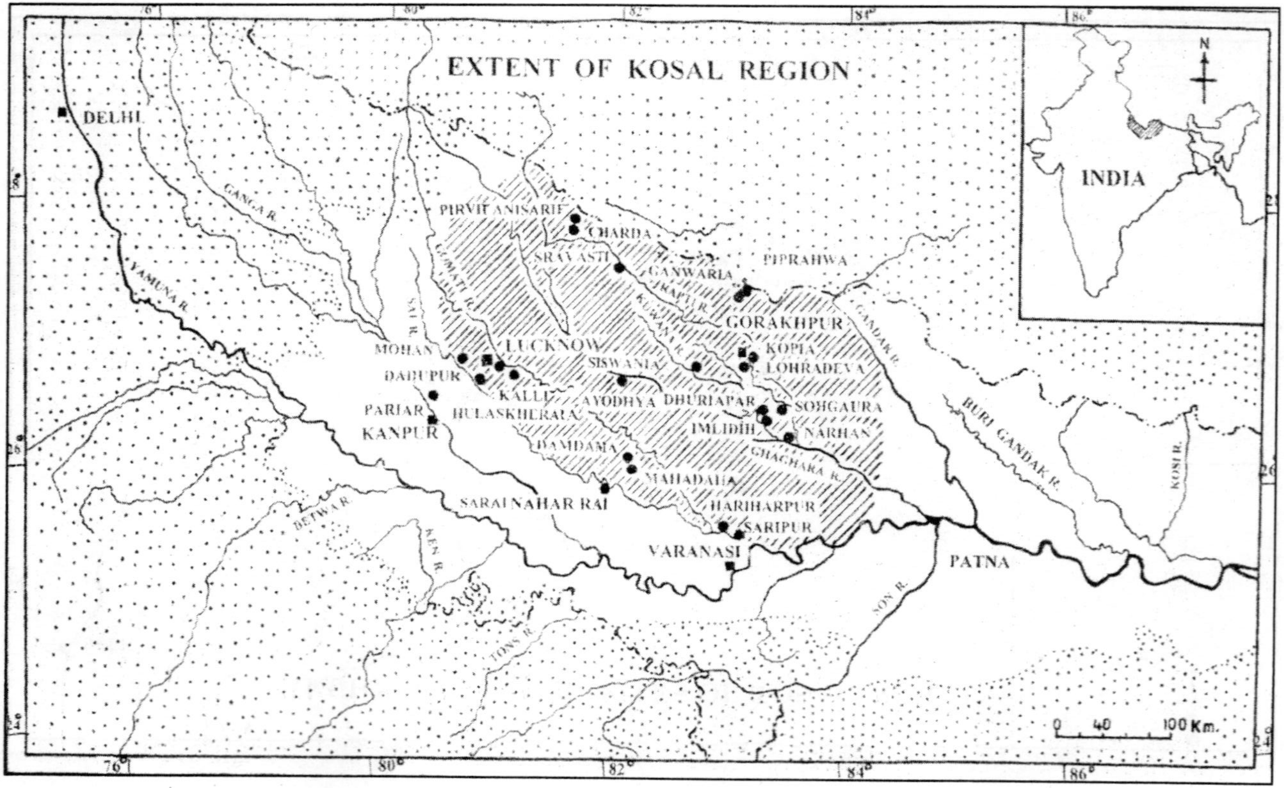
EXTENT OF KOSAL REGION
INDIA
N
DELHI
YAMUNA R.
GANGA R.
PIRVIT ANISARIF
CHARDA
SRAVASTI
GANWARIA
PIPRAHWA
GORAKHPUR
KOPIA
LOHRADEVA
MOHAN
LUCKNOW
DADUPUR
KALLI
SISWANIA
AYODHYA
DHURIAPAR
SOHGAURA
IMLIDIH
NARHAN
PARIAR
HULASKHERA
KANPUR
DAMDAMA
MAHADAHA
SARAI NAHAR RAI
HARIHARPUR
SARIPUR
VARANASI
PATNA
GOMATI R.
SAI R.
GHAGHARA R.
GANDAK R.
BURI GANDAK R.
KOSI R.
SON R.
TONS R.
KEN R.
BETWA R.
0 40 100 Km.
76°
80°
82°
84°
86°
26°
24°

Contents

1

Introduction

There is no reference of Kosal in the Rigveda, though two of its great conqueror kings, Iksvaku (X.60.4) and Mandhata (VIII.39.9), find mention in it. In the later Vedic age, there is a mention in the *Satapatha Brahmana* (1.4.1.14) of the river Sadanira, i.e. the great Gandaki as forming the boundary between the two Janpadas, Kosal and Videha. The *Atharvaveda* (X.2.32) describes the construction, wealth and greatness of Ayodhya, the first capital of Kosal, and it may be presumed that by the time of its composition Kosal had become fairly popular. Panini in his *Astadhyayi* (4.1.17) makes a mention of Kosal. In later Sanskrit works like *Mahabharata* (7.10.15, 7.101.50, 8.5.19, 8.33.22) and *Ramayana* (3.35.23, 2.43.7), albeit it was mentioned as country, but its geography is not properly defined. Kosal as one of the sixteen Mahajanpadas was for the first time mentioned in Buddhist Pali canonical *Anguttara-Nikaya* (I,213, IV,252, etc.) and later on in

Samyukta Nikaya (IV, 374) and *Majjhima Nikaya* (II, 124), etc. While in Jatakas (Alinacitta Jataka II, 19), Brahachatta Jataka (III, 115), Kunala Jataka (V, 425)., etc. simply abound in them. The *Sutta Nipata* also refers Kosal. The commentaries on these works, composed as late as the fifth century A.D., follow suit (*Sumanglavilasini*; *Papanca Sudani*; *Atthasalini*) and demonstrate beyond doubt that since quite long before the days of Buddha, Kosal had carved out for itself an important position as a political and cultural entity.

In global context it has been found that places, regions or even countries are sometimes named either after distinguished heroes of war or peace or the people inhabiting them. That does not seem to be true about Kosal since neither any distinguished hero nor any distinct people of that name like those of the Bharatas, Purus, Druhyus, Kurus, or the Mallas of the later times and the like is known to ancient Indian tradition "Kosalas", when used in the sense of a people, denotes the general mass of people and not any particular stock, which might have given its name to the Janapada. The *Digha Nikaya* commentary, *Sumangalavilasini*[1] says that the Janapada was named Kosal because of its having been the land of the Kosalan princes. But that does not carry us far about the knowledge of its nomenclature. It is thus, difficult to say as to when and how the name 'Kosal' got its currency.[2] Pargiter[3] believed that it was under King Dilipa II and his immediate successors that Janapada acquired that name.

Nowhere in Indian literature—Brahmanical or Buddhist, the exact and full extent of Kosal has been clearly stated. But through the method of deduction the boundary-lines of the kingdom can be satisfactorily drawn. If one starts from the west and north-west, it seems that the Panchala kingdom was the very next to it right from the Brahmanic period. The *Aitareya Brahmana* (VIII.14.3) mentions Kosal and Videha to the east of Panchala. It does not refer to any middle kingdom between Kosal and Panchala.

In the north, there is absolutely no doubt about the fact that the Kosalan territories touched the Himalayan hills. In the *Ramayana* (VR VII, ch. 102) it is said that the sons and nephews of Rama, with all the strength and prestigent Kosal at their command, conquered new territories in the west and north (Ch. V) and below the lofty Himalaya, what is now called the *terai*. Unlike other territories, which Bharata and Satrughna conquered in the north-west (VR VII, chs 100-101) and the western regions (VR, chs. 70-71), the conquests by the sons of Lakshmana below the foot of the Himalaya became its parts. They had been contiguous to what was the then Kosalan Kingdom. They were later, however, parceled out by Rama himself into different principalities (VR, VII, chs. 101-107). In the days of the Buddha the Sakyan Gana, though autonomous in its administration, was included in Kosal and the light the Pali literature throws on this fact is abundant.[4] Prasenajita[5] said that the Buddha was a Kosalan, a fact which the Lord himself accepted. Kapilavastu, the capital of the Sakyas itself has been said to have existed in Kosal.[6]

The *Aitareya Brahmana*[7] mentioned that Kosal bordered as far as the Sadanira, i.e. the great Gandaki in the east, which separated it from Videha. The latter lay to its east. In later times and perhaps since the days of Chandraketu, the Malla, who was the son of Laksmana and had been anointed as an independent ruler by Rama[8], the Mallas had become a separate entity.[9] But like some of their contemporary Ganas of North-east India, which were situated between Rapti and Sarayu on one side and the great Gandaki on the other, the Mallas had to probably accept the suzerainty of Kosal.[10] At any rate, like those of the Sakyas of Kapilavastu, the Mallian territories seem to have been included within the overall authority of Kosal.

It is difficult to demarcate the southern limit of Kosalan kingdom. Some light, however, is thrown on this problem by the *Ramayana*, where the route, which Rama selected for his exile-journey from Ayodhya to the Dandaka forest, has been described (VR, II, chs. 49). Starting from Ayodhya he took a southernly route, evidently on some good road (VR, II, 46.29) fit for royal chariots to be drive. His first halt was at the left bank of Tamasa, the modern Tonse.[11] Early in the morning on the second day he crossed it and after trying to delude the people, who were following him by taking a zig-zag route he again proceeded to the south (VR, II, Ch. 46). The second river, he crossed, was the Vedasruti[12] and further went to the direction, where lay the hermitage of sage Agastya. Then he crossed the Gomati, a river that bears that name even today. After Gomati, Rama had to cross Syamlika, identified with the Modern Sai[13] which joins the river Gomati in its north-easterly direction between Varanasi and Jaunpur. There Rama showed to Sita the vast tract of land, which Manu had given in ancient times to Iksvaku and which was vast in dimensions and encircled by Rastras (Rastravrtta), evidently other kingdoms (VR II, 49, 10.15). Rama uttered their some signs of pain born of separation from his own country (VR II. 59.15-18). He is then described by Valmiki to have gone beyond the long-stretched Kosala (VR II. 50-51). Having thus crossed Kosal, Rama proceeded towards the Ganga through the territories of other kings (VR I. 50.11-2). The exact points, where Rama crossed all these rivers, cannot be really determined. But it is certain from the above that the river Tons, Gomati and Syandika flowed through the Kosalan kingdom and it stretched on the right side of the modern Sai as well, where the vast tract of land given by Manu to Iksvaku was shown by Rama to Sita. That Kosal extended upto the Ganga, as is believed by many[14], is not warranted by the Ramayana, where it is said that Rama saw that river after traversing through the kingdoms of other kings. In the south Rama proceeded towards Sringaverpura[15], not very far from Prayaga and must have gone to the territories which later in the Mahajanapada period came to be known as the Vatsa Kingdom.[16] The boundary line between the two kingdoms cannot, however, be satisfactorily pointed out.

As noted earlier that Kosal was one of the sixteen (*Mahajanapada*) great countries of India as per Buddhist text of *Anguttara Nikaya* (I.213). Its earliest reference as mentioned in *Satpathabrahmana* (1.4.1.14-17), Kosal formed the eastern boundary of the land which the Aryan invaders had colonized for some time. It was bounded on the east by the river Sadanira, which is sometimes identified with the modern river Gandak. When semi-nomadic tribes of invaders settled in the fertile plain of the Ganga basin during the 8th and 7th century B.C., small settlements began to emerge especially along the rivers, which functioned as important routes of transport. Some of these developed into urban settlements in the 6th century B.C. Simultaneously with the transformation of the tribal countries (*Janpada*) into either kingdoms (*Mahajanpada*) or republics (*Ganrajya*). Thus the *janpada* of Kosal was transformed into *mahajanpada* of Kosal in the early historical period as per *Anguttar Nikaya*. In the days of the Buddha and Mahavira (the second half of the 6th and the beginning of the 5th century B.C.) the Kingdom of Kosal contained two important cities, Sravasti and Saket, both reckoned among the six great cities of the time. According to the Buddhist Pali canon, Sravasti (*Sāvatthi*) was the capital and residence of the King whereas the Jain canon mentions Saket (*Sāeya*) as the capital of Kosala. Modern historians are unanimous in considering Sravasti, which is identified with the site known today as Sahet-Mahet, 80 km. north of Ayodhya as the older capital of Kosal. The Jain canon may relate to a later period. In Sravasti resided the historical King of Kosal, Prasenjit (489 B.C.). The topographical indications in both heterodox canons as to the location of Saket confirm the identification of this town with Ayodhya and this localization is no longer questioned. Considerable difficulty, however, arises when examine the literary evidence regarding a place called Ayodhya. The relation between these two places has been investigated by many scholars, but no satisfying conclusions have been reached so far. Different resolutions have been suggested. According to Rhys Davids, who confined himself mainly to the evidence regarding the places Saket and Ayodhya, in early Buddhist sources, both cities were "adjoining like London and Westminster"[17]. No historical parallel of two adjoining cities in the sixth century B.C. India is known, and the argument is not very convincing. Both cities were taken to be the same by Cunningham[18] and

Kane[19] and considered to be virtually identical by B.C. Law[20] and Potech[21]. E.B. Joshi, however, thinks that the mention of both places as existing in Buddha's time precludes their identity (Faizabad District Gazetteer 31) and M.C. Joshi[22]. Recently the question has been taken up by Andre Bareau.[23] He points out that Ayojjha is only twice mentioned in the Pali canon, and in at least one of the *suttas* (*Sutta Nikaya*, 3.140 and 4.179) in which *Ayojja* figures the place is said to be situated on the bank of river Ganga. If Ayodhya indeed was a quarter of the town Saketa, one wonders why this name did not figure more often in Buddhist (or Jaina) description of the city and secondly, why all other Epic Sanskrit sources refer exclusively to this quarter and never to the town of Saketa. Evidently the first alternative proposed by Bareau to the effect that as far as the Pali canon is concerned, Saketa and Ayojjha refer to two different sites is more possible in the area of Kosal. There is no indication whatsoever that this "bourgade" on the Ganga river had anything in common with the Epic city of Ayodhya besides its name.

Kosal in different Literary Sources

A. Buddhist Canonical (Pali) Text

Kosal was one of the sixteen *Mahajanpadas (Anguttara Nikaya*, I, 213; IV, 252 etc.) ruled over by King Pasenadi (*Samyutta Nikaya* IV, 374, *Majjhima Nikaya* II,124 etc.)

Kosal was ruled over by King Dighiti (war with King Brahmadatta of Kasi) (*Vinaya Pittaka* I, 342). Kosal included

Kasi in the form of Kasi-Kosal (*Majjhima Nikaya* II.111; *Digha Nikaya* I,228; *Anguttara Nikaya* V, 59).

Buddha belong to Kosal i.e. Kapilavastu (*Majjhima Nikaya* II, 124; *Anguttara Nikaya* I, 276 and *Suttanipata* 405).

Reference of War between Pasenadi of Kosal and Ajatasattu of Magadha in which Kasi theatre of war (*Samyutta Nikaya* I, 82-85).

B. Buddhist Jatakas (Pali) Text

Reference of War between Kosala and Kasi (*Alinacitta Jataka* II, 14; *Brahachatta Jataka* V, 316 and *Kunala Jataka* V, 425)

Kosal was ruled by prince Dighavu and his war with Kasi, but the name of the King of Kasi is not mentioned (*Dighiti-Kosala Jataka*.II, 211f).

Kasi conquered by Dabhasena, King of Kosal (*Ekarāga Jataka* III,13).

Kasi conquered by king Vanka of Kosal (*Ghata Jataka* III.168f.)

Kosal encompassed the kingdom of Kasi and Pasenadi gave village in Kasi as dowry of his daughter to Bimbisara of Magadha (*Haritamata Jataka* II, 237; *Taccasukara Jataka* IV, 342).

C. Kosal in Early Jaina Canonical (Prakrit) Sources

Kosal as one of the sixteen Mahajanapadas (*Viyahapannatti*, VP, p. 219).

Kosal as Ariya country with Sageya as its capital (*Nayadhammakahad*, NK, p. 95; *Pannavana* PN SU.37, 55).

Reference of confederacy of 9 Kings of Kosal (Lecchai) fought together with 9 kings of Kasi (Mallai) against Kuniya Videhaputta in the war of the Big Stones i.e. *Mahashilakanka samgama* (Viyahapannatti, VP, p. 140); *Nirayavali* (NS, pp. 27-28). Sunakkhatta disciple of Mahavira hails from Kosal (*Viyahapannatti*, VP, p. 218).

D. Kosal in Early Sanskrit Sources

Kosal was referred as *Janapada* and most eastern Aryan region, before the occupation of Videha, border between these two is Sadanira-Gandaki (*Satapathbrahmana* 1.4.1.14-17).

Kosal was referred as *Janapada* (Panini, 4.1.77) and *Mahajanpada* in the form of Kasikosala in Mahabharata (7.10.15, 7.101.50 and 8.5.19, 7.33.22).

Kosal as country of Dasaratha and Ram in Ramayana, in which Dasarath is a *Kosalaraja* (*Ramayana* 3.35.23) and Rama is *Kosalesvara* (*Ramayana* 2.43.7).

Kosal is referred both as a country and its people in *Raghuvansa* (9.9;3.5; 6.71) and as couple of Magadh i.e. Magadhkosala in *Raghuvansa* (9.17).

Seven Kings ruled in Kosal, before the Guptas as per *Vayupurana* (2.37.377) and *Brahmapurana* (3.74.188).

In post-Gupta Sanskrit sources, the reference of Ayodhya-Saketa in couple form is prevailing feature, but reference of Kosal is very rare.

In Greek sources, the reference of Kosal is totally absent, but Saketa is referred as a country in the Ganga basin[24]. In Tibetan sources also Kosal is not reported, but reference of Saketa is present as "Originally King *KA-NI-KA* (the Kusan emperor Kaniska) and the King of *GUZAN* and the *Li* ruler king *VIJAYAKIRTI*, and others led an army into India and captured a city named *SO-KED* (Saket) on which occasion King Vijayakirti obtained many *sariras*, which he deposited within the Stupa of *PHRU-NO*.[25]

Like Greek and Tibetan sources, the Chinese sources also lack the reference of Kosal, but it frequently referred Saketa and Ayodhya.

... the great country of *SHA-CHI* (Saketa), Leving the southern gate of the capital city, on the east of the road, is a place where Buddha once dwelt. Here is a tree grown up from a willow stick used as Toothbrush by the Buddha. Here also they raised towers on places where the four Buddhas walked for exercise and sat down. The ruins still exist (*FA HSIEN 'FO' 'KWO' 'KI'* Ch. XIX) (A.D. 400).

-*MA-MING* (Asvaghosa) was a native of *SHA-KI-TA* (Saketa) of the country *SHA-YEI* (Sravasti) (6th century A.D.).

If we look any significant differences between those Sanskrit texts which refer to Saketa but omit Ayodhya and those that mention Ayodhya but omit Saketa in the area of Kosala, is due to the fact that the former texts are of a semi-scientific or factual nature, whereas the later (*Mahabharata,*

Ramayana and *Puranapancalaksana*) have basically a fictional character. This tallies with the intrinsic nature of the older parts of both heterodox canons, which primarily aimed at recording the actual deeds and technique teachings of the historical founders of both traditions and to which only Saketa was known.

Saketa in the area of Kosal remained admittedly a provincial town of secondary importance during the heyday of Mauryan rule, yet there are several indication that its importance increased reciprocally with the decline of central power, resulting finally in the establishment of a petty kingdom which was virtually independent. Saketa figures prominently in the important text of the *Yugapurana* and Patanjali's commentary on Panini's *Astadhyayi* which relates to the period of the downfall of the Mauryan empire, the incursion of the Greeks and the Sunga period. It is first mentioned as a residence of a governor then as being attacked by combined force of Greeks, Mathuras and Panchalas, and finally as being ruled by seven mighty kings. The historicity of these seven kings as per *Yugapurana* (11.117) (*Saket saptarajano bhavisyanti mahabalah*) is numismatically attested by the coins of Deva King found in Faizabad District. The coinage of five of these kings is known as Muladeva, Vayudeva, Visakhdeva, Patnadeva and Dhandeva[26]. On the basis of similarities of their coinage, it may be conjectured that Sivadatta succeeded Visakhdeva and from the time of Sunga upto coming of Kushana, the following kings ruled in Kosala:

1. Pusyamitra (*Circa* 187-151 B.C.)
2. Muladeva (possibly vassal of Pusyamitra)
3. Mitradeva (contemporary of Vasumitra Sunga` *circa* 140-130 B.C.)
4. Vayudeva
5. Pathdeva
6. Phalgudeva (Father of king 'Dana')
7. Dhanadeva (*circa* 50 B.C.)
8. Visakhadeva
9. Sivadatta
10. Jyesthdatta
11. Naradatta

During the reign of these kings, Saket in Kosal probably developed into a military stronghold, hereby eclipsing the old capital of Sravasti, which had according to Fa-hein sunk into insignificant around 400 A.D.[27]

The date of this Yavana incursion has been in debate. An early date i.e. 190 B.C. was proposed by J. Mitchiner, while later date of 150 B.C. has been proposed by A.K. Narain[28]. This so-called 'Yavan incursion' may well have hastened the end of the dying Maurya dynasty and facilitated the revolt of commander-in-chief (*senapati*) Pusyamitra Sunga.

After Pusyamitra Sunga, the political condition of the Kosal changed drastically. For the history of this period we have to rely mainly on numismatic sources, because in this area a mind in Saketa was in practice which issued the 'Ayodhya coins', whose date according to Allen goes back to third century B.C. But unfortunately the numismatics who deal with this period[29] hold widely differing and contradictory view. This is because of the fact that post-Maurya period witnessed the rise of a large number of ruling dynasties in several part of North India including Kosal too.

The chronological history of the area of Kosal roughly designated as the Kushan age (50-320 A.D.) is confounded by the controversy over the date of the Kanishka who introduced the Saka era of 78 A.D. has a direct bearing on the history of Saketa. P.L. Gupta (1968) supporting the later date of Kanishka (*circa* 140 A.D.), places the Mitra dynasty that is known from Ayodhya coins before the conquest of Kushana. Sircar[30] adhering to the early date of 78 AD, places these Mitra rulers between the Kushana and the Gupta i.e. 150-300 A.D. The Mitra dynasty, labeled as 'rulers of Ayodhya' is only known from its coinage.[31] Since during this period Mitra rulers are known from petty kingdoms Mathura, Ahicchatra (Panchal) and Kausambi, hence Kosal was also ruled by them, albeit their coins are reported only from Ayodhya. After this analysis of the sources the following course of events seems possible. From the middle of the first century A.D., the Dattas of Kosal were increasingly confronted with the menace of Kushana power in the West. This resulted in a siege of the capital by newly proclaimed emperor Kanishka, who aspired to add the eastern kingdom of his realm. As per Tibetan sources[32] of eleventh century the conquest of Saketa took place in the last quarter of the first century A.D. After the conquest of the capital the Kushana held sway over Kosal (including the country of Kasi) upto the 2nd half of the 2nd century A.D. From this period also dates the first archaeological evidence that testify to the actual name of the town 'Saketa' an inscription in the Late Kushan characters on the pedestal of Buddha image found in Stupa 9 in Sravasti records its gift by one Sihadeva of Saketa[33]. A general consensus hold that after the reign of King Vasudeva (146-176 A.D.), Kushana power rapidly declined, resulting in the re-emergence of local kingdom[34]. Thus rose the dynasty of the Mitra rulers of Kosala of whom, besides the data discussed above, nothing is known.

At the beginning of the 4th century A.D., the independent kingdom of Kosal was for the second time in its history confronted with the rising power of Magadha and for the second time it succumbed. The Mittras of Kosal had to face the imperialistic aspirations of the Gupta after the founder of the Gupta era, Chandragupta in 320 A.D. By the support of Licchavis, Chandragupta I extended his influence to the west. After what has been said about the strategic position of Kosal for defence of the western frontiers of the Magadh and Kasi country, it will not be surprising that Kosal were ruled over by the Gupta dynasty from the very beginning.[35] During the reign of Samudragupta, Kosal was placed under the direct rule of Pataliputra.[36]

The fifth century would appear to be crucial phase in the history of Kosal. It saw heyday of its prosperity and restored to its former glory as of the illustrious Ikshvaku Kings. It is true that after Gupta period majority of the cities of northern India in a final disappearance from the stage of history[37], but this area is recognized as the legendary town of the Ikshvakus, and most of all as the capital of Lord Vishnu (Ayodhya) himself in his incarnation of Rama, the town of Ayodhya in Kosal never fully disappeared from the purview of the Hindus, like Mathura and Varanasi which were practically abandoned after Gupta period. Other important towns of the area like Kausambi and Sravasti never recovered from this decay. Its geostrategic position in the Ganga Plain were another essential factors for its survival after Gupta period. And Ayodhya in the region of Kosal could once again become a provincial capital under the Delhi Sultanate of the thirteenth century A.D. But it is also a fact that when in later times the commercial and strategic functions were taken over by rival towns in the fifteenth century by Jaunpur, in the eighteenth century by Faizabad, and at the end of the eighteenth century and first half of the nineteenth century by Lucknow-Saket, Ayodhya in the region of Kosal, unlike Sravasti did not fall into decay, on the contrary those centuries in particular witnessed a flourishing of religious life in the city.

Difficulty was presented by the excavation of B.B. Lal as to the exact location of the Ayodhya in Kosal during the Gupta period.No Gupta layers were so far found among the strata of the Ramkot.[38] But this dark phase of the history of the area is fully enlightened by the recent excavation conducted by Archaeological Survey of India, under the direction of Hon'ble High Court of Lucknow 2002-03 in which a very thick deposit of culture was seen after Gupta period at Ayodhya, albeit at Mathura and Rajghat (ancient Varanasi) Gupta layers are poorly represented.

Soon after Fa hsien left India a new emperor ascended the Gupta throne, Kumargupta [(*circa* 415-455 A.D.) who was a half-brother of Prabhavatigupta which appears to have been one of the earliest known devotees of the Rama incarnation of Vishnu.[49] In conformity with the spirit of the time the period of Kumargupta's reign provides us with the first archaeological evidence of topographical details of Ayodhya in Kosal. The Karamadanda inscription perhaps supplies us with the name of the governor of the province of Kosal. The capital of this province is denoted as Ayodhya. The inscription was found 24 km south-west of Ayodhya, near village Karmadanda along the road from Faizabad to Inayatnagar and Rai Bareilly. The inscription informs us that in 436 A.D., the former 'minister' (*mantrin*) and 'governor' (*kumaramatya*) and at the time of 'superintendent of the office of the Commander-in-chief' (*mahabaladhikaranika*) of the emperor Kumargupta, Prithivisena made an offering to some Brahmins (?) hailing from Ayodhya on the occasion of an image-procession (*devadroni*) at Bharadi. Prthivisena was a devotee of Shiva, specially of Prthivisena, presumably his *ishtadevata* as the name would suggest (*linga*), and he recorded his offering, which might have consisted of the inscribed *linga* itself at Karmadanda, to the 'feet of the illustrious Mahadeva,' the Lord of the Himalaya (*bhagavacchailesvarasvamimahadevapadamule*).

From Chinese sources we know that King Vikramaditya, i.e. Skandagupta, had the royal court installed in Ayodhya[40], or country of Sravasti.[41] It is beyond doubt that the country of Sravasti refers Kosal, the capital of which was at the time of Saketa/Ayodhya, not Sravasti.[42] The possibility remains open that the royal court had already moved from Pataliputra to Saketa/Ayodhya during the reign of Kumaragupta. It is established by the fact that the first inscription featuring the name Ayodhya dated from the reign of Kumargupta preserved the last Gupta ruler of Pataliputra i.e. Chandragupta II, who was father of Kumargupta. There are indications that the capital Pataliputra was stricken by a calamity in the middle of the 5th century A.D., possibly a flood of Ganga.[43] Saket/ Ayodhya in Kosal offered a good alternative for the old capital. Since the reign of Kumargupta the empire had come under increasing pressure of Hunas on its western borders, and this made Saketa/Ayodhya strategically preferable to the eastern capital.[44] Seen in the perspective of the North Indian political configuration over a long period it would seem that the move of the court to Saketa was only a short interlude. The tendency to move the center of power from east to west, i.e. to that side from which again and again all North Indian empires were threatened by foreign armies, was further effectuated by the shift of power from Ayodhya/Saketa in the region of Kosal to Kanyakubja (Kanauj) directly after the dissolution of the Gupta empire, and it finally resulted in the declaration of Qutb-ud-din in 1193 A.D. of Lalkot (Delhi) as capital of the Sultanate. It may be noted incidentally that all cities successively raised to the status of capital were situated along the important east-west highway.

The region of Kosal-Saketa-Ayodhya was after Gupta period, it was again ruled temporarily by Kanauj during the reign of the Pratihara dynasty, notably of the kings Mihir Bhoja (836-885 A.D.) and his son Mahendrapala (885-904 A.D.). The Dighwa-Dubauli Plato inscription issued from Mahodaya (Kanauj?) by Mahendragupta, King of Kanauj, in 761-62 A.D., declares that a village in the district of Valayika belonging to the Sravasti bhukti in the Sravasti *mandala* was given to a learned man (*bhatta*).[45] From these centuries, however, no historical sources relating to Ayodhya-Saketa-Kosal have come to light. A new era in the history of the region was ushered in when the area again formed part of a kingdom of Kannauj in the second half of the 11th century A. D.

References

1. *Pali Text Society* (1855), ed. Vol. I, London, p. 239.
2. V. Pathak (1963), *History of Kosala*, Delhi, p. 37.
3. Pargiter, F.E. (1922), *Ancient Indian Historical Traditions*, Oxford University Press, London; Motilal Banarsidass, New Delhi, 1962, p. 275.
4. *Digha Nikaya* (PTS), Pt. III, p. 82, Jataka (Fausbolls' ed.), Vol IV, p.145.
5. *Majjhima Nikaya* (PTS), Pt. II, p.124. भगवाऽपि कोसलको अहम्पि कोसलको।
6. *Anguttara Nikaya* (PTS), Pt. I, p. 267.
7. VIII, 14.3; I.4, 11.3
8. *Valmiki Ramayana,* Vii, 102, 4-11.
9. *Anguttar Nikaya* (PTS), Pt. I, p. 213.
10. Ray Chaudhuri, H.C. (1950), *Political History of Ancient India*, ed., Calcutta University, p. 199.
11. Dey, N.L. (1927), *The Geographical Dictionary of Ancient and Medieval India*, 2nd ed. London: Luzac & Co., p. 202.
12. Identified with Bhaita between Tons and Gomati or Gumti river, *Geog. Dic.* By N.L. Dey, p. 200.
13. *Ibid.* 200.
14. Law, B.C. (1943), *Tribes in Ancient India*, Bhadarkar Oriental Series, No. 4, p. 119.

    He, however, seems to have changed his view, for he believes that Sarpika or Syandika (Sai) was Kosala's boundary on the south (*Classical Age*, p. 4.)

    Davids, Rhys (1922), *Cambridge History of India*, Cambridge, Vol. I (ed,. Rapson), Cambridge University Press, 1922, p. 178.

    Ray, Chaudhury H.C. (1950), *Political History of Ancient India* (V ed.), Calcutta University, p. 199.

15. Cunningham identified it with modern Singor or Singror, 22 miles to the north-west of Allahabad on the left bank of the Ganga, vide *Archaeological Survey of India Report,* Vol. XI, p. 62, Vol. XXI, p.11.
16. *Anguttar Nikaya* (PTS), Pt. I, p. 213.
17. Rhys Davids, F.W. (1903), *Buddhist India—The Story of the Nation,* London, Vol. 61.
18. Cunningham Alexander (Simla 1871; Calcutta 1987), 23 vols. (reprint Delhi, 1966-73, 21 vols.) *Archaeological Survey of India.*
19. Kane, P.V. *History of Dharmasastra (Ancient and Medieval), religious And Civil Law in India,* 5 Vols, Poona, Government Oriental Series, Clan B, No. 6; Vol. IV, Poona, p. 798.
20. Law, B.C. (1943), "Ayodhya in Ancient India" in *The Journal of Ganganath Jha Research Institute,* Vol. I, Allahabad, p. 423-443.
21. Petech, Luciano (1976),) *Indien bis zur Mitte des b. Jahrkunderts,* Berlin, p. 440
22. Joshi, M.C. (1978), "Archaeology and Indian Tradition: Some Observations" in *Puratattva,* Vol. 8, Delhi, 1975-76, p.98-102.
23. Bareau, Andre (1976), "Ayodhya et Mithila dans les texts canoniques du Bouddhism ancient" in *Indologica Taurinensia,* Vol. VII, p. 75-82.
24. Ptolemy. *Claudii Ptolemaei Geographica.* Edidit C.F. A. Nobbe cum introduction a Aubery Diller. Leipzig, Cap. 1, 719; Cap 2, 22, 1843-45.
25. Thomas, Edward J. (1949), *The Life of Buddha as Legend And History* London.
26. Allen, John (1936), "Catalogue of the Coins of Ancient India. *A Catalogue of the Indian Coins in the British Museum.*, London, p. xxxviii; Gupta, *IAR* 1976-77, p. 53.
27. Beal, S. (1884), *Si Yu Ki Buddhist records of the Western World. Translation from the Chinese of Hiuen Tsiang (AD 629),* London.
28. Narain, A.K. (1957), *The Indo-Greek,* Oxford, p. 88. Fleet, J.F. (1886), "Sanskrit and Old Kanarese Inscription" in *Journal Asiatique,* XV, p. 105-110.

29. Dasgupta, Ch. Ch. (1932), *Ancient Coins found in Panchala, Ayodhya, Kausambi and Mathura—A Study in Indian Historical Quarterly*, Vol. VIII, Calcutta, p. 549-564.

30. Sircar, D.C. (1951-77), *The History and Culture of Indian People*, Vol. II. Bombay, p. 113.

31. Thaplyal, Kiran Kumar (1972), *Studies in Ancient Indian Beals*, Lucknow, pp. 32-36.

32. Thomas, F.W. (1935), "Tibetan Literary Texts and Documents concerning Chinese Tuakestan," Selected and Translated. *Part D: Literary Texts, The Annals of the Li Country*, London, p. 119.

33. Mitra, Debala (1971), *Buddhist Monuments*, Calcutta, p. 78.

34. Majumdar, R.C. (ed.) (1951-1977), *The History and Culture of Indian People* (11 Vols), published by Bharatiya Vidya Bhavan, Bombay.

35. Pargiter, F.E. (1913), *The Purana Text of the Dynasties of Kali Age*, London, p.13

36. Majumdar, R.C. *op.cit.*, Part III, p. 13.

37. Sharma, R.S. (1973), "Decay of the Gangetic Town in Gupta and Post-Gupta Times" in *Journal of Indian History (Golden Jubilee Volume)*, Delhi, p. 135-150.

38. *I.A.R.*, 1976-77. p. 53.

39. Sircar, D.C. *History and Culture of Indian People*, Part III, Bombay, p. 180.

40. Takakusu, J. (1904), *The Life of Vasu-bandhu* by *Paramartha (AD 499-569)*, Japan, p. 283.

41. Beal, *op.cit.*, p.106.

42. Frauwallner, E. (1951), *On the Date of Buddhist Master of the Law 'Vasubandhu,' Serie Orientale*, Part III, Rome, p. 30.

43. Schlingloff, D. (1969), *Die altindische stadt. Sine vergleichende Untersuchung. Wiesbaden.* Abh. D. Ak. D. wirs. U.d. Lit. in *Mainz Geistes u. Cozial wiss.* K.I., p. 41.

44. Frauwallner, E. (1951), *op.cit.*, p. 31.

45. Fleet, J.F., *op.cit.*, p. 112. Tripathi, Ram Shankar, (1973) *History of Kannauj to the Muslim Conquest*, Banaras, p. 252.Vaidya, C.V., 1979. *History of Medieval Hindu India*, 3 Vols., Delhi.

2

Geo-Ecology of Kosal Region

The vast depression of the Quaternary period between the foothills of Himalaya in the north and Vindhyan ranges in the south which is filled by alluvium of the perennial Ganga known as Gangetic plain. The Ganga Plain occupies the central position in the Indo-Gangetic Plains, a peripheral foreland basin system. In the Pleistocene period it had come into existence in the form of a topographic depression of thousands of meters in which unvarying monotony, of Pleistocene-Holocene alluvial deposits of the rivers of Indo-Gangetic system emerged covering an area of 777,000 square km. from Sindh, northern Rajasthan, whole Punjab, Haryana, Uttar Pradesh, Bihar, Bengal and half portion of Assam. In the initial stages of its formation, around 20-15 Ma BP, in middle Miocene the Ganga Plain was narrow, with the alluvial plain directly abutting the rocks of the Lesser Himalayas. Later on, the northern part of the Ganga Plain was uplifted in several pulses forming the Siwalik hill ranges. Simultaneously, the basin shifted southwards in response to the thrust-sheet loading in the Himalaya.[1] The last major thrust-sheet event was the upliftment of Upper Siwalik rocks[2], which represent deposits of the northern part of the Ganga Plain. This upliftment took place around 500 Kyr B.P.. At the same time along the southern margin, the Ganga Plain expanded south by about 100 kilometres.

The foreland basin of Ganga Plain shows all the major components of an Orogensis by which deformed and uplifted foreland basin deposits adjacent to the Siwalik and mountain building of a depositional basin of Ganga Plain. The Ganga Plain has been subsiding since its inception around 15 Ma BP and has wedge shaped sediment accumulation, thickest close to the Himalaya and thinned-near the Craton in the South. The younger sediments have overlapped the older sediments towards the south; consequently in the southern part only the youngest sediments are present.[3]

The subsidence (settling downwards to a normal state) and sediment accumulation rates in the Ganga foreland basin have varied between a few millimeters per thousand years to a few metres per thousand years, varying in different parts and different geological times (last 15 Ma B.P.). In response to the subsidence the older sediments are buried near the young surface sediments. The Ganga Plain has a surface cover of Holocene sediments of variable thickness throughout.[4] The older sediments of the Ganga Plain are exposed as Siwalik deposits, ranging in age between about 15 Ma and 0.5 Ma. Thus geologically it was a deep basin in Pre-Tertiary Times which has been filled in by the Tertiary river-borne debris from the Peninsular and later supplemented by the upper and Post-Tertiary Himalayan debris known as alluvium. The Gangetic deposition started taking place during the last phase of the Siwalik formation and has all through Pleistocene up to the present. Here Gangetic river system is different from Indus river system by the fact that in the case of Indus, five rivers of the Punjab unite and form one river which flows through a desert without receiving any tributary, whereas the Ganga system is enriched by one confluent river after another and flows in the direction of increasing rainfall from West to East.

Earlier in Geographical literature, the Ganga Plain is subdivided into three parts, Upper Ganga Plain (Delhi-Allahabad), Middle Ganga Plain (Allahabad-Farakka) and Lower Ganga Plain (Ganga delta region from Farakka to the Bay of Bengal) but recently it is modified into three parts as Western Ganga Plain, Median Ganga Plain and Eastern Ganga Plain.

(1) Western Ganga Plain

The Western limit of the Ganga Plain is the Delhi-Aravalli (NE-SW) ridge and the Yamuna River, while the eastern limit is around Kanpur (25°26'-26°28'N; 79°31'-80°34'E) which is banded by the Ganga in the east and Yamuna in the west. The northern region of this part has a regional slope in a south-east direction of about 20 – 10 cm/km. The rivers from the Himalaya initially flow southward and then swing to the southeast. This region shows a number of abandoned channels of an ancient an astomosed system.

It exhibits prominent development of the Upland Terrace Surface T_2 (Bhangar or older alluvium of Middle Pleistocene) with undulatory areas of centripetal drainage. The main rivers, namely Ganga, Yamuna and Ramganga make conspicuous river Plain i.e. Khadar of newer in age. The relief is rugged T_2(Upland Interfluve surface), T_1 (River Valley Surface) and T_0 (Active Flood Plain Surface) surfaces show distinctive developments. The upland interfluve surface exhibits ponds, lakes, abandoned channel belts, aeolian sand ridges (bhur) and wetlands. North-south oriented abandoned channels are common in the northern part.

(2) Median Ganga Plain

This region marks the middle part of the Ganga Plain. This area is characterized by a number of south-east flowing rivers, separating large linear uplifted interfluve regions. The interfluve areas are characterized by mildly undulatory terrain with centripetal drainage systems. Lakes, ponds, abandoned channel belts and channel segments are common. In the northern part, the wide Ghaghara River Plain is present, with a dense network of river channels in different stage of evolution. This region extends between Kanpur in the west and Patna in the east. Geomorphologically, the rivers have been strongly influenced by the tectonic activity of the subsurface north-east extension of Faizabad ridge and Vindhyan Plateau. The southern part of the Ganga Plain shows evidence of upliftment by Bundelkhand Granite mass it during the Holocene. There is a northern slope component in the Central Alluvial plain with a distinct northern slope from Kanpur toward Faizabad (from Ganga towards the Ghaghara River). The slopes are highly variable ranging between 20 – 5 cm/km[6] due to its buried tectonic element. It may be mentioned that this area and the Vindhyan Hills towards its south are archaeologically most significant and have a large number of archaeological sites, ranging from Mesolithic to Medieval periods.

(3) Eastern Ganga Plain

It marks the eastern part of the Ganga Plain with maximum widens upto 400 km. in Bengal. This Plain covers most of the area of West Bengal and Bangladesh. Its eastern boundary is formed by the Naga-Lushi orogenic belt and on the west by the Peninsular shield composed of the Achaen basement complex on which lie patches of Gondwana sediments.

Geomorphology of the Ganga Plain

Geologically on the basis of morphostratigraphy the Ganga Plain has been divided into two units: (i) Older Alluvium of Middle Pleistocene age (*Bhangar = Bangar*) and (ii) Newer Alluvium of Holocene age (*Khadar*).[7] The older Alluvium marks the higher interfluve areas; while newer Alluvium forms deposits of major river channels.

Bhaber—it is a gravel talus with a somewhat steep slop fringing the outer margin of the Siwalik hills. It resembles the alluvial fans or dry delatas. The rivers in crossing them lose themselves by the abundant percolation in the loose absorbent gravels.

Terai—the densely forested and marshly zone below the *Bhaber*. In these tracts the water of the *Bhaber* slopes reappears and maintains them in a permanently marshy or swampy condition.

Bhur denotes an elevated piece of land situated along the banks of the Ganges and formed of accumulated wind-blown sands during the dry hot months of the year.

Usar are salt impregnated, or alkaline soils which form an important group of soil in southern portion of Ganga Plain. There are yet in these soils many undecomposed rock and mineral fragments, which with weathering liberate sodium, magnesium and calcium salts and sulphurous acid. Such alkaline soils are notably impervious and, therefore, have impeded drainage. Large areas, once fertile during Mesolithic period have become impregnated with these alkaline salts, destroying the agricultural value of the ground. The salts are confined to the top layers of the soils, being transferred from below by capillary action. The alkaline content is high and there is a large excess of fres, salts, combined with poverty in nitrogen and organic plant food material (humus).

But recently the remote sensing data provided regional synoptic geomorphic features of the Ganga Plain which is as given below[8]:–

1. *Upland Terrace Surface*

The large areas of Ganga Plain, north of the axial river are present as interfluve highland-area (Bhangar or Older

Alluvium).[9] It is the oldest alluvium surface, belongs to the Middle Pleistocene. This surface shows southern or south eastern regional slopes and is beyond the reach of floods created by overtroppy of the river channels. The active rivers are incised in this surface. Deposits of this surface are dominantly fine-grained sediments showing distinctive characteristics termed as *Doab* or upland interfluve deposits.[10] These deposits are exposed in cliff sections of the rivers and in the ravines. Its general level is 3-4 m. above the highest and 15-20 m. above the lowest level of the bed of Ganga. The $CaCO_3$ nodules (*kankar*) are found everywhere in *Bhangar* land from the surface down to 10-15 m. depth. The surface exhibits a large variety of alluvial features on micro- and macro-scale, namely gentle warps and undulations, abandoned channel belts and segments, sand ridges (*bhur*), ponds and lakes.

2. *Marginal Plain Upland Surface (M)*

The interfluve upland surface, south of the axial river (Marginal Alluvial Plain) is termed Marginal Plain Upland Surface, also designated as Banda Older Alluvium or Bhanger.

3. *Megafan Surface (MF)*

Synoptic remotely sensed data helped in identification of large megafan surfaces in the Kosal region which are associated with large Himalayan rivers, namely Ganga, Yamuna, Sarda (Ghaghara), megafans. At present, these megafans are inactive, only the surface is being modified by surfacial processes with mostly fine-grained sediments being deposited. This surface merges with the T_2 (Upland Interfluvial surface) and in small areas it is difficult to differentiate the two, as the megafan building processes ceased to operate. The Ganga River has incised into its megafan deposits exposing them in cliff sections.[11] The megafans of the Ganga Plain show evidence of smaller fans superimposed on the larger ones, indicating reducing fan building activity through time.

4. *River Valley Terrace Surface (T_1)*

Major rivers of the Ganga Plain show development of broad river valleys, which are entrenched into T_2 (Upland Interfluial surface), MF (Megafan surface). There is a prominent terrace T_1 (River Plain Terrace) Surface located several metres below the T_2 surface within the river valleys. This surface is younger than T_2 and MF surfaces. Within the T_1 surface, the active river channel with its active flood plain is incised by several metres. The term *Khadar* includes the deposits of river valleys, T_1 surface and T_0 (Active Flood Plain surface). The term Khadar includes the deposits of river valleys, T_1 –surface and T_0 –surface. The River Valley Terrace Surface (T_1) is also described as the older flood plain. Sometimes, the T_1 –surface shows several levels.[12] The T_1 –surface is generally beyond the reach of flood waters of the active river. However, back flooding in small channels and excessive rainfall can cause flooding of this surface. The T_1 –surface often shows abandoned channels, meander cutoffs, liver water bodies and alluvial ridges which are not directly related to the present day active-river Yazoo-type channels are characteristic feature of the T_1 – surface which may run parallel to the main rivers for tens of kilometers to hundred kilometres. Here yazoo is a deferred junction of a tributary, he name derived from the Yazoo river of lower Mississippi. Yazoo is a Tributary which flows for some distance parallel to the main Mississippi river before merging with it. The development of the T_1 surface indicates the present-day active rivers are underfit rivers and were larger, carrying much more water in an earlier humid climatic phase.

5. *Piedmont-Fan Surface (PF)*

A 10-50 km. broad belt of coalescing fan surfaces is developed along the Himalayan foothills. This surface shows high slopes of 3^0 - 4^0 and exhibits both diverging and converging drainages. It overlies and is younger than the T_2 MF and T_1 surfaces. This surface mostly shows ephemeral shallow channels. It includes the *Bhabar* and *Terai* zones. It has also been termed *Bhat* Alluvium.[1] This surface shows evidence of shrinkage of fan building activity, as smaller fans are superimposed on the larger fans. Fan is the alluvial deposit of a scream where it issues from a ravine or camupm amd drops its load on to a plain. Deposits of this surface consist of gravely sediments interfingering with muddy deposits.

6. *Active Flood Plain Surface (T_0)*

This surface consists of active river channels and their poorlydevelopedfloodplains,whicharenvariablyentrenched into the T_1 surface. Some of the river channels of the northern Ganga Plain show very little incision and mark large flood plains. Due to incision, the active rivers of the Ganga Plain show limited lateral shifts. However, the river channels of the northern Ganga Plain often show avulsion on a time scale of 1000-10000 years. It is the youngest geomorphic surface of the Ganga Plain, showing a variety of fluvial landforms, namely channel bar, natural lever, meander cutoff, swamps, crevasse, channels and flood plains. The deposits are seen in river bank and natural levee sections.

Singh[14] related the above formation of regional geomorphic surfaces of the Ganga Plain to climatic cycles of the Late Pleistoceno-Holocene, and accompanying base level changes due to sea-level fluctuations. Srivastava[15] dated the sediments of these surfaces and provided a chronology for the topmost deposits of these surfaces. The probable timing of formation and luminescence ages of different regional geomorphic surfaces are given below:-

(1) Upland Terrace Surface T_2 probable timing of formation, 128-74 kyrs, 015-5 Luminescence age of Upper Part – 76-32 kyr.

(2) Marginal Plain Upland Surface (MP) probable timing of formation, 128-74 Kyrs, 015-5 Luminescence age of Upper Part 76 – 32 Kyrs BP

(3) Megafan Surface (MF) probable timing of formation, 74 – 35 Kyr BP, 015-4 and part of 015-3 Luminescence age of Upper Part 26 – 22 Kyr BP

(4) River Valley Terrace Surface (T_L) probable timing of formation, 35-25 Kyr BP, part of 015-3 and 015-2 Luminescence age of Upper Part 5-2 Kyr BP.
(5) Piedmont Fan Surface (PF) probable timing of formation 25-10 Kyr BP, 015-2 Luminescence age of Upper Part 9-3 Kyr BP.
(6) Active Flood Plain Surface (T_0) probable timing of formation, 10 Kyr BP – present, 015-1 Luminescence age of Upper Part 0.5 – 0.2 Kyr BP.

But the Kosal region include the geomorphic surface of 1, 3, 4, 5, and 6 with a lack of marginal plain (25°10'-27°52'N; 80°12'-84°16'E) upland surface.

From amongst the one geomorphic surfaces the Kosal Region lack only marginal plain upland surface (MP) of the Ganga Plain with the following features:

(1) It is an active-foreland basin undergoing fast subsidence and accumulating sediments coming mostly from the Himalaya and less from Peninsular carton which was a stable block of the earth's crust which has remained relatively unaffected by organic activity for a very long period of time. The Siwalik foothills represent sediments deposited in the early phase of the formation of the base of the plain.
(2) It drained by a network of rivers originating in the Himalayas and alluvial plains where the Ganga and Ghaghara is the trunk river.

(3) The meteorology of the Kosal region is essentially controlled by the southwest monsoon with ha moderate rainfall and high coefficient of variation in atmospheric temperature.

(4) The fine geomorphic surface (T_2, MF, T_1, PF and T_0) have been identified in the Kosal region. They were formed during the Late Pleistocene-Holocene climatic cycles going back to 128 Kyr B.P. influenced by neotectonics and base-level changes. These surfaces are depositional and have a cover of sediment, younger than the time of their formation.

(5) The Kosal region shows several neotectonic features, causing disruption of small tributaries and formation of undulatory topography. It produced a large number of ponds and lakes and areas of centripetal drainage.

(6) The interfluve surface in the form of Bhangar is the most widespread region showing many microgeomorphic features, like abandoned channel belts, segments, lakes and ponds, swamps, wetlands and alkaline soils in southern part of the cited region. These features developed in response to climatic change and neotectonic activity during the latest Pleistocene-Holocene.

(7) Palynological studies of lake deposit profiles have helped in the reconstruction of the palaeovegitation which indicates that the region was open grassland with a few forest thickets.

(8) The climate was humid with a short cycles of dryness during 50-25 Kyr B.P.; low rainfall from 25-13 Kr B.P.; 13-11.5Kyr B.P. high rainfall; 11.5-10.5 Kyr BP low rainfall; 10.5-5 Kyr BP high rainfall; 5-3.5 Kyr BP low rainfall.

(9) Teeth enamel studies from neighbouring area of archaeological sites indicate that the climate was humid around 3.5-3.0 Kyr BP, 160-0-1400 Yrs BP and 1300 Yrs BP. There are century scale rainfall fluctuations in the last 3500 yrs BP. Each cultural event begins with a relatively humid climate and culminates with drier climate.

(10) Albeit the oldest record of human occupation in the region was untraceable, but the oldest archaeological evidence of cultivated rice dates back 8000 yr BP from Lahuradeva confirm the early beginning of agriculture and inobvious evidence of human activity.

Part II

Kosal, which is mentioned in Panini's *Astadhyayi* (4.1.171) was one of the sixteen countries (*Mahajanpada*) of India as per *Anguttar Nikaya* (U\I, 213), albeit *Vishnupurana* (Chapter 4, *Ansa* 4) and *Bhagavatpurana* (IX.120,20; IX.11,22; X.2,3; X.58,52; X.86,20; XII.12,24) refers to it as a country. It lies to the east of *Kurus* and *Panchalas* and to the west of *Videhas* from whom as per *Satapath Brahmana* (I,4,11) it was separated by the river *Sadanira*, probably the great *Gandak* which emerges through the Siwalik Ranges at *Tribeni* on Indo-Nepal border and it joins the Ganga near Patna. The literal meaning of Kosal is the land of treasure and this has now been amply proved with its high fertility index of the alluvial land where earliest evidence of cultivation of rice is now archaeologically established.

At present the Kosal region (25°10' – 27°52'N; 80°12' – 84°16'E) extends from eastern part of western Ganga plain to western part of median Ganga plain or middle Ganga plain comprising the districts of Bahraich, Sravasti, Balrampur, Gorakhpur, Gonda, Basti, Siddharthnagar, Maharajganj, Deoria, Sant Kabirnagar, Faizabad, Jaunpur, Sultanpur, Pratapgarh, Rai Bareilly, Barabanki, Lucknow, Unnao, and Sitapur of Uttar Pradesh.

Locational and physiographic factors of a region have generally influenced the environmental characteristics of the same in the past. In the present context region means an area of the earth's surface with one or more features or characteristics (material on the result of human activity) which gives it a measure of unity and make it differ from the areas surrounding it. According to criteria used in the differentiation, a region may be termed as cultural, economic, morphological, natural, physiographic, political etc. Here environment is that which surrounds the sum total of the conditions of the surroundings within which group of living organism including man exists. It differs from the climate which deals with the average weather conditions (a general term for the conditions prevailing in the layer near the ground surface of the earth i.e. troposphere) throughout the seasons over a fairly wide or very extensive area of the earth's surface.

As to the relative significance of the climatic elements over primary human activities, it may be remarked that humidity and temperature along with soil profile make an impediment to the early farming economy over a considerable expansion of time and space in a particular area. Disability to the early farming economy in the yore was caused by uneven spatial distribution of moisture and precipitation on the surface of the area.

Structurally the region of Kosal is a segment of the great Indo-Ganga trough (depression in the surface of the earth) which cover an area of both Saryupar plain and Ganga-Ghaghara doab. Here the broad relief features of the entire Saryupar have a series of alluvial cones formed by master streams along with intercones or intervening slopes between them. Generally and quite naturally the intercones have lower gradients than the cores. On the other hand, south of it Ghaghara-Gandak interfluve is diagonally divided by Rapti as master stream, while other subsidiary streams of Burhi Rapti, Kuwana, Choti Gandak etc. There are numerous oxbow lakes, tals and dead or deserted channels of rivers on their banks ancient settlement is reported. The northern portion of Saryupar in Kosal has a moist belt of marshy lands locally known as tarai. Since the general slope of the plain in Kosal is from north-west to south-east, thus its primary river Ghaghara is the recipient of all drainage of the Saryupar west of Gandaka through its tributaries like Kunna, Rapti, Choti Gandak and other smaller ones.

The Saryupar Plain or trans-Śaryu plain is bounded on the south by Ghaghara and on the west by Gandak, extends north into the foothills of the Himalayas and forms a distinct archaeological entity. The Saryupar plain included the districts of Gorakhpur, Gonda, Basti, Balrampur, Bahraich, Sravasti, Siddharthnagar, Sant Kabirnagar, Deoria of eastern Uttar Pradesh. The Ghaghara and Rapti emanate from the Himalayas. The Kuwano (Kuana) springs from a lake having its source in the east of Bahraich and it flows through Gonda and Basti. It separates Gorakhpur district from the Basti district and then passes through the west of Pargana Dhuriapar of Gorakhpur district to join the Ghaghara near Shahpur. It is a meandering slow flowing river with a deep channel. The little Gandak rises from the Siwalik ranges and has a narrow bed passing through stabld land.

The Ghaghara, a highly notorious for its floods and changing courses and capacity of rendering vast agricultural tracts into sand flats. Other streams of the area like Rapti, although equally notorious deposit fertile silt and provide highly fertile agricultural tracts. This notoriety of the Saryu river can be well tested in the form of extensive zone of *majha* (outer marches) which stretches over a distance of 5 km upto the municipality area of Faizabad which was erstwhile a part of Kosal. This uncertain behaviour of basin of the rivers in the area of Kosal may engulf many ancient settlements. Thus the wide riverine deposit in Kosal area disturbed especially small early farming settlements. If it was not so happened in the yore, the settlement statistics of the Kosal area must be much greater than that of the present. The river piracy of the primary rivers in Kosal area by which a river, by rapid headward erosion, captures and diverts to itself the headwaters of another stream, thereby enlarging its own drainage area and diminishing that of other also disturbed many ancient settlements in the area, especially when brick was not in use.

Gomati and Sai are other important rivers which drained the southern part of the Kosal region. Gomati and Sai join the master stream of the Ganga. Sai is originating from the depression of tal in the bhangur tracts, which is flowing through Pratapgarh and Jaunpur districts and join the Gomati between Jaunpur and Varanasi. River Gomati is flowing through Lucknow, Sultanpur and Jaunpur and merged into Ganga at Kaithi in Varanasi.

Geomorphology

Tthe Kosal region having geomorphic surfaces of Upland Terrace Surface (T_2), Megafan Surface (MF), River Valley Terrace Surface (T_1). Piedmont Fan Surface (PF) and Active Flood Plain (T_0). It indicated some neotectonic activity after the formation of Piedmont fans in the Middle-Late Holocene, although mostly Piedmont Fan surfaces post dates the T_1 surface. In the Piedmont zone, there is evidence of ridge formation, related to the activity of Himalayan Frontal Thrust. The basement high of Faizabad -Vindhyan ridge strongly affected the geomorphology of the southern margin of the Ganga Plain. There is a strong evidence of upliftment of the southern Ganga Plain in the middle part located over the Faizabad -Vindhyan ridge.[17]

The interfluve areas (tract of land between two adjacent river) are beyond the reach of floods in the active rivers, which are invariably incised to occupy lower levels. The interfluve areas are not monotonous flat plains, but exhibits changes in vertical relief of several meters and have a variety of alluvial geomorphic features. Topographically, the whole region is made up of higher grounds of varied origin where most of the population centres are located; along the lower grounds having wetlands, ponds, lakes and agricultural land. The higher grounds are mostly in the form of mounds which are out of reach of any type of floods. This form of landscape has made the Kosal Plain as one of the most densely populated region of India. The geomorphic features of the upland interfluve areas are bandoned channel belts, channel segments, lakes and ponds, swamps, wetlands, alkaline soils, mound and alluvial sand ridges (bhur). The features developed in response to climatic change and neotectonic activity during Pleistocene Holocene. Some of these features have been studied in detail and have helped in the geomorphic response of the upland interfluve areas to climatic change, level change and neotectonics in the last 20 kyr.

The upland interfluve areas are depositional areas; though not receiving any sediment contribution from incised major rivers. The deposits of the interfluve surface are exposed in cliff sections of the rivers and in the cliffs of ravines, where about 20-30 m thick successions can be exposed. These deposits are distinctive muddy deposits and do not relate to the channel processes of the incised major rivers. They have been designated as Doab or Upland interfluve deposits. These deposits show a 20-50 m thick succession, with distinctive facies formed in specific domains of the upland interfluve region, namely small channels, sloping surfaces, flat surfaces, small lakes and ponds. These deposits often contain bedded calcrete horizons. The Doab deposits in the central alluvial plain are dated back to 507 Kyr B.P. It also indicates that at least for the last 50 Kyr, the main rivers (Ganga-Yamuna etc.) are incised in their plains.

The Gomati-Sai interfluve of Kosal region shows that the central part of interfluve 27°0'80°45" - 27°0'81°15' and 26°15'80°45' - 26°15'81°15' does not show any tributaries network of river channels, but clusters of lakes and ponds. In such area, pediment-water movement is essentially as non-channelized sheetflow and by a few poorly defined gulleys and channels. Such segments are 10-100 km^2 in area and exhibit independent sediment-water movement system, mostly showing central low lying part with ponds and swamps, surrounded by slightly elevated high grounds. These features are upto 10 kms. undulations with higher warped areas showing gullying and low lying areas of ponds and wetlands. The undulations are distinctly noted on regional slope profile. They appear as semi-circular to oblong areas of centripetal drainage, the higher parts are gradually eroded, while the lower parts accumulate sediments.[18] A large part of the upland interfluve surface, at present is not contributing any sediment-water to the tributary network of the Ganga River system, but is accumulating sediments on this surface itself. Presently, only 30% of the interfluve surface is drained by small, highly sinuous, underfit streams and theii minor tributaries, that are incapable of transporting any appreciable quantities of sediment load. About 70% area of the interfluve surface is part of the centripetal drainage system, accumulating significant amount of sediment.[19]

There are a few well-defined abandoned channel belts on the upland Terrace surface of older alluvium occupying tens kms. wide areas and running for several hundred kilometres. Presently, part of these channel belts act as linear sinuous lakes of considerable dimensions. They also exhibit cūt-off meander and ox-bow lakes. They are large drainages which were abandoned sometimes in Late Pleistocene. A prominent channel is present on Ganga-Sai interfluve traceable for few hundred kilometres. Spread on the interfluve surface are areas showing segments of channels and cut off meanders. They must also be parts of a large ancient drainage system. At present, these channel segments act as ephemeral to perennial lakes. Lakes and ponds of varied shape and dimensions are present all over the interfluve surface, often occupying in groups and clusters. They are local sinks of segment and water. There is evidence that initial large linear lakes became segmented into smaller ponds and clusters of pond through time.[20]

The cluster of remnant of the ancient horse-shoe lakes appears on the confluence of Tambura nala, a tributary of Pili Nadi which itself is a tributary of the Sai. During the rainy season these serve as natural drainage for the area. There are a number of lakes like Sanai Tal in district Rae Bareilly, Basha lake in district Unnao, Misa Tal, Lucknow, Lahuradewa lake in district Sant Kabir Nagar which is of a palaeo-ecological importance. Studies of lakes and ponds of the intefluve indicate that they evolved from river channels and most of the lakes formed during 85 Kyr BP. Some of the lakes formed in Late Pleistocene. The Aeolian sand of the alluvial ridge mostly formed around 5 Kyr BP. It has been also confirmed that tectonic pulses between 8-5 Kyr BP produce surface undulations in interfluve areas causing disruption and abandonment of minor tributaries. These tributaries transformed into liner lakes and later to smaller ponds due to increased siltation. The dry climate around 5 Kyr BP caused deposition of Aeolian sand on disrupted channel segments to make bhur ridges. The dry climate of 5 Kyr BP led to lowering of ground water and in warped up regions caused precipitation of $CaCO_3$ to produce bedded calcrete horizons which are mostly dated 3-4 Kyr BP. Formation of the bedded calcrete in the subsurface and impeded drainage on the surface produced closed circulating system of water. This led to the development of alkaline soils in the southern portion of Kosal. The pollens of the aforesaid lake sediments indicates palaeo-environment activities in the area. Palaeovegetational that the area was open grassland with a few thickets. Locally there may have been some forested areas. The data on palaeovegetation is from areas between Shahjahanpur in the west and Sant Kabir Nagar in the east and from the southern Ganga Plain covers a time span of around 80 kyr B.P. It can be argued that during the Late Quarternay the Ganga Plain was a grass land throughout its expanse with only few thickets of forest.

Climate

The entire Ganga Plain including Kosal region is located in the sub-tropical climate zone where rainfall is essentially controlled by the monsoon system. Originally, monsoon is applied to the regular winds of the Arabian sea, blowing from the southwest. Now generally applied to these some other kinds that blow with considerable regularity at definite seasons of the year due to the seasonal reversal of pressure over land masses and their neighbouring oceans, combined with the influence of Jet Streams. The southwest monsoon system affecting the Indian subcontinent. The southwest monsoon system becomes active in early June in Bengal, moves westward and by middle July extends over the entire Ganga Plain and continues until October. There is a change in the amount of annual rainfall from east to west, from about 1600 mm in Bengal, 900 mm in Bihar and eastern Uttar Pradesh and about 500 mm in western Uttar Pradesh. 90-80% of the rainfall occurs in the months of July to September due to the southwest monsoon. The annual seasonality in the area of Kosal can be classified into three seasons[21] –

(1) **Warm rainy (monsoon) season**—It extends from July to October and is characterised by high rainfall due to the southwest monsoon system. The daily mean maximum temperature is about 30°C, the diurnal range (day and night) is usually 5 – 10°C.

(2) **Cold dry season**—It extends from November to February and is characterised by low temperatures and low rainfall. The maximum temperature is 20 – 30°C; minimum temperature is 5 – 12°C in January. Diurnal range of temperature is 15 – 20°C and rainfall takes place due to western disturbances.

(3) **Hot dry Season**—It extends from March-June and is marked by high temperatures. Values in May reach 40-46°C. The diurnal range of temperature is 15 – 25°C.

The northwest dry wind dominates, there may be thunderstorms and dust storms.

Soil

Soil is the loose material of the earth's surface in which terrestrial plants grow, usually formed from weathered rock or regolith changed by physical, chemical and biological processes. Thus the soil may be considered as an entity, quite apart from the rocks below it. It consists partly of mineral particles and partly, to a varying extent, of organic humus. The mineral particles can be graded according to the proportion of the grade present the terms clay, soil, sandy soil etc. are also applied. A soil is said to be mature if it has a fully developed soil profile (a vertical soil showing the sequence of soil horizon downwards from the surface to the parent material), immature if it lacks a well-developed profile; truncated if it has lost all or part of the upper soil horizons.

The soil of the Kosal region is, by and large, homogeneous. The alluvial soils (an azonal soil on newly deposited alluvium) with the variants, the *Usar* and *bhur*, depending on the drainage conditions, mechanical and chemical constituents and the climatic characteristics are observed in its different parts. In addition, there are minor variations in certain proportions. As stated earlier, the two common types—the *Khaddar* (newer alluvium) and *Bhangar* (older alluvium) with different local names, which sometimes stand for minute variations in properties, are quite widespread. The *khadar* soils of west area Ganga Plain (or eastern Upper Ganga Plain) relatively rich in plant nutrients, occupy the narrow frequent siltation tract in the flood plains of rivers. Neutral to alkaline in reaction (pH 8-9) these are deficient in organic material especially phosphorous, and are sandy to loamy in texture. In Upper Ganga Plain khadar soils have immature profiles with sandy to silty loam texture, lack of concretion, fair proportion of lime and other soluble salts and are alkaline in reaction (pH 8-9) with imperfect drainage.

The *Khadar* newer in age than the *Bhangar* covers the flood plains in the vicinity of rivers including the lower reaches of smaller rivers and also the old beds, and is replenished annually by new deposits. They naturally remain moist and derive moisture from the rivers through seepage in dry period and are capable of growing crops without irrigation. They mostly consist of fine silts but may be sandy in places, as along the Ghaghara and the Gandak. Because of the better drainage in Middle Ganga Plain, except in river beds, newer alluvial soil contains a low percentage of humus and nitrogen and little lime. Being more sandy or silty, it is highly friable and is rich for the *bhadai*, rabi and zaid (especially root) crops and such annulas as sugarcane. Where it is underlain by hard pan, and contains more silt than sand, it is also suitable for rice cultivation.

The *Bhangar* is the older alluvium and covers the upland tracts beyond the annual flood limit in the valley flats. The *bhangar* soils are more extensive in areal spread, occpying the interfluvial zones. Relative consistency in the factors responsible for the soil development has provided it a somewhat mature profile with varying colours. In general the soluble salts and lime are low and show neutral to slightly acidic (pH 6 – 7.5) reaction except in the low-lying areas prone to water logging. Illuviation is a common characteristic everywhere. Illumination is the process by which material removed in suspension or solution from the upper part of a illuvial soil horizon is washed down and deposited in the lower layers of illuvial horizons. Unlike the *Khadar*, it is under process of denudation and contains patches of *usar* infestations, increasing towards the western portion of the Ganga-Ghaghara Doab. The formation of *Kankar* or nodular lime concretions through capillary action is also noticeable. The *Bhangar* soils grade from balua or sandy to clayey loamy, but are often heavier with higher clay factor in depressions. As such, it is sticky and is usually not well drained; it is richer in lime content and *kankar* than the *khadar*. It is more suitable for rice cultivation as it holds water with its hard clay pan.

The *Bhat* or calcareous soil of the eastern Saryupar is a chemical variant of the alluvial soil. It is white in colour, riverine and low-lying but well drained, good for tilth and highly fertile, containing as high as 25 to 30% of lime, a particular asset for growing sugarcane. The sub-soil is infested with beds of kankar.

The another variant of the alluvial soil is the Tarai soil, extending from northern-most strip in Deoria, Gorakhpur, Basti and beyond to the west, sharing with Nepal Tarai down the pebbly Bhadar zone. Owing to high rainfall (over 120 cm.) and almost continuous seepage of water from the Bhabar zone and highly riverain nature of the tract, these soils have developed under constantly moist conditions. They are highly leached heavy clayey soils, and provide moist conditions for rich rice crops.

Natural Vegetation

The literary text[22] mentioned *Anjanvana*, which was located in *Saket* and *Mahavana* in Kapilvastu. As some distance from Kaushambi and near Sravasti were *Parileyyakavana*, which was inhabited by elephants. On the bank of Rohini, *Lumbinivana* was also a natural forest. *Devi Purana* referred *Naimisaranya* or Nimisha famous forest in Sitapur district and the hermitage of sage *Valmiki* on the bank of the Ganga in the area now a part of the Unnao district, Khandav of the Mahabharat and other such fragmentary reference throw sufficient light on the predominance of natural forest vegetation in the past. But today there exist a few small patches of woodland in the Kosal region.

These literary references do not show the area was covered with a continuing dense forest. Instead, some localized forests located at certain places. If there was a continuous forest spread, there would have been no need to specify different names. The locations of these forests indicate that most of them were in the northern and north-eastern parts of the Ganga Plain (Kosal region) which comprise the Himalayan foothills (Terai and Bhabar) and the middle Ganga Plain. The average annual rainfall (100 – 200 cm) in these areas is comparatively more than that of the Upper Ganga Plain (100 cm). In the district Bahraich of the Tarai region the forested area covers only 13% of the area.

The forests can be grouped as tropical moist deciduous, tropical wet and sub-tropical dry. Tropical moist deciduous forests are confined to the Tarai areas. The remnants of the once extensive *Sal* (Sakhu) forests are found in northern

Gorakhpur. Elsewhere, the induced vegetation is seen in the form of Savanna with grasses and bush (mainly xerophytes) land dotted with trees of different sizes. The village wastelands or vacant places are covered by naturally growing trees like the *peepal, banyan, tamarind, Babul, dhak*, date palm, etc. while such grasses as bher, moonj, kans, jhau etc. are forms in the diaras, Tarai or other low lying areas, and the more omnipotent dub, motha, and other less pervasive types are found in the cultivated fields and mounds or field boundaries and left over lands. The planted fruit orchards and groves of trees consist of *mango, jamun, guava, mahua, jack fruit, plums, lemon* etc. and also timber trees like *shisham* etc., while *bamboo* clumps grow around and within settlements. In most of the districts of Kosal region like Pratapgarh and Faizabad, the forest cover is negligible only 0.11%, Deoria 60.23%, Sultanpur 0.41%, Basti 0.91%. In the Saryupar, some parts of more humid and riverain, and other detached pockets of Gorakhpur, Gonda and Bahraich districts have appreciable forest cover and swell the district figures in percent of the total area of 8.7, 9.1 and 14.3, respectively. The district of Pratapgarh have remnant of Dhak and Sihore trees. The ancient site of Damdama was surrounded by patches of forest. On account of human encroachment the area at present is devoid of trees and it is getting converted into alkaline *usar* land. These *usar* soils have many undecomposed rock and mineral fragments, which with weathering liberate sodium, magnesium and calcium salts and sulphurous acid. By this fact the *usar* land are notably impervious and, therefore, have impeded drainage. Large areas, once fertile during Mesolithic phase have become impregnated with value of the ground.

The salts are confined on the top layers of the soil horizon, being transferred from below by capillary action.

Palaeoenvironment

The Pollen analysis of perennial lake Lahuradeva Lake[24] (26°46'N; 82°50'30"E) having cultural deposit from *circa* 2000 B.C. to Early Historic Period throw a fresh light on the palaeoenvironment of the Kosal area during Holocene period. Pollen analysis is the analysis of pollen grains[25] preserved in soil or peal and of fossil pollen and other microfossils highly resistant to acids found in sedimentary rocks of all ages, the findings providing valuable environmental indicators and aids to strategraphic correlation.

Pollen analysis of Holocene Period at Lahuradeva confirm both the presence of terrestrial (plants growing on land or to the earth surface) and aquatic (plants growing in or frequenting in water) plants in which aquatic plants and spores of ferns have local source of origin, while few of the terrestrial have not locally originated, but it migrated from other places, whose climatic condition is different from the climatic condition of Kosal. Five different Pollen zones from 2.80 meter deep to the surface of the earth have constructed and each zone is dated by radiocarbon method too. Thus this pollen sequence confirm the five type of minor climatic fluctuation in the area of Kosal since 10425 B.P. to 950 B.P. i.e. from *circa* 8000 B.C. to 1000 A.D. in a following manner:

Pollen Zone I (2.8 to 2.5 m. deep from the present center surface). The time span as per radiocarbon date of this deposit is from 10600 to 9250 B.P., means it covers early phase of Holocene. It has open vegetation dominated by grass (60 to 80%) and scattered trees. Presence of aquatic pollen of *Potamogrton Typha* and *Botryococcus* confirm the existence of lake in the area. Thus the climate during early phase of Holocene in area of Kosal was cool with reduced monsoon rainfall can be postulated on the presence of high frequency of gracers with less frequency of angiospermic[26] trees. Human activities in the vicinity of lake are inferred from the record of culture pollen texa viz. *Rumex, Artemisia, Chenopodiaceae*[27] / *Amaranthaceae*[28] which all are fruit producing plants.

Pollen Zone II (2.5 to 2.1 m from the present earth surface, above to the Pollen Zone I deposit). This zone covering a temporal range of 9,250 to 6400 BP as per caliberated radiocarbon dates. Grasses (61-70%) is again recorded with much higher frequencies like Pollen Zone I, whereas the other terrestrial plants remain the same as before. But this zone of pollen demonstrates the dominance of non-arboreals and sporadic presence of arboreals (climbing plants) confirm amelioration in climate, and in contrast to previous one, in this phase of time in the area of Kosal there is an increase in monsoon rainfall. This can be assumed by the fact that Lahuradeva Lake becomes wider as indicated by the preponderance of aquatic plants. First appearance of cereals around 7000 BP suggestive of agricultural activities.

Pollen Zone III (2.1 to 1.7 m. from the present earth surface which is above to the deposit of Pollen Zone II). This pollen zone encompassing the chronological range of 6400 to 4050 BP demonstrate further improvement in terrestrial plants i.e. trace. Among the non-arboreals grasses (57-34%) decline further in this pollen zone. The marshy elements decline considerably. Enhancement in agricultural practices is demonstrated by the marked increase in the cereal and other culture pollen taxa in 5000 BP. The presence of *Trapa* (Singhara) pollen in higher frequency in 5000 BP confirm further increase in monsoon rainfall than the previous one. By this fact aquatic plant fruits would have been a means of subsistence for settlers. Thus during this phase (6400-4060 BP) of Holocene, the region of Kosala have maximum monsoon rainfall by which alluvial deposit of the area become more thicker.

Pollen Zone IV (1.7 to 0.70 m. deep from the present earth surface, above to the deposit of Pollen Zone III) have time bracket of 4050 to 1300 BP depicts the maximum expansion of arboreals and contemporary decline of gracers (59-29%). Long distance transported pollen of *Pinus* (3-12%) has confirmed a high wind flows from north to south-east direction. Groves of forests turned more dense and diversified as demonstrated by the increased frequencies of tree taxa. Further acceleration in agricultural practice is demonstrated by marked increase in cereals and other related cultural pollen taxa. Since during this time of span, the monsoon rainfall is of moderate type by which Lahuradeva lake swamp transformed into sediments in their base. There is sharp reduction in aquatic plants which is also ample testimony of moderate rainfall. Thus from *Cica* 2000 B.C. to 700 A.D. the climate of Kosal was moderate for human habitation which is confirmed by the archaeological settlements of the area too.

Pollen Zone V (0.70 m deep from the earth surface) have time span of three hundred years from 1300 BP to 1040 BP, there is a sharp reduction in the frequency of arboreals and improvement in non-arboreals confirm a reduction in annual monsoon rainfall. Agricultural practice continued with same pace as before as no significant changes noticed in the cerial and other associated cultural pollen taxa. Lahuradeva lake shrunk and assumed the present ephemeral status as depicted by the meager aquatic vegetation. Since 1300 BP to the present time the decline in the frequency of trees barring the dry element in the climate of Kosal region. It is also confirmed by the arboreal vegetation became sparse in forest groves as a consequence of reduction in monsoon rainfall and human interference. The consistent occurrence of pollen of *Pinus* in high frequency along with other temperate elements *picea, Alnus, Rutula* and *Carpinus* indicates their transportation by wind from the nearby Himalayan region where all these plants are abundant.

References

1. Bajpai, V. (1989), "Surface and Subsurface Evidences of Neotectonic and Aquifer Deposition in Central Alluvial Terrain of Kanpur-Unnao Region in Uttar Pradesh, India," *Photonirvachak, Journal of the Indian Society of Remote Sensing*, 17: pp. 47-53.
2. Singh, I.B. (1999), "Tectonic Control of Sedimentation in Ganga Plain Foreland Basin: Constraints on Siwalik Sedimentation Models in Geodynamism of the NW Himalaya," *Gondwana Research Group Memoir* (A.K. Jain and R.M. Manickavasagam, eds.), 6, pp 247-262.
3. Singh, I.B. (1996), "Late Quaternary Sedimentation of Ganga Plain Foreland Basin," Proceeding. *Symposium NW Himalaya and Foredeep*, Feb. (1995) Geological Survey of India, Special Publication No. 21(1), pp. 161-172.

4. Singh, I.B. (2005), "Land Form Development and Palaeoenvironment Vegetation in Late Quaternary of Ganga Plain: Implications for Anthropogenic Activity," *Pragdhara*, 15, p.

5. Singh, R.L. (1973), (ed.). *India: A Regional Geography*. Varanasi: National Geographical Society of India.

6. Singh, I.B. (1999) *op.cit.*

7. Oldham, R.D. (1917), "The Structure of Himalayas and the Gangetic Plain as Elucidated by Geodetic Observations in India," *Memoirs, Geological Survey of India*, 42: p. 1-153.

   Pilgrim, G.E. (1919), "Suggestions Concerning the History of the Drainage of Northern India Arising Out of a Study of the Siwalik Boulder Conglomerate," *Journal of Asiatic Society of Bengal*, 15, pp. 81-99.

   Pascoe, E.H. (1973), *Manual of Geology of India and Burma* (Vol. I-III). Delhi: Government of India Publications.

8. Singh, I.B. and D.K. Ghosh (1992), "Interpretation of Late Quaternary Geomorphic and Tectonic Features of Gangetic Plain using Remote Sensing Techniques." Proceedings National Symposium on Remote Sensing and Sustainable Development, Lucknow.

9. Kumar, G., P.C. Khanna and S. Prasad (1996), "Sequence Stratigraphy of the Foredeep and the Evolution of Indo-Gangetic Plain, Uttar Pradesh." Proceedings of *Symposium NW Himalaya and Foredeep*, Feb. 1995, Geological Survey of India, Special Publication No. 21 (2), pp. 173-207.

10. Singh, I.B. (1999), *op.cit.*

11. Shukla, U.K., I.B. Singh, M. Sharma and S. Sharma (2001), "A Model of Alluvial Megafan Sedimentation: Ganga Megafan Sedimentary." *Geology*, 144, pp. 243-262.

12. Singh, I.B. (1996), "Geological Evolution of Ganga Plain—An Overview," *Journal of Paleoontological Society, India*, 41: pp. 99-137.

13. Kumar, G. (1996), *op.cit.*

14. Singh, I.B. (1987), "Sedimentological History of Quaternary Deposits in Gangetic Plain." *Indian Journal of Earth Sciences*, 14: pp. 272-282.

Srivastava, P., I.B. Singh, M. Sharma and A.K. Singhvi (2003a), "Luminescence Chronometry and Late Quaternary Geomorphic History of the Ganga Plain, India, "*Palaeogeography, Palaeoclimatology, Palaeoecology*, 197: pp. 15-41.

15. Singh, I.B. (2001), "Proxy Records of Neotectonics, Climate Changes and Anthropogenic Activity in the Late Quaternary of Ganga Plain." *National Symposium Role of Earth Sciences Integrated Development and Related Societal Issue*, Geological Survey of India, Special Publication, No. 65 (I) 2001: xxxiii-1.

16. "Siwalik Sedimentation Models in Geodiagrams of the NW Himalaya, Gondwana." *Research Groups Memoire* (A.K. Jain and R.M. Manickavasagam, eds.), 6, pp. 247-262.

17. Singh, I.B. (2004), "Late Quaternary History of the Ganga Plain," *Journal of Geological Society of India*, 64, pp. 431-454.

18. Srivastava, P. (1998), "Sedimentology and Geomorphology of Interfluve Areas of Central Ganga Plain," Ph.D. Thesis, Lucknow University.

Singh, I.B. (1999), "Tectonic Control of Sedimentation in Ganga Plain Foreland Basin. Constraints on

19. Sharma, M., H.J. Tobschall and I.B. Singh (2003), "Environmental Impact Assessment in Moradabad Industrial Area (River-Ramganga-Ganga Interfluve), Ganga Plain, India," *Environmental Geology* 43, pp. 957-967.

Singh, I.B. (2002), "Late Quaternary Evolution of Ganga Plain and Proxy Records of Climate Change and Anthropogenic Activity," *Pragdhara* 12 (2001-2002), p. 1-25.

20. Srivastava, P., I.B. Singh, S. Sharma, U.K. Shukla and A.K. Singhvi (2003b), "Late Pleistocene-Holocene Hydrologic Changes in the Interfluve Areas of Central Ganga Plain, India," *Geomorphology*, 54, pp. 279-292.

21. Singh, I.B. (2005), "Quaternary Paleoenvironments of the Ganga Plain and Anthropogenic Activity," *Man and Environment*, XXX (1), p. 14.
22. *Ibid.*, p. 5.
23. Tiwari, Rakesh (2004), "The Myth of Dense Forests and Human Occupation in the Ganga Plain." *Man and Environment*, XXIX (2), p. 105.
24. Chauhan, M.S., Pokharia A.K. and Singh, I.B. (2009), "Pollen Record of Holocene Vegitation Climate Change and Human Habitation from Lahuradeva Lake, Sant Kabir Nagar, District Uttar Pradesh," *Man and Environment* XXXIV (1), pp. 88-100.
25. Pollen in the very fine powder (microspores) carrying the male element of seed producing plants, each grain of pollen i.e. each microspore, containing a (much reduced) male gametophyte. The pollen grains are carried by wind, insects, birds or water to the female parts of the plant where pollen tubes containing the male nuclei develop and eventually penetrate the embryo sac.
26. Angiosperm is a group of plant producing seeds enclosed in an ovary (unlike a Gymnosperm). The angiosperms succeeded the gymnosperms in dominant land plants having gained ascendancy by the end of the cretaceous period. Most seed bearing plants today are angiosperms which grow in a moderate rainfall.
27. Chenopodiaceae is a family of the centrospermae in which stipule are absent. There are 3.5 lobes to the calyx which may be fused. There are no petals.

3

Archaeological Sites in Kosal Region

At present the Kosal region extends from eastern part of upper Ganga plain to western part of middle Ganga plain comprising the districts of Gorakhpur, Bahraich, Sravasti, Gonda, Sant Kabir Nagar, Balrampur, Basti, Deoria, Faizabad, Barabanki, Jaunpur, Pratapgarh, Sultanpur, Lucknow and Unnao. A large number of ancient settlements ranging from Mesolithic period to Medieval period have been reported from the Kosal region. But only twenty four settlements have been excavated so far and that too vertically. Although some of the extensively excavated sites throw ample light on the idea of the settlement-pattern of the region. The excavated settlements of the Kosal region are as follows:—

1. Narhan (26°19'N; 83°24'E)

Narhan[1] is located on the left bank of the Ghaghara river in the Gola, sub-division of Gorakhpur district in eastern Uttar Pradesh. The archaeological excavations were conducted during 1983-88 by the department of Ancient Indian History, Culture and Archaeology, Banaras Hindu University under the direction of Professor Purushottam Singh. The site has yielded a culture sequence divisible into five periods and ranging in date from the second millennium B.C. to the seventh century A.D..

Period I	-	Painted Black-and-Red ware (Narhan Culture) (1300 B.C. – 800 B.C.)
Period II	-	Black slipped and associated wares (800 B.C. – 600 B.C.)
Period III	-	Red ware, thick grey ware and Northern Black Polished Ware (600 B.C. – 200 B.C.)
Period IV	-	Shunga-Kushan Red ware (200 B.C. – 300 A.D.)
Period V	-	Red ware of Gupta Period and associated antiquities. (300 A.D. – 600 A.D.)

2. Imlidih Khurd (26°30'30"N; 83°12'5"E)

Imlidih Khurd[2] is situated in district Gorakhpur of Uttar Pradesh about 80 km. to the west of Narhan in the Sarayupar plain was excavated by Prof. Purushottam Singh of Dept. of A.I.H.C. & Arch, Banaras Hindu University in the year 1992. The ancient settlement has extended in an area of 15 to 20 acres, divided into three cultures—

Period I	-	Cord-impressed and the associated antiquities (Pre 1300 B.C.)
Period II	-	Narhan Culture (1300 – 800 B.C.)
Period III	-	The absence of Black-and-Red Ware, the dominance of Black Slipped Ware (comparable to that of period II of Narhan) (800-400 B.C.)

3. Dhuriapar (26°25’25”N; 83°14’30”E)

The ancient settlement of Dhuriapar[3] is located on the left bank of the Kuwano river about 46 km south of Gorakhpur and 25 km. west of Narhan. The ancient settlement presently spreads over a length of about 1.5 km, along the river bank and trial digging was carried out by Prof. P. Singh of Banaras Hindu University in April-May 1991. The excavation revealed a total cultural deposit of 2 to 5 m. which is divided into five periods—

Period I	-	Narhan Culture (1300 B.C. – 600 B.C.)
Period II	-	NBPW (600 B.C. - 200 B.C.)

Period III	-	Kushan-Gupta (200 B.C.- 500 A.D.)
Period IV	-	Early Medieval (900 A.D. - 1500 A.D.)
Period V	-	British period

4. Sohgaura (26°28'N; 83°47'E)

The site[4] is located on the confluence of river Rapti and Ami in district Gorakhpur of Uttar Pradesh. The site was excavated by Professor G.C. Pandey in 1961-62 and re-excavated by Dr. S.N. Chaturvedi of Gorakhpur University in 1974-75. The excavation yielded five cultural period is as follows—

Period I	-	Handmade pottery with matt mpressed
Period II	-	Plain and Painted Black Slipped Ware, Plain and Painted Black and Red Ware, Grey and Red Ware
Period III	-	NBPW
Period IV	-	Kushan
Period V	-	Medieval times

5. Lahuradeva (26°16'N; 82°57'E)

The ancient site of Lahuradeva [5] is located in the district of Sant Kabir Nagar in the Saryupar region. The site is in the form of a mound elevated to a height of about 400 m from the surrounding levels. A lake surrounds it from the north, the west and the south. The ground level of the lake is rising day by day due to siltation mainly caused by the agricultural activity in its dried up northern and southern portions. The western portion of the lake still comprises sufficient water in all the seasons. During the rainy season the lake is completely filled with water. The excess water of the lake spills over through a *nālā* into the Katanahia River, which flows about 1.0 to 0.5 km to the west of the lake. The Katanahia River emerges from a lake upstream and is a tributary of the Kuwano River, which meets the Gaghara River. Originally the mound of Lahuradeva would have extended over an area of about 500 m in east-west and about 200 m in north-south directions. A large portion in the east and small portion of the peripheral parts of the mound have been levelled in order to make agricultural fields. Presently the mound measures about 220 m in east-west and 140 m in north-south directions. The mound to the west of the village is well known because of a temple '*Samai mai-ka-than*' located on it. The Lahuradeva site is about 5 km south to the Bhujaini Crossing, is situated between Basti and Gorakhpur on National Highway No. 28 and comes under Khalilabad tahsil of the newly formed district of Sant Kabir Nagar. The site was excavated in 2002-3, 2003-4, 2005-6 by Dr. Rakesh Tiwari of U.P. State Archaeological Department, Lucknow. About 3 m. thick occupational deposit revealed five-fold cultural sequence—

Period I	-	Early Farming Phase
Period II	-	Developed Farming Phase
Period III		Advance Farming / Early Iron Age
Period IV		NBPW Phase
Period V		Early Historic (Early Centuries B.C./A.D.)

6. Sravasti (27°31'N; 82°2'E)

In the district of Sravasti[6] (formerly district Gonda-Bahraich), the capital of Kosal, a city intimately associated with the lives of Buddha and Mahavira when Prasenjit was the ruler. The ruins consists of two distinct units—Sahet, the Buddhist establishment, and Maheth to its n.e., a fortified city—separated from each other by a low-lying land probably an ancient bed of the Rapti, ancient *Achiravati*, on the bank of which Sravasti was situated. During the life time of Buddha his disciple *Sudatta-Anathapindaka* raised here a monastery, the *Jetavana-vihara*, for the residence of Buddha and that became the nucleus of the Buddhist establishment of the place. Ashoka is said to have put up two capital pillars near the e.gate of the Jetavana-vihara.

The site has attracted the attention of archaeologists right from the days of A. Cunningham. The excavation was conducted here by J. Ph. Vogel, J. Marshall and D. R. Sahni between 1907-08 and 1910-11, as a result of which numerous stupas, monasteries and temples, consistent with its sacredness to the Buddhists, have been exposed at Saheth within an irregular compound wall. The earliest of them go back to Kushan times; the latest datable object is a copper plate of *Gahadavala* ruler *Govindachandra* (12th century A.D.) granting land to the *Jetavana* monastery, which unassailably established once for all the identity of Saheth-Maheth with Sravasti.

Mahet, the city site, its rampart crescantic in shape, with a circuit of about 5 km. and a height of 18 m, lies about 1 km to the south of the Rapti. The prominent land marks here are the Sobhanath temple on a high mound believed to be the birth place of the tirthankara Sambhavanath, Pakki Kuti and Kacchi Kuti, the latter two perhaps originally Buddhist stupas but at least the second one converted into a Brahmanical temple in Gupta times, as is evident from the discovery of a large number of Ramayana panels from its debris.

Resumed excavation at Mahet in 1959-59 by the ASI under K.K. Sinha has yielded significant evidence on the antiquity of the city. The excavation revealed three periods—

Period I	-	6th century to 300 B.C,
Period II	-	early phase: 275 to 200 B.C.
		Middle phase 200 to 125 B.C.
		Late phase: 125 to 50 B.C.
Period III	-	early centuries of the Christian era.

Again this site was jointly excavated by Excavation Branch III, Archaeological Survey of India, Patna and Consai University, Suita, Osaka, Japan under B.S. Raman, Yoshinori Aboshi and others during field season 1986-87 and 1987-88. The excavations of both the seasons revealed the earliest material related to Sunga-Kushan period. Further excavation was jointly conducted by Excavation Banch III, Archaeological Survey of India, Patna and Consai University, Suita, Osaka, Japan under L.C. Singh, Yoshinori Aboshi and others during field season 1992-93. Four cultural deposits were recovered. Earliest culture i.e. Period I belongs to Pre-NBPW and Period II was associated with NBPW Period. During season 1993-94, the above team excavated the area and found late NBPW Periods as earliest deposit. Once again excavation in this area at Orajhar mound was conducted by Lucknow circle, Archaeological Survey of India during season 1999-2000 and 2000-2001. The excavation was conducted at Kushan Period's stupa.

7. Piprahwa (27°26'N; 83°7'E)

Piprahwa[7] is located in district Basti now in Siddharthnagar near the border of Nepal, well known for having yielded one of the earliest relic caskets with Brahmi inscription in the excavation by Peppe, an English zamindar of the area, who bored a shaft in the stupa in 1897-8. P.C. Mukherjee conducted limited excavation here in 1899. On the basis of the inscription on the casket, he felt that Kapilvastu, the capital of Sakyas to which clan Buddha belonged, should be sought not very far from it. Mitra in 1972 also declared that Piprahwa had a reasonable claim for being a part or suburb of Kapilvastu and its surrounding villages like Ganwaria being the site of Kapilvastu itself. Apart from the view of previous explorers, the inscription on the casket found by Peppe implied that the relic-yielding stupa was the same as the one that the Sakyas constructed at Kapilvastu over their share of the corporeal relics of Buddha received by them. Secondly, the distance of 9 miles (14.48 kim) from Kapilvastu to Lumbini as recorded by the Chinese traveller Fa Hein corresponds well to the distance from Piprahwa to Lumbini, the birth place of Buddha.

To settle the long-standing controversy, K.M. Srivastava started excavation at the site in 1971 on behalf of the A.S.I. In 1972 he came across fresh relic caskets contained in two burnt brick chambers at a depth of 6 m, i.e. further below the massive box found by Peppe. The two soapstone (steatite) caskets contained charred bones. The caskets were contemporaneous with the NBPW. In 1973 the cells and the veranda on the north side of the e-monastery yielded terracotta sealing with the legend Kapilavastu. The sealings have not been found in a hoard but occurring at difference levels and spot ranging between 1.05 and 1.75 m depth. The legend on the sealings in Brahmi characters of the 1st-2nd centuries A.D. can be classified into three groups. One of them reads *Devaputra vihara Kapilvastu-bhikkhusanghasa* and the second *Maha-Kapilvastu-bhiksusanghasa,* while the third carries name of monks one being *Sarandasa.* The inscription on the sealings and the lid was the deciding evidence in the identification of Kapilvastu. The excavation yielded the occupation approximately from the 5th century B.C. to 3rd century A.D.

8. Ganwaria (27°26'N; 83°7'E)

Ganwaria[8] is located 1 km. south-west of Piprahwa, plausibly identified with Kapilvastu, the capital of the Sakyas. This identification has been confirmed by the excavation of 1977-78 by K.M. Srivastava which yielded terracotta sealings and the lid of a pot with the legend *Kapilavastu*. The excavation also brought to light extensive structural remains and a rich assemblage of antiquities. The occupational deposit can be divided into four periods—

Period I	-	(c. 800 – 600 B.C.) BSW, fine grey ware, red ware
Period II	-	(c 600 to 200 B.C.) NBPW, red painted in Black Ware
Period III	-	(200 B.C. to the beginning of the Christian era);
Period IV	-	Kushan (beginning of the Christian era to the 4th century A.D.)

9. Siswania (26°45'N; 82°46'E)

The archaeological site of Siswania[9] is located in district Basti of Uttar Pradesh. The site was identified in 1991 and excavated by Dr. B.R. Mani, Director, Institute of Archaeology, New Delhi, in 1995-96 and 1996-97 with ancient city of Setavya.. The extension of Siswania mound from village Deoraon in the north upto villages Tarijot and Pachisa in the south along the left bank of river Kuwano or Kuwana, a tributary of Sarayu (Ghaghara) and the proximity of much revered river shrine of Bhadreswarnatha where the river forming a loop flows to some distance towards north (*Uttar vahini*) and then turns to south-east, definitely indicates great importance of the site. The famous *Payasisutta* of the *Dighanikaya* mentions about the discourse by *Kumara Kassapa* to *Payasi Rajanya* on the rebirth and karma in the Simsapavana to the north of *Setavya nagara* in Kosala kingdom; the name of Simsapavana or the grove of Simsapa or Sisam tree (*Dalbergia Sisu*) is still preserved in the name of the place Siswania, 9 km towards south east of Basti city on the left bank of Kuwano. Three mounds in a series are found along the river in north-south orientation in an area of approximately 1000 x 300 m, and have been designated as SWN-1, SWN-2 and SWN-3.

Setavya is also mentioned in the *Vatthugatha* of the *Parayanavagga* of Sutta-Nipata in the context of Bavaris story who despatched a group of scholars to get answers to some metaphysical questions from Buddha, who travelled to *Savatthi* (Sravasti) and then to *Setavya*, *Kapilvastu* (Kapilvastu), *Kusinara*, *Pava* and *Vaisali*.

The aforementioned areas of SWN-1, SWN-2 and SWN-3 separated by water-channels along the River Kuwano in north-south orientation Mounds at SWN-2 and SWN-3 were found badly damaged due to extensive cultivation and levelling of the area. The main mound at SWN-1 was found in better state of preservation than the others, although the top layers have suffered some damage due to the levelling of the ground for cultivation and some building activities in late

Medieval Period. The deposits revealed a sequence of four cultural periods—

Period I	-	Pre-NBPW (circa 10th-9th century BCE)
Period II	-	NBPW (circa 9th-3rd century BCE)
Period III	-	Sunga Period (circa 2nd – 1st century BCE)
Period IV	-	Kushan period (circa 1st – 3rd century CE)

10. Charda (27°56'45"N; 81°36'40"E)

The mound of Charda[10] Jamogh is situated on Babaganj-Malhipur road, at a distance of about 3 km from Dabaganj, a local market on Bahraich-Rupaidiha road. It is 48 km. north of District headquarters Bahraich, 16 km. from Tehsil headquarters Nanpara. It is spread over an area of 470 x 312 m, and about 7 meters high from the surrounding surface. It is bow shaped and resembles with the shape of Mahet of Sravasti in its plan which is called the Karmuk type of settlement[11]. The site was reported by A. Fuherer[12] with an additional name Chahardah as ruins of Buddhist city. According to the local tradition this was fourteenth of the chain of forts which accounts for the name of the place Charda. Like all the other remains of the district, it is assigned to Raja Suhel Deo[2] , the opponent of Sayid Salar, but it is assigned to Raja Suhel Deo, the opponent of Sayid Salar, but it is evidently of earlier origin, and its construction may be assigned to the Buddhist.

The site is located on the alluvial plain land of Himalayan *terai* near the international boundary of India and Nepal. Geologically it is a part of Gangetic alluvium. The ranges of Himalayan foothills are about 20 km towards north and north-east and are visible from the site after rains. The main river of the area is Rapti, which after flowing through Nepal, about 152 km, enters in pargana Charda, of Bahraich district to the east of village Kundwa and demarcates the international boundary between India and Nepal. The site was excavated by Prof. D.P. Tiwari of Department of A.I.H. & Archaeology, Lucknow University in 1999-2000. The entire habitational deposit at Charda has been divided into four periods viz.

Period I	-	Pre-NBPW (ninth-tenth century B.C.)
Period II A	-	NBPW (eight to second Century B.C.)
Period II B	-	Absence of NBPW (Second Century B.C, to First Cent. A.D.)
Period III	-	Kushan-Gupta (1st to sixth centuiry A.D.)
Period IV	-	Post-Gupta and Early Medieval (sixth to 10th Cent. A.D.)

11. Pirvitanisarif-Trilokpur (27°50'30-50"N; 81°36'40-50"E)

The mound of Trilokpur[13] locally known as Pirvitanisarif/Takia is situated on the border of Sravasti and Bahraich districts of Uttar Pradesh. Although the whole area was under Bahraich district but its tahsils viz. Ikauna, Bhinga and Payagpur were merged in Sravasti, a newly constituted district. The district boundary line passes through this mound. Consequently the major area of Pirvitanisarif and nearby village Takia lie in Nanpara tahsil of Bahraich district and Trilokpur lies in Jamunaha block of Bhinga tahsil of Sravasti district. The place Pirvitanisarif was named after Pir Vitan Shah, a soldier of Sayid Salar Masud, who was slain here. The mound lies in Rapti-Ghaghara doab near the foothills of Himalaya Shiwaliks. The mound is five meters high from the surrounding ground level. A small lake known as Karbala Jhil lies in the east to the mound. The site was excavated in 2000-2001 by Dr. Devi Prasad Tiwari of the Department of A.I.H. & Archaeology, Lucknow University. The maximum thickness of the deposit on the site was recorded 4.54 m in trench A1 laid on the highest and central part of the mound. The entire deposit was divided into five cultural periods:

Period I	NBPW
Period II	Shunga
Period III	Kushan
Period IV	Gupta
Period V	Medieval

12. Ayodhya (26°48'N; 82°14'E)

Ayodhya[14] is situated in district Faizabad, Uttar Pradesh, on the right bank of River Saryu. Ayodhya was the capital of the Kosala kingdom, one of the kings of which was Rama regarded by Hindus as an incarnation of Vishnu. The city also finds reference in Buddhist and Jaina texts. It is believed to have been the birthplace of the first and fourth Jaina Tirthankaras and Buddha is also stated to have stayed here for some time. Thus, traditional and literary associations have cast a halo around the place. To check up archaeologically the antiquity of Ayodhya and other sites associated with the Ramayana story the ASI and the Indian Institute of Advanced Study under the direction of Prof. B.B. Lal Ayodhya was excavated in 1978. Earlier the Banaras Hindu University had also laid a couple of trenches here. The site was again re-excavated by the order of Hon'ble High Court of Lucknow in the year of 2003 under the direction of Sri Hari Manjhi and Dr. B.R. Mani of A.S.I.

The ruins at Ayodhya have a circuit of about 4 to 5 km and rise at places to a height of about 10 m. above the surrounding ground level. Exploratory trenches laid down about half a dozen spots which include the famous Janmabhumi area and lands close to Hanumangarhi, Sita-ki Rasoi, Asharji Mahal etc. Earlier excavation which was done by Prof. B.B. Lal revealed the ancient habitation was started here since Northern Black Polished and continued upto 11th Century A.D. The aim of the excavation of 2003 by Archaeological Survey of India is to confirm the anomaly of the GPR Survey comprises in 132 trenches, but cutting 90 trenches of 5 x 5 meter. The eight working floor and 22 pillar bases which were expected by GPR anomalies was confirmed by the excavation *in situ*. The cultured sequence of the working floor is as follows—

Period VI (11-12th Century A.D.) ⟶ First Floor
Period VII A (12th Century A.D.) ⟶ Second Floor
Period VII B (13th Century A.D.) ⟶ Third Floor
Period VII C (14 - 15th Century A.D.) ⟶ Fourth Floor
Period VIII (Mughal Period) ⟶ Fifth and Sixth Floor
Period IX (Late Mughal Period) ⟶ Seventh and Eighth Floor

The cultural sequence of Ayodhya, as per its excavation in 2005 by the order of the Hon'ble High Court, Lucknow is as follows—

Period IX (Late and Post-Mughal) ⟶ Glazed Ware, Red Ware, Black Slipped Ware

Period VIII (Mughal) ⟶ Glazed Ware, Red Ware, Black Slipped Ware

Period VIII (Medieval, 1200 A.D. - 1600 A.D.) ⟶ Glazed Ware, Red Ware, Black Slipped Ware

Period VI (Sultan Period, 1000 A.D.-1200 A.D.) ⟶ Red Ware, Black Slipped Ware, Grey Ware

Period V (Post Gupta-Rajput, 700 A.D. - 1000 A.D.) ⟶ Red Ware, Grey Ware, NBPW

Period IV (Gupta, 400 A.D.-600 A.D.) ⟶ Red Ware, Black Slipped Ware, NBPW

Period III (Kushan, 100 AD – 300 AD) ⟶ Red Ware, Black Slipped Ware, NBPW

Period II (Sunga, 300 BC – 100 BC) ⟶ NBPW, Red Ware, Grey Ware, Black Slipped Ware

Period I (1000 BC – 300 BC) ⟶ NBPW, Black Slipped Ware, Grey Ware

The only date of Period I is based on radiocarbon dating which confirm the earliest evidence of NBPW in Ganga plain. During and after Kushan period, there was large scale structural activity and rising and leveling of platform started. All structural activity after Period III (Kushan) at Ayodhya is non-residential in nature which is also confirmed by the fact that during and after Period IV (Gupta) at Ayodhya, household potteries are totally missing.

13. Hariharpur (25°36'23"N; 82°58'20"E)

This ancient settlement is situated on the left bank of Gomati River and is approximately 3 km west from Chandwak market situated on Azamgarh-Varanasi Road. This site is excavated by department of Ancient History, Culture & Archaeology, Banaras Hindu University, Varanasi during session 2006-07 under the supervision of Prof. Vibha Tripathi. The excavation revealed following cultural sequence[15]

Period I	Chalcolithic
Period II	NBPW culture
Period III	Kushan

14. Saripur (25°29'40"N; 83°01'39"E)

The ancient site of Saripur [16] is located on the bank of Gomati river, about 6 km south-east of Chandwak in district Jaunpur. The mound extends more than half a kilometer along the river. The department of Ancient Indian History, Culture & Archaeology, Banaras Hindu University conducted in limited excavation at Saripur, under the direction of Prof. P.N. Singh in January-March, 2009. Excavation provided a sequence of cultures starting from pre-NBPW period to early medieval periods.

Period I	-	**Pre NBPW**
Period II	-	**NBPW**
Period III	-	**Shunga-Kushan**
Period IV	-	**Gupta**
Period V	-	**Post- and Early Medieval**

15. Sarai Nahar Rai (25°48'N; 81°50'E)

The Mesolithic site of Sarai-Nahar Rai [17] is situated on the bank of a horse-shoe lake at a distance of 15 km. from Pratapgarh in south-westerly direction. The major portion of lake has been filled. The total area occupied by the Mesolithic people at the site measures 1,800 sq. metres and it is littered with microliths. Besides the tools, the complex contains hearth and graves. The site was excavated by the department of Ancient History, Culture and Archaeology, University of Allahabad in 1973 under the direction of Prof. G.R. Sharma.

16. Mahadaha (25°29'2"N; 82°11'30"E)

The site of Mahadaha[18] is situated at a distance of 5 km north of Patti which is 31 km to the north-east of Pratapgarh district of Uttar Pradesh. The settlement lies on the western bank of an ancient lake to the east of modern village Mahadaha. The site, including a part of the ancient lake, measures about 3937.5 square metres. The Jaunpur Minor Canal about 7.5 m. width running north-south passes through the site disturbing the settlement about 363.75 sq.m. area. The main area of the settlement, measuring about 2,400 sq.m, is located to the west, while the remaining to the east of the canal. There are two culverters adjacent to each other at the southern fringe of the site. The site was excavated by Prof. G.R. Sharma in 1978 by the department of Ancient History, Culture & Aechaeology, Allahabad University, Allahabad.

17. Damdama (26°10'N; 82°20'36"E)

It is situated at a distance of 36 km north-east of Pratapgarh and 5 km north-west of Mahadaha in Patti sub-division of Pratapgarh district. The site was discovered in 1978. It was further extensively explored in 1978 and 1982. The Mesolithic site of Damdama roughly circular in shape is at a slightly raised ground on the confluence of the two branches of Tambura Nala, a tributary of Pili Nadi which itself is a tributary of the Sai. These Nalas, it appears, are the remnant of the ancient horse shoe lakes. During the rainy season, these serve as a natural drainage for the area. The Mesolithic site is not flooded by water even during the rainy season and it looks like an island. It appears that the Mesolithic people on account of its strategic location selected it for settlement.[19]

As the site was away from the village it remained undisturbed. The circular mound of Damdama sloping towards periphery measures 8750 square m. It was excavated for the five seasons from 1982-83 to 1986-87 (Mishra 1988; Pal 1985-86, 1988, 1994, 2002a, 2000b) by Prof V.D. Mishra and Prof. J.N. Pal. The excavated area measures 550 square m. Excavation at the site revealed 1.5 m. thick cultural deposit divisible into 10 layers. Incidentally it may be pointed out that this is the maximum thickness of the Mesolithic strata encountered at any site in the Gangetic Plain.

18. Hulaskhera (26°41'N; 81°1'E)

Hulaskhera[20] is located in district Lucknow under Mohenlalganj tehsil on Lucknow-Raibareilly road which is about 20 km east to the district headquarter. The distance between tehsil headquarter and Hulaskhera is 6 km. The Hulaskhera village is settled on the south-eastern side of a lake, known as Karela jheel. A large mound covering an area of about 80 acres is situated to the north of Hulaskhera village. It is about 6 m. high from the surrounding levels and surrounded by the lake. Rainy season turns this mound in a small island. The north-eastern side of the mound is comparatively lower and under cultivation. The site was excavated in 1978-79 under the direction of R.C. Singh assisted by Hemraj and R.K. Srivastava in 1983-84 and in 1986-87 the site was again excavated by R. Tiwari, Director of U.P. State Archaeology Department. The excavations provided the following sequence from bottom upwards—

Period IA	Black Slipped Ware, Black and Red Ware, Red Ware 1000-700 B.C.
Period IB	PGW, besides the above
Period II	NBPW 700 – 300 B.C.
Period III	Shunga Kushan 200 B.C. – 200 A.D.
Period IV	Gupta & Post Gupta 200 A.D. – 700 A.D.
Period V	700 A.D. to late Medieval

19. Dadupur (26°42'N; 80°49'E)

The site[21] is located about 1.0 km west to Banthara, on Lucknow-Kanpur road (National Highway 40.25) and is 23 km south-west of Lucknow. The ancient site of Dadupur village is across the Nagwa nālā to the east of modern habitation area. It extends over an area measuring about 250 m. east-west and about 150 m. north-south-west. Its height from the surrounding level is over 4 m. The Nagwa nālā emerges near Mohan in district Unnao and after flowing in district Lucknow meets river Sai (ancient Syandika) at Bani, flows along the northern and western sides of the mound. The site is excavated in 1999-2000-2001 under the supervision of Dr. Rakesh Tiwari, Director of State Archaeology Department and assisted by R.K. Srivastava and K.K. Singh. The excavations yielded three-fold cultural sequence—

Period I	Red ware, BSW, BRW, broken kiln, burnt bricks and Iron (1600 B.C.)
Period II	Marked by the presence of PGW sherd, BRW, BSW and associated red ware
Period III	Marked by the presence of NBPW.

20. Pariyar

It is the most famous site[22] on the left bank of the Ganga just opposite to Bithur. It is about 10 kms.south of Chaka-lavansi (i.e. Chak-lava-kusi) and about 23 kms. north-west of Unnao. There was a large forest (Maharanya) in its neighbourhood in the past. The hermitage of Rishi Valmiki was also there. It was here Sita, the consort of Rama, was abandoned by Lakshmana at the behest of his elder brother. Sita gave birth to her sons—Lova and Kusa[23]—in the hermitage of Rishi Valmiki, who made them well versed in his Ramayana, which they recited in the presence of Rama at Naimisharanya.[24] Tradition goes that the *Asvamedha* horse of Rama was also seized by these two young but gallant boys, who defeated the armed batallions of Rama that escorted the *Asvamedha* horse.

Pariyar may be equated with Parihar (to abandon) denoting thereby the place, across the Ganga, where Sita was abandoned by Lakshmana. There is in the Ramayana a very touching graphic description of Sita's exile in the Valmiki Ashram, which was amidst a thick forest across the

Ganges.[25] The Ramayama tells us that following the order of his elder brother Lakshmana asked Sita to get ready for the forest across the Ganga, where she desired to see the hermitage of the Rishis.[26] Sita readily agreed and set out for the excursion riding on a beautiful chariot. After a long journey they stopped on the bank of the Gomati[27] (probably near Lakshmana Tila at Lucknow) and passed the night. Next day, they started to the banks of the Ganga and by mid-day they reached there. Then, they crossed the Ganges by boat and reached the southern bank of the Ganges from where Lakshmana having left her crying and weeping alone, returned to the northern bank of the Ganga by the same boat.[28] Thus, it appears that Lakshmaṇa took the road to Pariyar via Mohan from Lucknow. He reached the northern bank of the Ganges somewhere near modern Makhi-Korari or Antava, from where he took a boat, and crossing the Ganges, reached the Maharanya, where Rishi Valmiki lived. While dealing with the old course of the Ganga, it has already been stated that in the ancient time Ganga flowed along the old banks on which the modern villages of Antava, Korari and Makhi, etc. are situated. An on-the-spot-study of the topography of that area testifies the hypothesis stipulated above. It should also be noted here that Makhi-Korari is only 50 km. west of Lucknow; and this distance can easily be covered by mid-day sitting in a fast moving chariot drawn by swift steeds. Thus, the description as given in the Ramayana is in conformity with the identification of the present site of Pariyar, where there is a temple of Balakandesvara Mahadeva, the old lingam of which is said to have been installed by Lava-Kusa.

The site[29] was excavated in 1978-79 under the project of 'Archaeology of the Ramayana Sites', the Excavation Branch (II) of the Survey, in collaboration with the Indian Institute of Advanced Study, Shimla. The work was jointly directed by Professor B.B. Lal of the Institute and Shri K.N. Dikshit of the Survey. The excavation revealed sequence from O.C.P. to Shunga Kushan period.

Period I	OCP
Period II	PGW
Period III	NBPW
Period IV	Shunga-Kushan

22. Sanchankot

The imposing mound[30] with a vast stretch of structural remains scattered throughout the wide expanse of land measuring about 4 km, dominates the surrounding landscape. The serpentine river Sai or Syandika that washes the two fringes of the citadel, which is the highest landmark on the mound itself, makes it look more imposing, and the small village perched on it 'reminds one much of that of Sravasti'.

Sanchankot, which is also known as Ramkot is 55 km north-west of Unnao. It is situated on the ancient Kannauj-Ayodhya highway about 15 km. N-E of Bangarmanu. Making it a central point one can radially pin-point Naimishranya 53 km. orth-east; Lucknow, 53 km. east-north-east; Pariyar, 47 km. south and S-W as the crow flies; and Kannauj, 54 km. west-north-west. Thus, in the light of its key position amidst the well-known sites of great antiquity it has assumed great archaeological importance. It is, therefore, worthwhile to determine its antiquity on the basis of legendary-literary, archaeological and structural evidences.

Traditionally, Sanchankot is known as Ramkot, i.e. the 'Kota' or fort of Rama, the son of Dasharatha of Ikshvaku dynasty.[31] The relation of this place with Ikshvakus and especially with Rama sounds plausible for many other places related with the same illustrious figure, i.e. Rama, are situated not far off from this place. For example, 'Pariyar', where Sita was abandoned and Naimisharanya where Rama had performed his 'Ashvamedha' sacrifice have already been referred to.

Later, the site was known as Sujatakota or Sujankota. Sujata was, according to the Buddhist Text Mahavastu, the Ikshvaku King of its great city of Suket.[32] It appears that during the life of Lord Buddha, it was known by the name of Saket[33] and was regarded as one of the three major towns of Kotala, viz. Sravasti, Ayodhya and Saksi. In Buddhist literature Ayodhya and Saket have been described as two distinct places.[34] Sometimes Saket has been described as the capital of Kosala. It was Saket and not Ayodhya that is called one of the six great cities of India.[35] Thus, this place appears to have flourished and developed into a magnificent township where Lord Buddha stayed and preached while on his way to Rajgriha[36] from Navadevakula, i.e. modern Newal.

Fa-Hien, the famous Chinese traveller who visited India between A.D. 400 and 411 while going to "*Sha-Che*"Ayodhya from Kannauj writes:

> Going South-East from this place (Kannauj) ten yojanas we arrive at the great country Sha-che.

> Leaving the southern gate of the capital city, on the east side of the road, is a place where Buddha once dwelt. Whilst here he bit (a piece from) the willow stick and fixed it in the earth; immediately it grew up seven feet high, neither more nor less. The unbelievers and Brahamanas, filled with jealousy, cut it down and scattered the leaves far and wide, but yet it always sprung up again in the same place as before. Here also they raised towers on places where the four Buddhas walked for exercise and sat down. The ruins still exist.[37]

Thus, the capital city, which Fa-Hien came across after leaving Kannauj was Shache.[38] According to Fuhrer the position of this great mound (i.e. Sanchankot) on the highway between ancient Kannauj and Ayodhya has its bearing on the identification of Sanchankot with the capital of the Sache visited by Fa-Hien.[39]

This identification is placed beyond doubt by the existence of a Stupa on the south-east of the opening which seems to mark the south gate of the city, and four other marked eminences in other places. During his itinerary to the Buddhist sites Cunningham visited this site and found the aforesaid stupas badly rummaged for bricks. According to him the Zamindar who got it excavated made the statement that he found 'a round pot containing bones and nothing else but on a further enquiry he was told by the local people that thre were five relic boxes inside the pot, four of which were of black stone and one of white stone (most probably they were all of steatite i.e. soap stone). In the black casket there were some rotten pearls and in the white casket there were a large piece of amethyst-coloured quartz. This K.S. Shukla[40] has got. It is one inch long and three-fourth of an inch thick with a hole through the middle.[41] Thus, it is clear that Cunningham found the stupa though excavated for bricks by the local people, yet it was certainly the same mentioned by the Chinese travller. According to him it was only 18½ feet in diameter but it stood on a lofty terrace, 60 feet square and 15 feet above the fields with a wall of 6 feet thick, all round It was built entirely of very large wedge-shaped bricks measuring 17½" x 11½"x 4".[42] The present Sanchankot was identified with *Sa-che* of Fa-Hien.

The earliest known pottery found at this site is black-painted red ware, Black-and-Red ware and P.G. ware. The specimens of these ceramic wares were discovered by K.S. Shukla from the lowest-levels while a well was being dug on the lofty mound which is generally known as the 'quila' or the 'fort'. Apart from these wares, N.B.P. ware in different shades is profusely found. Sanchankol has been excavated by Prof. D.P. Tewari[43] of Ancient Indian History and Archaeology department of University of Lucknow.

23. Kopia (26°51'N; 83°4'50"E)

Kopia[45] is located on the Khalilabad-Bakhira road at a distance of about 12 km north of Khalilabad town in Sant Kabir Nagar district (erstwhile part of district Basti), Uttar Pradesh. The archaeological site, consisting of a prominent mound is located on the western fringe of the village. It extends over an area of about 1 sq.km. and has a height of about 12 m from the surrounding ground level. This early historic site is reported by many since early last century, as a site which produced glass in large quantity. The mound is fortified and surrounded by moat. The mound is partly inhabited with houses built of bricks removed from the mound, and the rest of it under intensive cultivation, leaving only an area of about 200 sq.m intact. Though the bed of the Ami has moved far more or less away, when the site was occupied it was flowing near the settlement.

This archaeological site of Kopia is on the right bank and 3.5 km away from the present channel of Ami river. It is on the flood plain between river Churma in the east and river Ami in the west. The mound is close to a dried up lake, which was a part of an ox-bow lake. It is clear after image processing that the site is on the right bank of a cut-off horse shoe shaped meander. The cut-off meander represents the palaeo-channel of the Ami. The present channel is very narrow but perennial. The mound is located on a higher surface, which separates the Ami basin from the Rapti river.

This site was excavated by A.K. Kanungo and V.N. Mishra in 2003-2004 and in 2006 by A.K. Kanungo of Deccan College, Pune. The findings of the excavation are of much archaeological and historical interest. Though complete stratification could not be obtained, the earliest evidence seems to be that of Northern Black Polished Ware (NBPW) of about 6th century B.C. Over this layer is Sunga-Kushana occupation and sporadic evidence of Muslim period.

24. Kalli-Pachchhim (26°43'N; 88°57'E)

Kalli-Pachchhim is situated in district Lucknow of Uttar Pradesh. The mound of Kalli-Pachchhim covering an area of about 200 x 200 m is about 8 m. high from surrounding ground. The Kalli-Pachchhim locality is located on the natural level of a meander lake. This is few meter high level by the side of lake provided an ideal site for the human settlement. The site was reported for the first time by Singhs.[45] Kalli-Pachchhim[46] site was excavated by Prof. D.P. Tewari of the Department of Ancient Indian History Culture & Archaeology, Lucknow University in 1997-98 and 1998-99.

References

1. Singh, P. (1994), *Excavations at Narhan (1984-89).* Varanasi, pp.1-345.
2. Singh, P., A.K. Singh, Indrajeet Singh (1991-92), "Excavations at Imlidih Khurd," *Puratattva*, No. 2, pp. 120-122.
3. Singh, P., Ashok Singh, Indrajeet Singh (1991-92), "Trial Digging at Dhuriapar," *Pragdhara*, No. 02, pp. 55-58.
4. *Indian Archaeology, 1974-75—A Review*, p. 48.
5. Tewari, Rakesh, R.K. Srivastav, K.K. Singh, K.S. Saraswat and I.B. Singh (2002-2003), "Preliminary Report of Excavation at Lahuradeva, District Sant Kabir Nagar, U.P., 2001-2002: Wider Archaeological Implications," *Pragdhara*, No. 13, pp. 37-58.

   Tewari, Rakesh, R.K. Srivastava, K.K. Singh, K.S. Saraswat (2005-06), "Further Excavations at Lahuradeva, District Sant Kabir Nagar (U.P.): Preliminary Observations," *Puratattva* No. 36, pp. 68-75.
6. Sinha, K.K. (1967), *Excavations at Srvasti—1959*, Varanasi, pp.1-77.

7. Ghosh, A. (1989), *An Encyclopaedia of Indian Archaeology*, New Delhi, pp. 345-346.

8. *Ibid.*, p. 143.

9. Mani, B.R. (2003-04), "Excavations at Siswania (District Basti, U.P.) 1995-1997," *Puratattva No. 34*, pp. 100-105.

10. Tewari, D.P. (2002), *Excavations at Charda*, Lucknow, pp. 1-197.

11. Acharya, Prasanna Kumar (1981), *A Dictionary of Hindu Architecture*, Mansara Series, Vol. I, Second Edition, New Delhi, p. 129, 180-87.

12. Fuhrer, A., *Archaeological Survey of India* (New Series), Vol. I.XII, North-Western Provinces and Oudh , Monumental Antiquities and Inscriptions, p. 293.

13. Tewari, D.P. (2006), *Excavations at Pirvitanisarif-Trilokpur*, Lucknow, pp. 1-229.

14. Ghosh, A. (1989), *op.cit.*, pp. 31-32.

15. Tripathi, Vibha (2007-08), "Excavations at Hariharpur, District Jaunpur," *Purarattva*, No. 38, pp. 205-209.

16. Singh, P.N., R.N. Singh & Ashok Kumar Singh (2008-09), "Archaeology of Gomati Basin with Special Reference to Excavations at Saripur, District Jaunpur,: *Bharti*, Vol. 33, pp. 1-30.

17. Mishra, V.D. (1977), *Some Aspects of Indian Archaeology*, Allahabad, p. 99.

    Sharma, G.R. (1973), "Mesolithic Lake Cultures in the Ganga Valley," Proceedings of the Prehistory Society XXXIX.

18. Sharma, G.R., V.D. Mishra, D. Mandal, B.B. Mishra and J.N. Pal (1980), "From Hunting and Food Gatherings to Demestication of Plants and Animals," *Beginnings of Agriculture* (Epi-Palaeolithic to Neolithic Excavations at Chopani-Mando, Mahadaha and Mahagara), pp. 110-131.

19. Robbins, Giwen, V.D. Mishra, J.N. Pal and M.C. Gupta (2003) *Mesolithic Damdama: Dental Histology and Age Estimation*, p.1-116.

20. Tewari, Rakesh, Hemraj, Rakesh Kumar Srivastav (1995-96), "Excavations at Hulaskhera," *Pragdhara*, No. 6, pp. 97-133.

21. Tewari, Rakesh, R.K. Srivastava, K.K. Singh (2001-02), "Dadupur Excavations 1999-2000-2001, District Lucknow, Uttar Pradesh: A Preliminary Report," *Pragdhara,* No. 12, pp. 99-113.
22. Shukla, K.S. (1986), *Archaeology of Unnao District*, Delhi, p. 34.
23. *V. Ramayana*, VII, chs. 94-97.
24. *Ibid.*,
25. *V.* Ramayana, *Uttarkhand,* chs. 46-49 (Hindi Tr. Chaturvedi, D.S.).
26. *Ibid.*, 46.8.
27. *Ibid.*, 46.19.
28. *Ibid.*, 49.23.
29. *I.*A.R.
30. Fuhrer, A., *ASI* (New Series), Vol. II (1891) pp. 274-75.
31. Pargiter, F.R. (1922), *Ancient Indian Historical Tradition*, p. 147.
32. *Mahavastu*, Vol. 348, 10-11.
33. Majumdar, R.C. & Pusalkar (1953), *The Age of Imperial Unity*, Bombay, p. 4.
34. *Digha Nikaya* (1957), Pt. II, p. 116 (Bombay University publication) Rhys Davids, *Buddhist India*, p. 20.
35. *Mahavastu*, I, 348, *Jataka* III, 270.
36. Rahul Sankrityayana, *Buddhacharya*, p. 502.
37. Beal, S. (1884), *Buddhist Records of the Western World*, p. xliii.
38. J. Legge (1971), *Trvels of Fa-Hien*, p. 54 (Delhi).
39. Fuhrer, A. (1890), *op.cit.*, Vol. I, p. 318, Vol. II (1891), p. 275.
40. Shukla, K.S. (1986), *op.cit.*, p. 34.
41. Cunningham, *ASIR*, Vol. XI, p. 54.
42. *Ibid.*, p. 53.
43. Shukla, K.S. (1986), *op.cit.*, p. 36.
44. Kanungo, A.K. and V.N. Mishra (2003-2004), "Excavation at Kopia: A Preliminary Report," *Puratattva*, No. 36, pp. 116-123.
45. Singh, S.D. and S.B. Singh, (1970), *The Archaeology of Lucknow Region*, p. 26.
46. Tewari, D.P. (1999), *Antiquarian Remains from Kalli Pachchhim Excavations*, Lucknow, pp. 1-136.

4

The Mesolithic Culture in Kosal Region

The Mesolithic period falling in between the Palaeolithic and Neolithic coincides on the onset of the Holocene geological period, after circa 10,000 years ago and is characterized by societies continuing to practice a hunting and gathering economy by using microlith throughout the world. Both climatically and culturally, it marks a definite stage in the history of men's development. With the withdrawal of glaciers, the ice sheets, which had covered the surface of the earth during the Pleistocene, retreated and the waterlogged regions in tropical zones were fast becoming habitable on account of inter-pluvial conditions. The earth attained its present form and more fertile zones with better living conditions became available for habitation. On account of better climatic conditions there was a lot of movement of men and animal from one zone to another. The population, too, increased considerably. In order to cope with the changing ecological and environment conditions man also changed the pattern of his life in contrast to its past.

Mesolithic sites have a wide distribution in India and cover almost the entire country, except a few areas like most of the Indo-Ganga Plains, Assam and most of the West coast. In the Indo-Ganga Plains their absence is easily explained by the lack and remoteness of the primary raw material i.e. stone for making tools. Assam and the W. coast were probably not much inhabited because of the very high rainfall and dense vegetation. Some regions like Gujarat-plains, Marwar and Mewar have a denser concentration of sites than others. But this uneven distribution of sites would appear largely due to differential pace of research in different parts of the country. Though most of India had been occupied during the Lower Palaeolithic and successive Palaeolithic periods, the Mesolithic people significantly extended this process of colonization. They ventured into the Ganga Valley also.

Settlement Pattern

The Mesolithic people of the Ganga Plain was seasonally migrated from the Vindhyan region due to hot climatic condition. Although the exodus from the Vindhyan to the Ganga Region beginning from the Epi-Palaeolithic and the maximum period of intensity of migration was reached in the first half of the Mesolithic and it gradually declined in the later half of the Mesolithic. Explorations have brought to light about 195 Mesolithic sites in the Pratapgarh and Jaunpur districts of the Kosal region. Out of 181 sites of Pratapgarh, 174 sites are located on lake side and remaining sites are located on the river bank. In the Pratapgarh district 15% sites belong to non-geometric microliths (Phase IIA) and 16 geometirc microliths (Phase IIB). Out of 14 Mesolithic sites 11 are non-geometrical microliths and 3 are geometrical microlith sites in the Jaunpur district. The district of Sultanpur yielded only 05 non-geometric microlithic sites (Phase IIA).

The migrating indigenous mass from the Vindhyas made their settlements on the bank of the lakes formed by abandoned meander of changing river courses. Here the settlers had ample food supplies from the lakes as well as the dense primeval forests of the fertile alluvial plains. These people came during the summer when there was acute scarcity of food and water in the Vindhyas, a recurrent phenomena even now.

In the Kosal region, as stated earlier, a large number of sites ranging from Epi-Palaeolithic to Mesolithic have been discovered. These sites are found scattered in Pratapgarh, Sultanpur and Jaunpur, out of which maximum sites are located in Pratapgarh district, where three of such sites i.e. Sarai-Nahar Rai, Mahadaha and Damdama have been excavated extensively. In this connection it is interesting to note that all the three sites are located on the bank of horse shoe lakes. Mesolithic people selected these sites because of not only the availability of food, but the consideration of security was also a controlling factor. These two sites are surrounded on all sides by lakes, the access to them being controlled by a narrow strip of land. The migration appears to be seasonal in character and the sites were never occupied continuously for a long time, confirmed by the fact that occupational debris being very thin. But the situation of these sites were so alluring that the migrating people came again and again and selected the same spot (Sarai-Nahar Rai) which is considerably eroded, offers evidence of settlement at least twice as illustrated by the evidence of hearths and Mahadaha was occupied at least four times.[1] Excavations have also offered conclusive evidence that the new-comers were not aware of the existence of earlier settlement. The migrating people brought the raw material from the Vindhyas and manufactured the tools locally is fully documented by evidence from each sites. Cores in different stages of manufacture, debitage, rejected flakes and tools, though heavily patinated, have been discovered in very well preserved and fresh form with all the corners and angle intact. Since the stone material is not available in the Ganga Plain, north of the river, these people were actually conscious of the scarcity of the material, so vital for their survival and also of the need for extreme economy in its use. The consequence of this was a reduction in tool size and the use of cores till they became non-functional. The above phenomenon is fully documented by the analysis of the material whereas the proportional variation in sizes of tools from the Epi-Palaeolithic to the Mesolithic corresponds to that of the Vindhyas and reflects a corresponding development in tools technology, the sharp reduction in sizes in all the periods in the Ganga Valley is due to the scarcity of raw material. The phenomenon of reduction in the tools of the early Mesolithic in comparison to the Epi-Palaeolithic period of the Vindhyas holds equally true in the case of sites from the Ganga Plain.

The excavated Mesolithic sites of Kosal region i.e. Sarai-Nahar Rai, Mahadaha and Damdama throw some light on the pattern of life of the early Holocene folk. The Mesolithic site of Damdama roughly circular in shape is at a slightly raised ground on the confluence of the two branches of Tambura Nala, a tributary of Pili Nadi which itself is a tributary of the Sai.[2] These Nalas, it appears, are the remanent of the ancient horseshoe lakes. During the rainy season these serve as a natural drainage for the area. The Mesolithic site is not flooded by water even during the rainy season and it looks like an island. It appears that the Mesolithic inhabitants on account of its strategic location selected it for settlement. The circular mound of Damdama sloping towards periphery measures 8750 square meter. Excavation at the site revealed 1.5 m thick cultural deposit. Incidentally, it may be pointed out that this is the maximum thickness of the Mesolithic strata encountered at any site in the Gangetic Plain.[3] At Sarai Nahar Rai Mesolithic horizon was confined to 6 cm only while at Mahadaha it measured 8000 sq. m. and depth upto 60 cm. Thickness of cultural deposit at Damdama would clearly indicate that in comparison to Sarai Nahar Rai and Mahadaha it might have been occupied for a much longer period of time. The Mesolithic site of Sarai Nahar Rai is located on flat and the total area covered by Mesolithic people at the site measuresI 1800 sq.m.

Subsistence Pattern

The Mesolithic culture is generally associated with hunting, fishing and intensive collecting economy. They were considered to be nomadic who moved from one place to another in search of food and made microlithic tools for hunting. But excavations at different places make it clear that there was a lot of regional variation in the life pattern of the Mesolithic folk. The environmental factors also played an important role in the formation of their economical pattern of the different regions.

The subsistence economy of the Mesolithic folk depended on hunting and gathering as it was attested by the evidence of floral, faunal, lithic and bone implements of Sarai-Nahar Rai, Mahadaha and Damdama. At Damdama 90% of the animal bones obtained at the site are charred or semi-charred suggesting their use in the dietary item.[4] The excavations have yielded animal bones in appreciable number. More than 30 species of animals, comprising mammals, reptiles, birds, fish and molluses have been identified. The mammals include six species of deer including mouse deer and musk deer, nilgai, black buck, chinkara, wild pig, etc. There are also a few large mammals like elephant, rhinoceros, gaur, wild buffalo and possibly wild cattle. The species of carnivores (wolf, Jackal and fox) are also included. Hare and porcupins are represented by few bones. Birds, tortoise, fish, molluses and the other reptiles like *Trionyx gangtics*, *Varanul* sp. and *Colotes versicolour* also had their share in the food economy at the site.[5] All the animal species pertained to wild variety. A large number of animal bones were recovered from Sarai-Nahar Rai in charred, semi-charred and uncharred condition. The faunal remains[6] were collected in the form of bones at Sarai Nahar-Rai from hearths and floor area. Those recovered from the hearths were in different stages of roasting with extensive deposition of soot around them. Those collected from the floor area had a layer of earthy encrustration. The bones recovered from the site indicated the presence of cattle including bison (*Bos indicus* and *Bos gaurus*), hippopotamus (*Hippopotamus palaeindicus*), sheep or goat (*Ovis vignei blyth – Capra hircus aegarus*), deer and stag (*Cervus duvauceli—Cervus axis*), elephant (*Elephas indicus*) and tortoise (*chelonia*). At Sarai Nahar Rai the find of large number of bones of animals of wild variety confirms that they were hunted. The identification of roasting, chopping and extraction of marrow from these in an indication of their use for purpose of food. In the collection of bones from Sarai Nahar Rai chopping marks are visible on bones collected from the hearth and floor area. On the long bones chopping marks are visible at either ends, where muscles are generally attached, thus giving a hint that the operation was entirely food-oriented.

At Mahadaha[7] 768 specimens were examined in which 319 belong to the lake area, 165 to the butchery area and 284 to the cemetry-cum-habitational area. The animal identified from the bonal segment are—cattle (*Bos* indicus), sheep/goat (*Ovidae*/capridae), Antelop and deer (Cervidae), Bison (*Bos* gaurus), Hippopotamus (*Hippotamus* palaeindicus), Swine (*sus* scrofa), Horse (Equidae), Carnivores (Carnivoridae), Rat (*Rattus* rattus), Tortoise (chelonian), Fish and Birds (*Gallus* galeiformes).

Large number of hearths at Sarai-Nahar Rai, Mahadaha and Damdama, full of buried clay lumps, ash and charred animal bones demonstrate that the animal flesh was roasted in these hearths with grass and leaves. The clay lumps referred to above when put on grass and leaves covering the flesh might have helped in better roasting of the meat. At Sarai Nahar Rai eight small hearths and one community hearth were also exposed. The smaller hearths were circular, oval or of indeterminate shape.[8] At all places they are of the pit hearth type and only slightly vary in diameter and depth. The size of small hearth ranges being 1.02 to 0.45 m. on plan at the bottom and 1.49 to 0.70 m at the top. At Mahadaha eight hearths, one circular and seven oval have been reported from the different phases[9]—

Phase I (Hearth I), Phase II (Hearths 2, 3, 4), Phase III (Hearth 5, 6) and Phase IV (Hearth 7,8). These hearths are distributed throughout the cemetery-cum-habitation area. In the butchery complex area, some of the bones were also in a semi-charred conditions were found. At Damdama pit hearths constitute an important feature of the Mesolithic Culture of the site. As many as 31 hearths were opened. These are circular or oblong on plan. Their presence is indicated by the concentration of burnt clay lumps. These hearths may be divided into two groups: simple shallow pit hearths and hearths with clay plastering on the side wall or bottom or both. The hearths were found filled with burnt clay lumps, charred and semi-charred bone fragments of animals and ash. Charcoal was not obtained from any of the hearths. These hearths were evidently used for roasting the animal flesh, birds and acquatic creatures like fish, turtles etc. Absence of human bones from any of the hearths excludes the possibility of cannibalism in the Mesolithic society. The aforesaid description of the hearths in the Mesolithic sites indicated that the Mesolithic people of the Kosal region were well acquainted with the use of fire.

The occurrence of the fragments of a large number of querns, mullers, saddle at Mahadaha, Damdama & Sarai Nahar Rai would indicate the gathering of wild grains and other edibles had started playing some role in the life of the Mesolithic people at the sites otherwise the presence of food processing equipments could not be easily explained. It is worth-mentioning that for manufacturing these equipments, sand stone and quartzite, had to be obtained only from the Vindhyan area, as stone was not available in the Gangetic Plain. The Mesolithic people got some pits plastered with thick clay solution, sometimes more than one coating has been done for plastering the pits. Some plastered pits are completely baked or semi-baked. Some of such pits are devoid of burnt clay lumps, animal bones and ash. About the function of such hearths are not very sure. These shallow plastered pits may have been used as site pits for storage of the wild grains. Thus along with hunting wild animals, collecting acquatic creatures and killing birds, these people were augmenting their dietary items with the wild edible grains as well.

Structural Activity

Evidence of structural activity in the form of hutments, paved floor or windscreen comes from Damdama, Mahadaha and Sarai Nahar Rai. The excavations of Damdama brought to light circular or semi-circular burnt and plastered floors occasionally with multiple layers of plaster. The evidence of burnt plastered floors is present throughout the Mesolithic occupation. Outlines of two floors were completely cleared. One floor measured 5.35 m. on the northsouth and 5.39 m. on the east-west axis. Microliths, querns, a burnt clay lumps and animal bones fragments were found scattered on the floor. The second floor, elliptical on plan, measured 5.63 m. on the longer axis (north-west to south-east) and 4.20 m. on the shorter axis. As many as five post holes were located around the periphery of the floor. Microliths, a bone arrowhead and fragments of querns were obtained from the surface of the floor. Such plastered floors with fire places in the centre were used for living purposes. The fire places on the floor were occasionally used for roasting the animal flesh as is evident by the occurrence of charred animal bones on the floors. It is not unlikely that these places also served the purpose of working floor for the Mesolithic people as is suggested by the occurrence of microliths and bone objects scattered on them. At Mahadaha, the structural activity indicated by only a community hearth enclosed by four post holes and subsequently covered by a circular floor paved with burnt clay lump. The evidence of post holes around an oblong community hearth found at Sarai-Nahar-Rai seems to reflect the memory of huts constructed by these people in the Vindhyan area. This indicates that the area of settlement was used both for manufacturing tools and preparing food.

Material Culture

Stone objects

The microlithic tools were used for hunting and for cutting the wild grass by the Mesolithic folk of Sarai-Nahar Rai, Damdama and Mahadaha. At Mahadaha and Damdama large number of bone tools have been found which also served the same purpose. At Damdama both surface exploration and excavation at the site yielded a rich crop of tools and weapons fashioned out of stone and bone Microliths fashioned on chert, chalcodony, agate, carnelian and quartz are divided mainly into two categories[10] : (1) Unmodified waste and (ii) Finished and utilized artifacts. The unmodified waste includes blades, blade fragments, flakes, flake fragments, cores, core trimming flakes and core requvenating flakes. These are unretouched and unutilized. The finished tools and utilized artifacts include utilized blades/blade fragments, normal retouched blades/blade fragments, inversely retouched blades / blade fragments, normal and inversely retouched blades / blade fragments, onchtata retouched blades / blade fragments, convex backed blades / blade fragments, concave backed blades / blade fragments, partly backed and retouched blades / blade fragments, double backed blades / blade fragments, backed and truncated blades / blade fragments, scalene triangles, isosceles triangles, trapezoids, trapezes, lunates, perscoirs, drills, transverse arrowheads, tip of a triangle / miscellaneous utilized flakes, normal scrapers, concave scrapers, convex scrapers, notch scrapers and microburins.

The preliminary study of microlithic assemblade of Damdama indicates that unmodified waste constitutes 88.28% while the finished tools and utilized artifacts are only 11.72%. The most popular raw material was chalcedony represented by 71.53% followed by chert (24.934%), quartz (1.76%), agate (1.457%) and carnelian (0.310%). As per the same preliminary study the lunates and the backed blades start coming from the lowest level i.e. layer 10, triangles both scalene and isosceles, and perscoir from layer 9. The first appearance of trapeze is reported from layer 5. The microlithic industry of the site often exhibits an excellent workmanship.[11]

At Damdama the blade tools in a largest percentage of assemblage i.e. 58.93%, followed by triangular microliths. The raw material chalcodony and chert for spare tool production is found at a distance of 100 km. from the site and economy was vital to their production with every workable fragment having been used as a tool. Heavily worn grinding stones and sickles were recovered and the use-wear analysis of the heavily polished blades suggests use in cutting grasses and plants. Manuports were also used as querns and mullers for processing vegetal foods. Luckacs, Pal and Mishra attempted dietary reconstruction based on the carbon and nitrogen stable isotopes in bio-apatite samples from Damdama and Lekhaia. The change in carbon-13 ratio for Damdama were less negative than those for Lekhaia, meaning that the people of Damdama may have been eating more C4 foods (grassy plants)[12], while the population at Lekhaia (a Mesolithic site in the Vindhyan Hills to the south) were possibly concentrating mainly on meat and C3 plants (trees, shrubs and tubers).[13]

Among the food-processing equipments, mention may be made of quern and mullers made of quartzite and sandstone. Wear and tear on working surface on the querns indicated their long and constant use. Hammer stones, anvils and sharpness made on quartzite and sandstone have also been found in good number at Damdama.

The lithic industry of Mahadaha is marked by its small size due to the extreme economy which was compulsive necessity on account of the scarcity of raw material. The lack of rolling and the retention of sharp edges of the tools on the one hand, and the abundance of flakes and debitage on the other, furnish proof of the manufacture of tools at the site. The tools included 31.03% parallel sided blades, 19.54% blunted back blades, 9.19% lunates, 9.19% scrapers, 3.44% Triangles, 2.29% Trapeze. The microliths of Mahadaha are fashioned on 53.39% Chert, 35.81% Chalcedony, 6.19% Carnelian, 2.46% Agate,1.73% Quartz, Crystal 0.39%. From the relative percentage of cherty and more fine grained material like Chalcodony, etc., it can be inferred that source of supply was not only the Belan Valley but also some other areas where the Mesolithic group were making use of non-cherty material in a large measure. It may indicate arrival of Mesolithic group on these lake sites in the Kosal region of Ganga Plain from different areas of the Vindhyas. Other stone objects at Mahadaha yielded food processing tools. The assemblage consists of Quern 63.45%, Muller 8.30%, Anvil 1.32%, Muller-cum-anvil 0.66%, Hammer 1.99%, Sling ball 0.99%, Sharpener 23.25%.

Bone Objects

At Mahadaha the bone objects have been divided into 3 group: (i) Implements, (ii) Ornaments, and (iii) Utensils. The implements comprises arrowheads, points, blades, knives, chisel wrapper, saw etc. The arrowhead included 48.8%, Point 28.8%, Blade2.2%, Knife 4.4% and others 6.6%. For manufacturing the bone implements generally tubular bones have been used. These were split and subsequently rubbed. Besides small sized horn cores, mostly of sheep and goat, but occasionally of stag also have been used. Some of implements have shining surface, possibly on account of their constant use. The evidence of blunting and sharpening is also discernible, particularly in the case of blades and knives. The working edges of some of the implements are retouched, while in some other cases, these are serrated. The bone arrowheads which recovered from Mahadaha is the earliest bone arrowhead discovered in India so far.[14] At Damdama bone arrowheads, both long and small are found. Besides bone arrowhead, an ivory quiver having two perforations and some other objects were also found from the site. At the Mesolithic site of Damdama also the bone industry constitutes a salient feature of the culture. In this connection it may be pertinent to point out here that in the Vindhyas, the bone tools are rare in the Mesolithic context. However, in the Ganga Plain, the non-availability of raw material for manufacturing microliths might have forced the Mesolithic folk for the search of unconventional raw material. Bone industry[15] was the outcome of the search. The Butchering complex of the Mahadaha was also used as workshop for fabricating bone tools and ornaments. The animal species comprised bos, bos gaurus, hippopotamus, deer, stag, sus and chelonia. The majority of bones belonged to stag and deer. The Sarai Nahar Rai has yielded geometric microliths (only triangles) and not a single piece of trapeze.

Aesthetic Activities (Ornaments)

The men decorated themselves with ornaments such as ear-rings and necklaces. Earrings and necklaces have been recovered from three graves at Mahadaha. Of these, as many as nineteen are in finished form and the remaining seven are unfinished and are in various stages of manufacture. All the ornaments whether finished or unfinished are made from antler. The grave VII yielded two small sized rings. These measures 1.1 cm in diameter and 0.2 cm in thickness, the diameter of perforation being 0.7 cm. From Grave V were obtained both earrings and necklace. The earring (Kundal) is open at one end probably for getting inserted in the lobe of the ear. It measures 5.1 cm in diameter, and 0.6 cm in thickness. Presumably part of a nceklace eleven small rings each measuring 3.6 cm in diameter, 0.5 cm in thickness with the diameter of the perforated portions 2.3 cm were also found around the neck of the same individual. The grave IV yielded five small rings, the outer and inner diameters being 2.6 cm, and 1.8cm respectively and the thickness measuring 0.4 cm. A number of antler have incisions and deep groves. After the pieces were detached from antler, these were rubbed from all sides for getting the desired shape of the ornament.[16] At Damdama (grave VII) the burial was found with a carved ivory pendant[17]. It is interesting to note that ornaments have been found only on male skeletons. Does this indicate that men dominated the Mesolithic society? Are these ornaments the indicators of social status. Does it indicate that some sort of leadership principle had evolved?

Burials

The burials have greater significance for the inference of social structure of the Mesolithic people. The Mesolithic people buried their dead in the same area where they were living and performing several activities of their daily life. In the Ganga Plain at Sarai Nahar-Rai, Mahadaha and Damdama burials and pit hearths are in the same area. At Mahadaha the site yielded 28 skeletons associated with 35 pit hearths microliths, burnt clay lumps, rubbed ochre, quern and muller fragments, hammer stone fragments and rubbed hematite pieces.[18] The skeletons from Mahadaha are well preserved. The burials have been assigned to four phases of the Mesolithic based on stratigraphic associations.[19] The shallow, oblong graves were filled with material from the hearths and there was 4-6 cm thick soil cushion lining. All the burials were single individuals in a supine position except for burial I, which contained a male and a female buried side by side the female being on the left of male and burial V, which contained two individuals, one laying in a prone position on top of the other in a supine position.[20] The Mahadaha skeletons were oriented west-east with the heads towards the west. The remaining two skeletons nos. 9 and 15 of Phase III and Phase IV respectively had roughly east-west orientation. Some graves included bone rings and jewellery, rubbed ochre, microliths and charred and semi-charred animal bone fragments, shells, bone arrowhead, etc. As stated earlier, bone ornaments were found in grave No. V and Grave No. IV, the former containing skeletal remains of two individuals one male and one female. The skeleton of the male individual of the double burial was having pendant and necklace made of bone. The individual buried in Grave No. IV, again a male, was found adorned with bone necklace. Curiously enough, all the female skeletons exposed at the site were without any ornament. Besides, a few bone rings have also been obtained from Grave No. IX.

Sarai Nahar Rai was the first 'Mesolithic' site on the Gangetic Plain in which burials were discovered.[21] The dead were buried in shallow oblong grave pits with a west-east orientation, the skull lying towards the west. The grave was carefully prepared by laying a soil cushion 3-4 cm. thick.[22] Microliths and a particular type of shell seen to have been placed as offering goods.[23] The graves contained fifteen adult skeletons associated eight pit hearths.[24] The skeletons were in extended and supine position.[25] In placing the hand of the dead, care was taken to keep one along the body while the other across the abdomen. In filling the graves the material of hearth was also used as is indicated by the presence of burial clay and animal bones in the graves. With the exception of one (VII), all the graves of Sarai Nahar Rai contained single individual. In one grave as many as four were individuals, two males and two females who appear to have been buried at the same time.[26]

At Damdama four phases of burial activity were discovered and 47 individuals were recovered from the western and central areas of the site.[27] The graves were located in what has been called the habitation area due to the presence of hearths, material from which was used as fill.[28] The graves were shallow and oblong, resembling burial customs at Sarai Nahar Rai and Mahadaha. The majority of burials were single (41), oriented east to west with the skull to the west. However, Damdama is exceptional in that there were five double burials (in grave Nos. VI, XX, XXVI, XXX and XXXVI) and one grave (XVIII) contained a triple burial with two males and one female.[29] Forty one individuals were in an extended supine position, two were in a flexed prone position, and one was simply flexed.[30] About half of the skeletons were oriented east to west. Grave goods include bone arrowheads, microliths (in grave VII, XVI and XVIII) and a perforated ivory pendant (quiver) in grave VII.[31] Damdama is unique in that burials were marked with a stone tumulus[32] Similarities in the orientation, positioning and contents of the graves at Damdama, Mahadaha and Sarai Nahar Rai have been interpreted to represent a cultural tradition common the region in the Mesolithic.[33] The double burials of Mahadaha, Damdama have been found in pairs of male and female having almost equal age. This suggests emergence of a concept of family life. When placed side by side in the double burial the female skeleton has been found placed to the left. It is tempting to suggest that the placing of wife to the left of husband in Hindu religious ceremonies can be traced back at least to the Mesolithic time if not earlier. It seems that the Mesolithic folk had developed some belief in life beyond death because Sarai Nahar Rai, Mahadaha and Damdama have the evidence of grave goods with the skeletons. The orientation of the graves towards west-east at Sarai Nahar Rai, Mahadaha and Damdama is so perfect that it requires closer thinking. There is any hardly any doubt in the fact that the direction must have been guided by the direction of the sun. The variation is only of a few degrees which may be on account of the variation in the position of the Sun at different times of the year. The Sun must have attracted them and they must have been aware of the life giving qualities of the Sun. Will it be wrong to trace sun worship from the Mesolithic period?[34] Another opinion is that this directional divergence in human burials is linked with two distinct tribes.

The Age of the largest number of skeletons ranges between 17 and 45 years. At Mahadaha two burials of children (one male child of about 6 years and other female child of about 4 years) and a burial of an old woman (nearly 50 years) have been obtained. At Sarai Nahar Rai the excavated skeletons fall within the age group of 16 to 39 years with the exception of one which may be of a person of more than 30 years of age at the time of death.

The skeletal morphology of the Gangetic Plains populations of Damdama, Mahadaha and Sarai Nahar Rai appears to be relatively homogeneous: tall, robust people with well developed masculature on the appendicular skeleton.[35] The height of male measures 1.80 m and slightly less than it in the case of female at Sarai Nahar Rai.[36] The tallest figure at Mahadaha measures about 1.80 m. The cranial morphology and odontometric profiles further indicate that they may share genetic affinities.[37] Gene flow between these groups has not been positively established but it is possible, given cultural similarities and that they are thought to be roughly contemporaneous.[38] There are few apparent biological affinities between these population and later Indian peoples, with the possible exception of the people who inhabited Neolithic Mehargarh.[39]

Palaeobotanical Remains

The Indian Mesolithic sites had very scanty evidence of palaeobotanical remains. However, Kajale[40] analyzed some palaeobotanical remainsof Damdama and identified six plant—three to species including: buck wheat (*Poly gonaceae* sp.), mint (*Labiatae*), nightshade (*Solanaceae* sp.), wild grasses (*Heteropogon contortus*, H. sp.), goose foot (*Chenopodium album*), and Purslane (*Portulaca oleracia*). There is also evidence for the presence of the Indian jujube (*Ziziphus*), which is very common in the tropical regions of India. Impressions of caryopsis, glumes, ziziphus and the charcoal from bamboo have been discovered at Mahadaha and impressions of wild rice husks (*Oryza rufipogon* and *Oryza spontanea*) have been reported from Mahadaha.[41]

Palaeoenvironment

For the reconstruction of the palaeoenvironment of the Mesolithic culture of Mahadaha, Damdama and Sarai Nahar Rai, the palaeozoological and palaeobotanical remains could be helpful. The wild animal species comprises cattle (*Bos indicus*), sheep and goat (*Ovidae* and *capridae*), antelope and deer (*cervidae*), Bison (*Bos gaurus*), Hioppopotamus (*palaeindicus*), suine (*Sus scroffa*), horse (*Equidae*) etc. have been reported from Mahadaha.[42] Such type of animal remains also reported from Damdama. There is a few large mammals like elephant, rhinoceros, gam, wild buffalo at Damdama. From the Mesolithic site of Sarai Nahar Rai situated in the same area, bones of elephant have also been obtained. Of the animals mentioned above, bison, elephant and hippopotamus would require more humid climate than the one prevailing in the area at present. This would indicate a greater incidence of rainfall and swampy condition during the Mesolithic period in the Ganga Plain.

The pedological studies are very much useful for the reconstruction of the past environment of the Kosal region during Mesolithic period. A few soil samples were collected from the Mesolithic layers in the lake areas of Mahadaha and Damdama for the investigation of the palaeoenvironment in the area. Preliminary identifications revealed the presence of pollen grains gramineal, fungal spores and pinus indicating grassland vegetation.[43] The palaynological study of H.P. Gupta at the horse shoe lake at Newari (Lat. 25°41'N; Long 81°31'20"E) near Sarai Nahar Rai also confirm this. A bore to a depth of 3.30 m was made for collecting pollen from the lake at Newari. On the basis of the texture and colour of the sediments three distinct lithozones were identified. The Lithozone I (6-70 cm) was compact grey clay with fine sand and silica). Lithozone II (71-250 cm) consisted of dark black organic mud with very fine silt. The Lithozone III (251-330 cm) was made of grey sticky clay with very fine silt. The Lithozone III (251 – 330 cm) was made of grey sticky clay with coarse sand and irregular kankar nodules more frequent towards the lower limit.[44]

Biostratigraphy and Lithostratigraphy indicate a fourfold climatic fluctuation from very arid to semi-arid through arid and semi-arid. The Lithozone II witnessed a climatic oscillation from semi-arid to semi-humid. In this connection it is worth mentioning that layer Nos. 9 and 8 of Mahadaha are quite identical both in colour and composition to Lithozone II of Nevari. The climatic condition during which this formation took place might have been semi-arid to semi-humid.

Chronology

The term Mesolithic is conventionally applied in India to denote the cultural stage represented by microlithic industries, belongs to the early part of the Holocene geological period, starting at 10,000 B.P. and extending to the present day during which *homo sapiens sapiens* (technical name of the modern man), which evolved in the Upper Palaeolithic culture is in full swing. The oldest human skeletal remains of *Homo sapiens sapiens* yet known in India came from the Mesolithic levels of Sarai Nahar Rai and about dozen of C^{14} and thermoluminescence dates from the area give us a clear idea of the duration of the Mesolithic period in the region of Kosala. It represents the beginning of subsistence strategies that eventually led to the domestication of plants and animals and other technological patterns that can be linked to later cultural developments of Kosal.

Three C^{14} date is obtained from Mesolithic level of Sarai Nahar Rai, out of which average one is 8395 ± 110 B.C. is most reliable date by the scholars.[45] The absence of pottery at Sarai Nahar Rai indirectly confirm its earlier antiquity. The excavators of Sarai Nahar Rai had the opinion that it was a temporary settlement of Vindhyan mesolithic peopled population in summer, when climate of Vindhyan region was very hot. Thus during this phase, the area of Kosal was favourable for human settlement. This phase of Kosal (*circa* 8000 B.C.) was cool with reduced monsoon rainfall as per pollen analysis of Lahuradeva (Pollen Zone I, 8600 BC – 7250 BC). A thermoluminescence date from pit-hearth at Damdama[46] would suggest its time span from *circa* 7000 and 5000 B.C. Two C^{14} dates from Damdama[47] based on isotopes[48] of carbon having 14 and 13 weight are 6690 ± 65 BC and 6915 ± 65 BC. Thus the scientific date confirm that southern portion of Kosal region was occupied by Mesolithic people from *Circa* 8000 BC to 5000 BC.

Albeit there is no chronometric dates is reported from Mahadaha but their comparative study of microlithis from Sarai Nahar Rai confirm that it is much later than that of Sarai Nahar Rai. The human skeletal remains of both the sites (Sarai Nahar Rai and Mahadaha) are almost alike and both have pit hearths. But Mahadaha have advanced Mesolithic tools like trapeze, which totally absent at Sarai Nahar Rai. In contrast to it Sarai Nahar Rai have only triangle, which is technologically much inferior than that of trapeze of Mahadaha. This assumption is based on the fact that at Lekhaia and Chopani-Mando, stratigraphically triangle move forward in the upper strata where trapeze is reported. In the light of above facts, a slightly later date may be proposed for the Mesolithic settlement of Mahadaha, from Sarai Nahar Rai, whose chronometric dates confirm to its existence during *Circa* 8000 B.C.

References

1. Sharma, G.R., V.N. Mishra, D. Mandal, B.B. Mishra and J.N. Pal (1980), *Beginning of Agriculture* (Epi Palaeolithic to Mesolithic), Allahabad, p. 9.
2. Varma, R.K., V.D. Mishra, J.N. Pandey and J.N. Pal (1985), "A Preliminary Report on the Excavations at Damdama (1982-84)," *Man and Environment*, IX: 45-65.
3. Robbins Gwen, V.D. Mishra, J.B. Pal and M.C. Gupta (2003), *Mesolithic Damdama: Dental Histology And Age Estimation*, Allahabad, p. 8
4. *Ibid.*, p. 25.
5. Thomas, P.K., P.P. Joglekar, V.D. Mishra, J.N. Pandey and J.N. Pal (1995), A Preliminary Report on the Faunal Remains from Damdama," *Man and Environment*, XX(1), pp. 29-36

   - Thomas, P.R., Jogelkar, V.D. Mishra, J.N. Pandey and J.N. Pal (1996), "Faunal Evidence for the Mesolithic Food Economy of the Gangetic Plain with Special Reference to Damdama", in *Bioarchaeology of Mesolithic India: An Integrated Approach*, Colloquium XXXIII of the International Union of Prehistoric and Protohistoric Sciences (G.E. Ajanaser, S. Cleuziou, J.R. Lukacs and M. Tosi, eds.), pp. 255-266. Forli: ABA Co, Edizioni.

   - Thomas, P.K., P.P. Jodlekar, V.D. Mishra, J.N. Pandey and J.N. Pal (2002), "Faunal Remains from Damdama: Evidence for the Mesolithic Food Economy of the Gangetic Plain," in *Mesolithic India* (V.D. Mishra and J.N. Pal, eds.), pp. 366-380. Allahabad, Department of Ancient History, Culture & Archaeology, University of Allahabad.

6. Alur, K.R. "Faunal Remains from the Vindhyas and the Ganga Valley" in G.R. Sharma, V.D. Mishra, D. Mandal, B.B. Mishra and J.N. Pal (1980), *Beginnings of Agriculture*, Allahabad, pp. 207-208.
7. *Ibid.*, p. 211.
8. Mishra, V.D. (1977), *Some Aspects of Indian Archaeology.* Allahabad, p. 71.
9. Sharma, G.R. *et al.*, (1980) *op.cit.*, p. 98.
10. Pal, J.N. (1985-86), "Microlithic Industry of Damdama," *Puratattva*, No. 16, pp. 1-5.
11. Robbins Gwen, *et* al.. (2003) *op.cit.*, p. 18.
12. Pal, J.N. (1996), "Lithic Use Wear Analysis and Subsistence Activities Among the Mesolithic. People of North India in he Pre-History of Asia and Oceania: Colloquium, XXXIII, *Bioarchaeology of Mesolithic India: An Integrated Approach,* pp. 267-277.
13. Kennedy, K.A.R. (2000), *Gods Apes and Fossil Men: Palaeoanthropology in South Asia.* Ann Arbor: University of Michigan Press.
14. Sharma, G.R., *et al.* (1980), *op.cit.*, p. 108.
15. Robbins, Gwen, *et* al. (2003), *op.cit.*, p. 18.
16. Sharma, G.R. (1980), *op.cit.*, pp. 108-109.
17. Verma, R.K. (1985), "The Mesolithic Culture of India," *Puratattva*, No. 13 & 14.
18. Pal, J.N. (1992), "Burial Practices and Archaeological Recovery," in Kennedy, K.A.R., *Human Skeletal Remains from Mahadaha: A Gangetic Mesolithic Site,* South Asia Occasional Papers and thesis No. 11, Cornell University, New York, pp. 25-60.
19. *Ibid.*
20. Pandey, J.N. (1996), "Burial Practices and Funerary Practices of Mesolithic India," in *The Prehistory of Asia and Ocenia : Colloquium XXXIII* Bioarchaeology of Mesolithic India: An Integrated Approach, pp. 279-290.
21. Lukacs, J.R. and J.N. Pal (1993), "Mesolithic Subsistence in North India: Inferences from Dental Attributes," *Curr. Anthro.* 34 (5), pp. 745-765.

22. Kennedy, K.A.R. (2000), *God Apes and Fossil Men: Palaeoanthropology in South Asia*. Ann Arbor: University of Michigan Press.
23. Mishra, V.D. (1977) *op.cit.* , p. 100.
24. *Ibid.*
25. Kennedy, K.A.R., J.R. Lukacs, R.F. Pastor, T.L. Johnston, N.C. Lorell, J.N. Pal, B.E. Hemphill and C.B. Burrow (1992), *Human Skeletal Remains from Mahadaha: A Gangetic Mesolithic Site*, South Asia Occasional Papers and Thesis No. 11. Cornell University, New York.
26. Mishra, V.D. *op.cit.*, p. 100; Kennedy, K.A.R. 1986, (2000) *op.cit.*
27. Pal, J.N. (1988), "Mesolithic Double Burials from, Damdama," *Man and Environment*, Vol. 13, pp. 115-122.
28. Pal, J.N. (1992a), *op.cit.*
29. Pal, J.N. (1988), Kennedy, K.A.R., (2000) *op.cit.*
30. *Ibid.*
31. Pal, J.N. (1992a), *op.cit.*
32. Kennedy, K.A.R. (2000), *op.cit.*
33. Kennedy, K.A.R. (1986), *op.cit.*
34. Verma, R.K. "The Mesolithic Cultures of India" in K.N. Dikshit (ed.), *Archaeological Perspectives of India Since Independence*, New Delhi.
35. Lukacs, J.R. (1992b), *et al. op.cit*; Kennedy, K.A.R., (2000) *op.cit.*, pp. 745-765.
36. Mishra, V.D. (1977), *op.cit.*, p. 100.
37. Lukacs, J.R., *et al.* (1993b), *op.cit.*
38. *Ibid.*
39. Lukacs, J.R., J.N. Pal, and V.D. Mishra (1996), "Chronology and Diet in Mesolithic North India: A Preliminary Report of New AMS C-14 dates, Delta C-13 Isotope Values, and their significance", in *The Prehistory of Asia and Oceania: Colloquium XXXIII*, Bioarchaeology of Mesolithic India: An Integrated Approach, pp. 301-311.
40. Kajale, M.D. (1996), "Plant Resources and Diet among the Mesolithic Hunters and Foragers," in *The Pre-history of Asia and*

Oceania: Colloquium XXXIII, Bioarchaeology of Mesolithic India: An Integrated Approach, pp. 251-253.

41. *Ibid.*
42. Sharma, G.R. (1980), *op.cit.*, p. 110.
43. Pant, D.D. and Rekha Pant. "Preliminary Observations on Pollen Flora of Chopani-Mando (Vindhyas) and Mahadaha (Ganga Valey)" in G.R. Sharma (1980), *op.cit.*, p. 229.

    Kajale, M.D. and B.C. Deotare (1988), "Pollen Analysis and Chemical Examinations of a Prehistoric Lake Site at Damdama," *Puratattva* No. 19, pp. 28-30.
44. Gupta, H.P. (1976), "Holocene Palynology from Meander Lake in the Ganga Valley, District Pratapgarh, U.P.," *The Palaeobotanist*, Vol. 25, pp. 109-19.
45. Sharma, G.R. (1975), "Presidential Address to the *Indian Prehistoric Society*, Vol. 39, pp. Delhi, 129-44 and Agrawal, D.P. (Delhi, 1984), *Archaeology of India*, p. 67.
46. Warikalan, Luckacs J.R, and Pal, N.J. (1993), "Mesolithic Subsistance in Northern India: Inference from Atributes" in *Current Anthropology*, Vol. 34, No. 5, p. 749.
47. Luckacs, J.R., Pal, J.N. and Mishra, V.D. (1996), "Chronology and Diet in Mesolithic North India: A Preliminary Report of new AMS C^{14} dates - C^{13} isotope values and their significance and Bioarchaeology of Mesolithic India: An Integrated Approach, *Colloquim XXXIII of International Union of Prehistoric and Protohistoric Sciences,* (eds.) Ajanasa, S. Cleuziore, J.R. Luckacs and M. Tori), pp. 11-30.
48. Elements (or atoms) which have the same atomic number and therefore, similar chemical properties but different atomic weight are called isotopes, e.g. $Carbon^{12}$ have two isotopes of $carbon^{13}$ and $carbon^{14}$.

5

The Early Farming / Neolithic Culture in Kosal Region

Settlement Pattern

In the Kosal region, there is no typical Neolithic assemblage has been reported so far. Although Neolithic settlements yielded mostly handmade coarse variety of red ware bearing cord impressions on their exterior surface. Another characteristic of the Neolithic culture was present in the Kosal region i.e. early farming. Hence, the excavator of the Lahuradeva called its Period IA as Early Farming Phase instead of Neolithic which is contemporary to Early Food Producing Era of Mehargarh (7000 – 6500 B.C.E.) in the Indus region.

Regarding the settlement pattern it may be mentioned that all the excavated sites are located on the banks of rivers or on horse-shoe lake as in the case of Lahuradeva. Easy availability of water, cultivable land and also easy availability of food in the form of suitable vegetation, animals and aquatic creatures was the prime consideration for selecting a site for settlement.

Only three early farming settlements have been excavated so far in the said region i.e. Lahuradeva (Period IA), Imlidih Khurd (Period I, pre-Narhan Culture) and Sohgaura (Period I). The early farming phase of Imlidih-Khurd, Lahuradeva and Sohagaura yielded 50-60, 68 and 60 cm. thick cultural deposit respectively.

Subsistence Pattern

The subsistence pattern of the Neolithic Culture was mainly based on agriculture supplemented by hunting-gathering. Carbonised material of Lahuradeva Period IA contains grains of cultivated rice (*Oryza sativa*) and wild rice (*Oryza rufipogon*), which corroborates the beginning of rice based agriculture at the site at least around middle of the seventh millennium B.C.E.[1]

The Period I of Imlidih Khurd[2] confirm that the agriculture was a stable and rewarding economy. The universal and abundant occurrence of the remains of cereals and pulses as compared with the other finds suggests that their major role in the subsistence economy. By far the majority of cereal grains have lost their pales or husk by heat and wear, but the impress of pales is present. Maximum representation is of rice kernels during this period. The variation in their shape renders no help in determining the species, although they appear to be of cultivated form of *Oryza sativa.* Husk imprints in the potsherds and plaster-pieces collected from period I, however, confirm that rice was major crop cultivated throughout the occupational period of Imlidih-Khurd.

Next to the rice grains of wheat and barley from the Period I give clear indication of their relative importance. In this period grains of bread wheat (*Triticum aestivum*) and dwarf wheat (*Triticum sphaerococcum*) were found. Whole or fragmentary grains of hulled and six row barley (*Hordeum vulgare*) and jowar millet (*Sorghum bicolor*) and pearl-millet-bajra (*Pennisetum typhoides*) were also found.

The remains of pulses constituted a conspicuous proportion of vegetable food. This may in part be due to their comparatively high content of proteins which enables them to serve as a cheaper substitute for meal. The pulses include lentil (*Lense culinaris*), field peas (*Pisum arvense*), grass pea or Khesari (*Lathyrus sativus*), green gram or Mung (*Vigna radiate*).

Three seeds of field brassica (*Brassica juncea*) and single seed of sesame or til (*Sesamum indiam*) witness testimony to the cultivation of oliferous crops in the cord impressed Red Ware Culture.

The settlers of Period I also exploited fruits like wild jujube (*Ziziphus nummularia*), anwala (*Emlica officinalis*) and grape (*Vitis vinifera*).

At Lahuradeva Period I charred and uncharred bones and the turtle shell found in a broken condition which were also a part of their subsistence.[3] The excavation of Imlidih Khurd Period I yielded remains of cattle which often bear characteristic butcher marks. The aquatic resources comprise two species of fresh water turtle, fish by small and medium size and fresh water mollusca.[4]

Structural Activities

The structural remains[5] of Sub-Period IA of Lahuradeva are represented by burnt clay chunks and nodules bearing reed and straw marks, which indicate that the houses of this period was made of wattle and daub. The wattle and daub huts having screens made of reeds or other similar material enforced by a clay plaster on their exterior to prevent wind and water from the open slits left between the reeds.

Another important feature of this period is an irregular channel[6] running north to south from lakeside towards the central part of mound. It has been traced for a length of 12 m, which is about 30-50 cm broad at upper level and about 50-60 cm deep. Subsequently, it became broader due to siltation and overflow of water in it. Finally, the drain got filled up and became defunct. The post holes found on the surface of the sealing level of the drain clearly show that when the surface became flat, a wattle and daub structure was constructed over it. Two successive floors prepared with clay-bearing an armed clay hearth based on each of them is also reported.

The inhabitants of Period I of Imlidih Khurd lived also in wattle-and-daub huts represented by reed marks in large numbers. Several floors made of mud, ovens and chulah marked the other structural activity. An almost circular pit with a diameter of 1.95 meter was found to have been excavated in the natural soil. A circular structure with an internal diameter of 85 cm. could have been made a grain silo or bin. The thickness of its walls was approximately 7 cm. Remains of a mud floor, with an average thickness of 25-30 cm was also found.[7]

Material Culture

Pottery

Ceramic industries of Period IA of Lahuradeva[8] consisting mainly red ware and black-and-red ware, which include handmade and wheel turned (slow wheel) varieties. The proposition of black and-red ware sherds is as high as about 50% of the pottery assemblage. More than two-third of the thickness of their inner core is generally black, while a thin portion of the exterior part is red. The thickness of the outer red surface is, however, more than that of red wash and slip often applied on the exterior surface. Some of the black-and-red ware and red ware potsherds bear black and red slip respectively on their interior and exterior surface. Burnishing is also evident, in addition to slip treatment in many examples. In a few cases, red slip is remarkably fine. Generally the pottery is ill-fired having coarse and porous surface and uneven, sometimes gritty, core. The clay used for pottery making exhibits husk and straw marks and is not well-levigated. A good number of potsherds are decorated with cord impressions. Applied decoration showing primitive type of rope pattern is also found. The main shapes include convex-sided bowl, pedestal bowl, knobbed vessel, miniature bowl and vase. The high proportion of coarse variety of black-and-red ware is significant. Most of the pots are made in two stages, the lower and rim portions are prepared separately, thereafter the rim portion is pinched with the lower one.

Sohgaura[9] Period I is represented by handmade pottery with mat impressions on the exterior. The pottery is invariably made of coarse clay and is ill-baked showing unoxidized core.

The pottery of pre-Narhan Culture of Imlidih Khurd[10] is essentially a crude red ware, some it bearing cord impression on the exterior of the pots and hence termed 'corded ware', the others being vessels of plain red ware. In both cases the clay contains good amount of degraissent which got burnt firing and it resulted into a porous surface. Most vessels, particularly the globular vases have thin, sandy, fiable core, some of them having mica pieces. The vessels are generally ill-fired, leaving a black core.

Corded Ware

The principle shapes of the corded ware is the spherical, ovaloid and sub-ovaloid bowls with incurved rim and a pedestal base. The pots bear cord-impression on the exterior of which at least a dozen patterns have been noted. These include rope patterns, criss-cross design and excised notches. After making these patterns a thick paste has been applied in the pre-firing stage with the result that the cord patterns got subdued. The pedestal of such bowls was made separately, presumably on wheel or by turnette method and it was affixed to the body of the pot. The rim of such bowl is almost always inturned and there is an impression that a wicker like rim was made by coil method separately and attached to the body of the vessel. The height of a complete bowl is 7 cm. and the diameter of the rim is 16 cm. It was observed that while the selection of the clay and the firing did not reach the desired level of efficiency, the potters of this phase had perfected the art of applying a bright slip in the interior of the bowl and the exterior of other types of vessels and burnished it to such an extent that a shining surface with individual burnished strokes is visible even today. As a result the bowl became non-porous and any liquid could be stored in them without the fear of the loss of the contents; as the absorption capacity of clay is greatly reduced or almost eliminated. It is believed that perhaps a burnisher of bone or a very fine grained stone was used. The functional aspect of these bowls seems to be complicated as ethnographic parallels are not available at the moment. The interior of these bowls has hues of red (from bright red to biscuit red or even orange to buff colours) but occasionally the interior is black also. Another noteworthy feature of the bowls is a raised dot or ridge on the rim, the purpose of which remains to be ascertained.

The second type of vessel is the vase, typologically similar to some of the vases of the succeeding Narhan culture but the special feature of pre-Narhan vases is that below the flaring rim the body suddenly expands and it has cording pattern all over the body of the vessel starting just after the neck on the exterior. The thick coating of clay on the exterior is similar to that of the bowl subduing to a great extent the corded patterns. The section of such vessel is very thin and the pots are generally under fired. Because of this defect, these vessels are found in a shattered condition.

The third vessel in pre-Narhan Red Ware is a handi like cooking vessel with out-turned or inturned rim, constricted neck, expanding shoulders, carinated sides and a sagger base. Some of these vessels bear appliqué band just below the shoulder having chain pattern, rope pattern or incised decoration, made on the appliqué band. A large handi with a diameter of the mouth of 29 cm is a noteworthy find. The maximum diameter of the body of this vessel is 41 cms. It bears a bright red slip on the neck and shoulder (which has peeled off at places) and a corded pattern below the carinated neck. It has a small spout luted at the shoulder.

Besides, about a dozen tubular spouts have been found from various levels ranging in length from 5.14 cm to 6.57 cm and they invariably bear a bright red slip on the exterior. These spouts were luted to the carinated handi but besides these, to which other types of vessels they were luted, is not certain. It may be added here that a few pieces of the neck and rim of a vessel having arrow opening like the present day surahis of this area were also found. Presumably they had a globular body and some of the spouts might have been luted to this type of vessel.

Decoration of the Pottery

In addition to the various types of corded patterns there are two other methods of decorating the pottery vessels. The first method comprises post-firing scratching by a sharp instrument which essentially includes geometrical patterns (opposed triangles etc. within concentric circles). A few floral motifs have been noticed in a few cases. It is noteworthy that post firing scratched designs have not been documented so far on the potteries of Middle Ganga Plain.

The second method of decorating a vessel was by painting the pot with dots and dashes in red colour over a bright red surface. The painting seems to have been executed by multiple brush technique.

Applique Design

The appliqué method of decoration is confined to the handis only. A strip of clay was generally affixed on the exterior of the vessel at the point of carination below the shoulder and by cutting, incising and other methods, various types of rope and chain patterns were executed on the added strip of clay. Below the carination, the handis generally have a corded exterior.

2. *Beads and Ornaments*

Beads[11] made of steatite, carnelian and sempricious stones have been reported from Lahuradeva Period IA. The presence of wafer think micro disc beads of steatie is important finding. Elongated tubular and circular types of beads are also found in the Period IA of Lahuradeva. A small chunk of dried steatite and a terracotta beads are also found. Several micro beads of steatite, other beads of terracotta, agate and faience have been recorded from Imlidih Khurd Period I.[12]

3. *Bone, Stone and Other Terracotta Objects*

Bone objects such as bone points and arrowheads are reported from Lahuradeva[13] Period IA and Imlidih Khurd Period I.[14] Sling ball[15] has been reported from Lahuradeva Period IA whereas at Imlidih-Khurd in Period I pottery discs[16] have been reported. The presence of a rock piece[17] in Period IA of Lahuradeva is also significant. This rock piece appears to be a micaceous metamorphic rock, and possibly coming from the gneisses and schists of the Himalaya. Neither this type of rock nor any other rocks are present in the vicinity of the Lahuradeva. The nearest source of the rock found could be gravely rivers flowing from the Himalaya into the Terai and Bhabar belt. The presence of this rock piece at Lahuradeva thereby suggests its deliberate transportation by man and some sort of interaction with that area. The usage of this rock piece is not clear.

Chronology

In the Kosal region, the early farming culture was concentrated in the northern part whereas the medolithic culture i.e. Foraging was concentrated in its southern part. Stratigraphically Early Farming Culture/Neolithic Culture have no lower strata of Mesolithic Culture *in situ*, while at the same time Mesolithic sites have no upper strata of Neolithic Culture *in situ* in the area of Kosal. The Early Farming Culture is represented primarily at the site of Lahuradeva, Sohagaura and Pre-Narhan phase at Imlidh Khurd.

Three C^{14} dates along with an AMS C^{14} date of a carbonized domesticated rice from the level of Neolithic/ Early Farming strata[18] is reported—

5320	±	90 BP (BS 1951),
	±	160 BP (BS 1966)

AMS C^{14} date of domesticated rice is 6442 – 6376 BC since all the three dates at Lahuradeva is reported from the upper level of Early Farming Strata, therefore its antiquity push back to 7th millennium B.C. and continued to the end of the 4th millennium BC. It is important to note here that in the region of at the site of Mehargarh[19], the date of Early Food Producing Era ranges from 7000 – 5500 BC where there is evidence of domesticated wheat and barley. These evidences confirm the two epicenters of early farming culture of rice and wheat-barley in South Asia.

At Sohgaura the lowermost deposit of Neolithic/Early Farming phase containing handmade coarse variety of red ware bearing cord impressions on their exterior surface itself confirm its primitive form. On above the Neolithic/ Early Farming deposit at Sohgaura, a chalcolithic deposit is present which is marked by plain and painted Black Slipped and Black-and-Red Wares. The radiocarbon dates available from the late phase of Chalcolithic Period III is 1410 ± 130 BC (PRL 179) and 1490 ± 110 BC (PRL 178).[20] By this fact the lower level of Chalcolithic II at Sohgaura was assessed to be around 1900 BC and the beginning of the preceding Neolithic/Early Farming Period at Sohgaura during first half of the third millennium BC.[21] Thus the early date of Early

Farming Culture at Sohgaura is later on confirmly supported by the discovery of Lahuradeva in the region of Kosal.

References

1. Tiwari, Rakesh *et* el.(2005-06), *op.cit.*, p. 70.
   Tiwari, Rakesh *et al.* (2002-03), *op.cit.*, pp. 39-40.
2. *I.A.R.* 1974-75, p. 47.
3. Singh, Purushottam (1992), *op.cit.*, pp. 23-28.
4. Tiwari, Rakesh *et al.* (2001-02), *op.cit.*, p. 55.
5. *Ibid.*
6. Singh, Purushottam (1992), *op.cit.*, p. 30.
7. Tiwari, Rakesh *et al.*(2005-06) *op.cit.*, p. 70.
8. Saraswat, K.S. (1991-92), "Seed and Gruit Remains at Ancient Imlidih-Khurd, Gorakhpur: A Preliminary Report," *Pragdhara*, No. 3, p. 38.
9. Tiwari, Rakesh *et al.* (2005-06), *op.cit.*, p. 73.
10. Singh, Purushottam (1992), *op.cit.*, p. 31.
11. Tiwari, Rakesh *et al.* (2005-06), *op.cit.*, p. 70.
12. Singh, Purushottam (1992), *op.cit.*, p. 120.
13. Tiwari, Rakesh *et al.* (2001-02), *op.cit.*, p. 55.
14. Singh, Purushottam (1992), *op.cit.*, p. 120.
15. Tiwari, Rakesh *et al.* (2001-2002), *op.cit.*, p. 46.
16. Singh, Purushottam (1992) *op.cit.*, p. 120.
17. Tiwari, Rakesh, *et al.* (2002-03), *op.cit.*, p. 43.
18. *Ibid* (2004-05), p. 40.
19. Mark Kenoyer Jonathan (2006), "Cultures and Societies of thc Indus Tradition" in *India: Historical Beginnings and the Concept of the Aryan* Delhi, p. 53.
20. Possehl, G.L. and Rissman, P.C. (1992), 'The Chronology of Prehistoric India: From Earliest Times to the Iron Age' in *Chronology in Old World*, ed. Eurich Robert, Chicago, p. 463.

21. Chaturvedi, S.N. (1985), 'Advance of Vindhyan Neolithic and Chalcolithic Culture of the Himalayan Tarai: Exploration and Excavation in the Saryupar Region of Uttar Pradesh', *Man and Environment*, IX, Pune, pp. 100-101.

6

The Chalcolithic Culture in Kosal Region

Settlement Pattern

Explorations in the Kosal region have brought into light a number of Chalcolithic settlements in the district of Jaunpur, Pratapgarh, Sultanpur, Gonda, Bahraich, Sravasti, Siddharthnagar, Sant Kabir Nagar, Gorakhpur, Basti. The settlements are located either on the bank of Ghaghara, Gomati rivers and its tributaries, nala or on the lake sides. The rivers, nalas and lakes provided water and food in the form of aquatic animals like fish, tortoise, etc. In the selection of sites in the yore for settlements the main consideration was the availability of fertile land for cultivation. Hence, the favourable ecological conditions including alluvial soil, climate, accessibility of natural resources were largely responsible for the growth, maturity and expansion of Chalcolithic Culture in the Kosal region.

The excavated Chalcolithic settlements of Trans-Ghaghara region are Narhan (Period I), Dhuriapar (Period I), Imlidih Khurd (Period II), Sohagaura (Period II), Lahuradeva (Period IB & II). They are all rural settlements characterized by mud architecture, plain and painted pottery stone and bone tools with restricted use of copper. Their mixed economy was based on agriculture, stock raising and hunting-fishing.

The thickness of the Chalcolithic deposit shows that in comparison to the only farming Neolithic Culture it was survived very long span of time. The thickness of Chalcolithic strata at Narhan is 1 m, Lahuradeva Period IB is 50 cm.

In the Saryupar region, the Chalcolithic culture is called as 'Nrhan Culture' because at the type site Narhan there is no lithic assemblage has been reported. Hence, the excavation of the Narhan had given the nomenclature as "Narhan Culture" instead of Chalcolithic Culture.[1] The sites of Narhan Culture (1300-800 B.C.) are reported from several other sites of the Kosal region i.e. Dhuriapar and Imlidih-Khurd, etc.

Another important Chalcolithic site of Trans-Ghaghara region is the Lahuradeva[12]. Its Period IB (Early Farming Phase) and Period II (Developed Farming Phase) are associated with Chalcolithic Culture. The beginning of this sub-period (IB) is marked by the appearance of barley and dish/bowl on stand. Associated ceramic industries include red, black-and-red, black and grey wares. The main shapes comprise perforated legged bowl, lipped or channeled bowl, water vessels, pedestal bowl, spouted vessel, bowl/dish on stand, etc. The most important aspect of this sub-period is the appearance of a copper arrowhead made of sheet metal and a fishing hook from the lower levels. The finds may be placed in early 3rd millennium B.C.E. and represent earliest known copper artifacts in the Ganga Plain. Typologically, these finds are similar to those found in the Early and Mature Harappan contexts at Harappa, Lothal, Banawali, etc. by which excavator suggests some contact between Middle Ganga Plain and Harappa region during the Sub-period IB of Lahuradeva.[13]

Subsistence Pattern

The economy of the Narhan Culture was primarily based on the agriculture. Meat was the staple component of their diet. At Narhan, a good quantity of archaeobotanical remains obtained by flotation technique which give a fair idea of the agricultural practices of these people.[14] Cereal grains of hulled and six row barley (*Hordum vulgare*), Club wheat (*Triticum compactum*), bread wheat (*Triticum aestivum*), dwarf wheat (*Triticum sphaeorococcum*), pearl millet or bajra (*Pennisetum typhoides*), Kondon millet (*Paspalum scrobi culatum*), cultivated rice (*Oryza sativa*) have been identified. The pulses include field pea (*Pisum sativum*), green gram (mung, *Vigna radiata*), gram/chick pea (*Cicer arietinum*), Khesari or grass pea (*Lathyrus sativus*), and Lentil (*Lens culinaris*), besides mustard oilseeds (some form of *Brassica campastris*) and flax/linseed (*Linum usitatissium*). The find of mustard from Narhan is the first record of this oilseed in the Indian sub-continent. Carbonised seeds and cotyledons of jack fruit or Katahal (*Artocarpus heterophyllus*) is also an important discovery. At Imlidih Khurd, the inhabitants of Period II, cultivated rice (*Oryza sativa*), bread wheat (*Triticum aestivum*), dwarf wheat (*Triticum sphaerococcum*), hulled and six row barley (*Hordeum vulgare*) and Kondon-millet (*Paspalum scrobi culatum*). The remains of pulses constituted a conspicuous proportion of vegetal food. This may in part be due to their comparatively high content of proteins which enables them to as a cheaper substitute for meat. The pulses included lentil (*Lens culinaris*), cotyledons of green gram (*Vigna radiata*) and chick pea (*Cicer arientinum*). The people of Narhan culture at Imlidih Khurd exploited local fruits like wild jujube (*Ziziphus nummularia*) and *anwala* (*Emblica officinalis*). The Black & Red Ware culture of Narhan and Imlidih Khurd, both in the same region of Gorakhpur district seem to have shared much the same kind of crop economy and enjoyed mutual contacts. Lahuradeva is another important site of Trans-Ghaghara Plain of Saryupar region in which Period IB and period II yielded the remains of barley (*Hordeum vulgare*), rice (*Oryza sativa*), wheat (*Triticum aestivum*), lentil (*Lens culinaris*), field pea (*Pisum arvense*). The introduction of the crops of wheat, barley, lentil, field pea etc. has also been evidenced to form an established double cropping system in this region of settlement. Rice, bajra, kondon-millet, horse gram, green gram, moth-bean are usually grown in warm-rainy season, while wheat, barley, gram, khesari, lentil and field pea are the winter crops. Chenopodium album (locally known as *bathua*) and Setaria (S. glauca) are common weeds of cultivation and in all likelihood were used for food because of their large nutritious seeds.[15] The weeds of both were reported from the

Black-and-Red ware phase of Imlidih Khurd and Narhan. The seeds and leaves of Amranthus (locally known as *Chaulai*) also reported from Imlidih Khurd and Narhan. The above plant species are eaten as vegetables.

Pulses[16] constitute a group of the Legume family which, with the help of bacteria in their root nodules, fix atmospheric nitrogen and improve soil fertility. Their ability to thrive under a wide range of soil and climatic conditions resulted pulse crops finding an important place in the agricultural economy in Narhan, Imlidih Khurd, Lahuradeva and surrounding area of Kosal. *Kharif* crops of moth-bean, green gram, mung serve as a good cover crop under a taller growing associated crops of millets like jowar and bajra. It may reasonably be presumed that the settlers of Black-and-Red ware culture of Saryupar region may have practised the mixed cultivation of cereals and pulses, during the summer-rainy seasons. The nitrogen compounds formed in the roots of the legume crops pass into the soil in the vicinity of roots. When the non-leguminous plants are grown in association with legumes, they obtain a direct advantage. The fundamental practices of growing the cereal and pulse crops seem to have remained the same, as indeed there are in the present times.

Although the settlers of the Narhan culture practised agriculture but the meat was an important component of their diet as is evident from the presence of a large number of charred animal bones and antlers, some of them having cut mark. At Narhan only 15% of animal bones were collected from the excavation of Period I. The animal bones of humped Indian cattle (*Bos indicus*), sheep goat (*Ovis/capra*), wild ruminant like deer or anteope (*Axis* sp.) and horse (*Equus* sp.) have been identified.[17] That the ancient settlers subsisted on fish to supplement their protein requirement is suggested by the discovery of an impression of a fishing hook with part of a thread on a mud clod. A minute fragment of fibre recovered from the surface of thread impression. The faunal remains of Period II of Imlidih Khurd comprise domisticated cattle, goat/sheep, horse and dog. The wild fauna comprises boar, hog deer, chital or spotted deer and barasingha or swamp deer. The horse remains comprise a mandible with first and second premoters and an isolated molar/premolar.[18] This animal, medium to large in size, is of domestic type and similar to those presented from Narhan Culture. The aquatic resources comprise two species of fresh water turtle, fish of small and medium size. The Lahuradeva Pd IB comprises cattle (*Bos indicus*) and buffalo (*Bubalus babalis*) and presence of charred bone of a large cat is especially notable. The presence of charred bones shows the consumption of non-vegetarian, along with vegetarian food and in Period II the large quantity of charred and uncharred bones, antlers are found.[19]

Structural Activities

During chalcolithic period the settlers lived in wattle-and-daub houses. At Narhan the remains of post-holes and reed marks in burnt clay lumps. Successive floors made of beaten mud, occasional post-holes, ovens and hearths have been found. A large floor made of clay mixed with pot-sherds was exposed in an area of roughly 13.5 m × 5 m. However, the complete house-plan could not be reconstructed because of limited nature of excavation.[20] At Lahuradeva the structural activities of the chalcolithic period are mainly represented by post-holes, rammed earthen floors, a mud-wall, burnt clay nodules often bearing reed marks, hearths and bins. Post-holes appear to form circular alignment. Their mud plastered screens made of reeds or similar material are represented by the burnt clay chunks bearing reed like impressions. Hearths are of two kinds: pit hearths dug below the surface or floor, and clay hearths made of clay and placed on the floor. The floors were made of rammed clay procured from the adjoining lake and were generally 5.0 to 7.0 cm thick.[21] A few notable structures, almost circular in plan, are found to have been excavated either below the surface or in natural soil. Their internal surface is sometimes coated with clay-plaster. These structures seem to have been used as grain silo or bins and are comparable to similar structures found in the excavation at Imlidih-Khurd[22] of pre-Narhan period. The diameter of one of the silo is 85 cm and the internal depth is about 70 cm. The internal surface of this structure is plastered with a thick coat of yellowish clay. Though the plaster was found badly damaged, the remaining portion of it was quite apparent to elaborate its nature. The thickness of the remaining plaster varied between 2.5 to 8.0 cm. Incidentally, the measurements and shape of this silo compares well with that of found at Imlidih Khurd, having 85 cm internal diameter and about 7.0 cm thick wall.[23] The diameter of another bin was about 78 cm and its depth was 44 cm from the surface. The clay plaster applied on its internal surface could be traced intact, the thickness of this coating was 7-8 cm. Its shape resembles with a particular type of container made of *munja* or *sarpata* (straw) being used in the nearby villages and locally known as *dauri*. It is interesting to note that the excavators of Mahadaha, a Mesolithic site in district Pratapgarh have also reported the presence of a few shallow pits, plastered with thick clay solution like Imlidih-Khurd. Sometimes more than one coating of clay has been used for plastering the pits. Some of these pits were possibly used for storing surplus grains.[24] It shows that this type of earthen storage pits were a common feature in a larger area of the Indian sub-continent during the period beginning from the Mesolithic stage to subsequent periods. Another interesting feature of Lahuradeva (Pd. II) structural activity is a partially broken flat and rectangular terracotta specimen[25] of tiles which measures about 34 cm in length, 15 cm in breadth and about 2.50 – 3.00 cm in thickness. Curious enough is a downward projection along one of the longer sides. It appears similar to the baked tiles, and in all likelihood to cover some structures. It may also be noted that this type of terracotta objects has been found in a sufficient quantity from the trenches located in both the areas, the western and eastern portions of the mound.

Material Culture

The material culture of the Chalcolithic settlers were found in the form of pottery, beads & ornaments, bone, metal terracotta and stone objects.

Pottery

The main ceramic[26] industries of the Narhan are the white painted Black-and-Red Ware (57.77%), Black-Slipped ware with occasional painting in white (8.01%), Red Slipped Ware (8.84%) and plain Red ware (25.38%). The principal pottery types in Black-and Red ware are bowls (66.90%), basin (11%) and vases (22.09%).

However, the conspicuous absence of dishes is the salient featurein the Black-and-Red ware. More than 20% sherds in the fine and medium fabrics of the Black-and-Red ware are painted. The principal types in the Black Slipped ware consist of bowls (83.71%), dishes (14.95%) and vases (1.21%). The quantity of basins and vases is extremely limited. In the Red Slipped ware the dominant category is that of bowls (66.74%), followed by basins (23.89%), vases (7.32%) and dishes (2.04%). The Red Ware has bowls (50.18%), vases (29.86%), basins (15.51%) and dishes (4.44%).

The wares of Narhan Culture is also reported from the Dhuriapar (Period I) and Imlidikh Khurd (Period II) of Narhan phase. The characteristic pottery of this period is the white painted Black-and-Red ware, so well documented at the type site, located about 30 km east-south-east of Imlidih. The white painted Black-and-Red ware is numerically dominant ceramic industry at Imlidih Khurd also, but it differs from that of Narhan in the following ways[27]—

(1) Here only coarse and medium fabrics are present.

(2) In the medium fabric of Black-and-Red ware pots are generally thicker as compared to Narhan and the pottery has a unique look. It also has more of degraissand in the body clay which generally includes paddy husk and grains etc. and these

have burnt off in the firing process leaving a pours core.

(3) Burnished Black-and-Red ware which was very rare at Narhan (not more than a dozen sherds) is more prolific at Imlidih. The slip which is generally peeled off at places has a smooth burnishing particularly in the interior of bowls/pedestal bowls.

(4) Pedestal bowls generally have two perforations at the pedestal presumably for the suspension/ hanging of the pot on a peg when not in use. This feature was totally absent at Narhan.

(5) Paintings in Black-and-Red ware are comparatively rare. Whereas at Narhan the painted pots account for as much as 20% of Black-and-Red ware vessels at Imlidih it may be even less than one per cent of the total black and red ware pots. The paintings include only linear motifs and very few pots have paintings executed on both sides.

(6) Typologically in the dish-on-stand the stem is little more elongated raising the height of the pot.

(7) The bowls are comparatively more shallow and some of these look like plates or saucers.

(8) Basin with averted rim and corrugation below the rim/shoulders, which was a hallmark of Red Slipped ware at Narhan is now repeated in Black-and-Red ware lending support to the hypothesis that Red Slipped Ware of Narhan may not be an independent industry and it is the firing condition/ application of organic material on the body of clay

which resulted into different surface colours of the pots.

Coarse Black-and-Red Ware

The vases of various thickness of the rim are present at Imlidih Khurd also in large numbers, in addition to the Black-and-Red Ware, the Black-slipped Ware and Plain Red Ware. The Red-Slipped Ware was present at the Narhan in limited quantities is totally absent at Imlidih Khurd.

Black-Slipped Ware

Although comparatively less in number as compared to Narhan, such characteristic shapes as long beakers with external grooves at the waist are present at Imlidih also. Some vessels of this shape have thick fabric as compared to Narhan.

Besides, a completely new shape recorded at Imlidih is the *Lota* in Black-Slipped Ware of which about a dozen specimens have been found. They have a globular body, constricted neck and flaring rim with shining black slip on the exterior. Some of these specimens have vertical linear paintings originating from the rim and going downwards.

Plain Red Ware

In the Red Ware an important shape is the perforated vessel having four legs. These occur at the type site of Narhan as well. These vessels seem to be essentially bowls with 9 to 12 perforations in the bottom and they stand on four legs.

The fabric is thick and sturdy and the vessels bear a bright red slip on the interior.[28]

Period IB of Lahuradeva is marked by the appearance of dish/bowl-on-stand in red ware. Although the associated ceramic industries from the earlier sub period (IA) show continuity and include red, Black-and-Red, Black, and Grey wares. The main shapes comprise perforated legged-bowl, lipped or channelled vessel, bowl/dish-on-stand, etc. Decorative patterns of earlier sub-period also continue. The fabric of pottery improves from coarse to medium, and proportion of painted pottery also increases.[29]

The period II of Lahuradeva is marked by the appearance of painted and plain Black-Slipped ware in a considerable proportion. Other ceramics include Red (plain and painted), Black-and-Red (plain and painted), Black, and Grey wares. The bulk of the painted pot-sherds of this period are dominated by the Black Slipped ware which shows that this ware is one of the most distinct characteristic of this period.[30] The colours used are mostly white to creamy white. Some examples of Black and Ochre-Coloured paintings have also been recovered. Their workmanship is apparetly improved. The decorative patterns of Period I continue and show some innovations. The paintings include dotted, circular and linear designs. Some of which are very artistically executed. Incised and applique decorations continued in small proportion. It may be emphasised here that the white and black painted Black Slipped ware has been found from the chalcolithic deposits (Developed Farming Phase) of the other sites of the region such as Sohgaura[31], Imlidih Khurd[32] , Narhan[33] , etc. which shows that this pottery is the hallmark of the Developed

Farming Phase of the middle Ganga plain. Corded pattern of decoration also continued. Its proportion in comparison to other ceramic and that of Period I, however, is reduced. Quantity of slipped and burnished pottery, besides certain shapes such as dish-on-stand, bowl-on-stand, pedestal bowl, perforated bowl, button based lids and spouts enhanced in a good proportion.[34] Negligible occurrence of convex sided dish to be noted.

A broken spout of a red ware pot is unique for its painting at Lahuradeva. It is treated with brownish red slip on exterior, which is decorated with linear design in black pigment. Its extant length is about 5.9 cm. At an average it is about 2.2 cm broad. The respective internal and external diameters are 2.9 and 1.8 cm. This is the only example found in the excavation till date at Lahuradeva which bears painted decoration, not known so far from any other site of the Ganga Plain. Presence of thick red ware pot-sherds having bold perforations across the core of their body remains is of the Harappan tradition. One such example was also found at Waina in district Ballia. Though the perforated pottery is considered related mainly with Harappa culture, its manufacture by the early Aharians and Chalcolithic people of the adjoining areas is also well evident.[35] It is also observed that the non Harppaan perforated ware is unmistakably identical to that of Harppans. It shows that the practice of perforating certain pots were prevalent in a much larger areas during third millennium B.C. However, the shapes of such pots selected in different areas may be due to varying regional styles.

Period II of Sohgaura is characterized by the introduction of potter's wheel[36]. Although the handmade pottery of the earlier tradition continued, new ceramics were introduced which include plain and painted Black-Slipped ware, plain and painted Black-and-Red ware, Red ware and coarse Grey ware. Black-slipped ware is generally of medium fabric and is represented by bowls and miniature vases. A few sherds[37] were found to be painted with black pigment showing vertical, horizontal and curved lines. In Red Ware a number of sherds show a burnished surface. Applique decoration and graffiti are also seen on some of the pots. In the black-and-red ware, some sherds bear painted designs in white pigment. The usual shapes are bowls, dishes and globular vases. The linear patterns are sometimes painted both on the exterior as well as interior. The uniformity in the delineation of the linear patterns suggests that some sort of stencil device must have been used in drawing them. Sometimes the designs are picked up in the reserved technique.

Beads & Ornaments

The people of the Narhan Culture had the aesthetic sense which indicated by the use of different types of beads. The type site Narhan[39] yielded 12 terracotta beads of Arecanut shaped (Flat based 2), Arecanut shaped with incised line and striatation marks on the body, and elongated Ghata shaped with concave base in Period I. Most of the arecanut shaped beads are made of fine clay on a fast wheel and baked very hard at a high temperature. Probably these beads were fired in closed kilns under reducing condition, resulting in a black of smoky grey colour. Generally they are devoid of any surface treatment. A few of these have two parallel lines incised all round the body while in motion on wheel. Other sites of Narhan Culture also include terracotta beads i.e. Imlidih Khurd and Dhuriapar. Lahuradeva comprises not only the beads of terracotta but semi-precious stones and steatite (?) beads.[40] The beads recovered from the deposits of this period (II) are of various sizes and shapes. Most notable amongst them are creamish white coloured micro to medium sized beads found in a large quantity. Such beads have also been recovered in the excavation at Sohgaura, Imlidih Khurd of Trans-Ghaghara region. Their shape, size and manufacturing technique is similar to those of micro to medium sized circular disc shaped steatite beads found a Harappan sites in abundance. Considering their similarity with the Harappan beads, the beads found at the sites mentioned above are also generally believed to be made of steatite. Two copper beads are reported from Imlidkh Khurd[41] from Pd II. Beads of jasper and agate have been reported from Sohgaura[42] excavations.

Apart from beads broken bangle of bone or anteler have been reported from Dhuriapar.[43] The copper antimony rod is reported from Lahuradeva Pd II. The Narhan Period I yielded one terracotta and one glass bangle A copper bangle is reported from Lahuradeva in Pd II also.

Bone Objects

The excavation of Narhan yielded arrowheads and points made of bone and ivory. The technique of manufacture was quite simple and involved flaking a piece of bone to the desired shape with retouches at the tips for sharpening. The Period I of Narhan[44] include 23 bone points and 15 arrowheads of tanged type. Bone points of Narhan Culture are crudely made from long bones of animals while few of them are made of ivory. The tanged types of arrowheads are well-finished. Some arrowheads are made of ivory whereas the rest are made of animal bones. Bone arrowheads and points reported from the excavations of Lahuradeva (Period II) also. Some of the very well made ground, polished and decorated bone arrowheads of tanged, barbed and socketed varieties, often bearing punctured circlets, are worth mentioning for their quality workmanship.[45] A bone stylus or shuttle has been reported from Sohagaura in Period II.

Metal Objects

The copper fish hooks comes from Period I of Narhan[46], suggesting that fish was an important component of their dietary system. One copper ring is also reported from the same place. A copper arrowhead is reported from the excavation of Imlidih Khurd[47] in Period II, typographically similar to the copper arrowheads of Ganeshwar (Rajasthan) datable to the third millennium B.C.E.. Like those of Ganeshwar the copper arrowhead is also made by cutting from a thin copper sheet. In Period I, the most important aspect of the sub Period I of Lahuradeva[48] is the appearance of a copper arrowhead (3.0 × 1.4 cm) made of sheet metal and a fishing hook (1.5 × 1.0 cm) from the lower levels. These finds may be placed in early 3rd millennium B.C. and represent the earliest known copper artefacts in the Ganga Plain.

At Narhan[40] a mud clad, found in the upper levels of Period I (*Circa* 1300-800 B.C.E.) has provided an evidence of iron fishing hook, in the form of its impression showing some grains of iron rust.

Stone and other Terracotta Objects

A small stone scraper (2.4 × 1.3 cm) is reported from Period IB, Celts, muller and hammer have been reported from Period II of Lahuradeva. A stone anvil is also reported from the same place in Period II. Terracotta balls have been reported from Period I of Dhuriapar. Terracotta discs have been reported from Imlidih Khurd (Period II) and Dhuriapar (Period I). Terracotta wheels are reported from Period II of Lahuradeva. The material remains suggest that they were common village folk.

Chronology

By computing the chronology Chalcolithic chronology in the area of Kosal, several chronometric dates in the form of radiocarbon have been obtained from Sohgaura, Narahan and Lahuradeva which is as given below.

1.	Sohagaura	Lab No	C^{14} dates	Caliberated dates
	(Chalcolithic Phase)	PRL-179	1230 ± 130 BC	1410 ± 130 BC
	PRL-178	1330 ± 110 BC	1490 ± 110 BC	–
2.	Lahuradeva	BS – 1938		1519 BC
	(Chalcolithic Phase)	BS – 2150	2012 BC	

3.	Narhan	BS – 850	1123 ± 110 BC	1380 ± 110 BC
	(Chalcolithic Phase)	BS – 852	1133 ± 110 BC	1340 ± 110 BC

On the basis of aforesaid dates the beginning of Chalcolithic Culture in the area of Kosal goes back to early phase of 2nd millennium BC. This can be counter-supported by the early Chalcolithic dates of Chirand (3600 ± 100 B.P.) in Saran district which is situated east to the Kosal. On the basis of Narhan its terminal date goes back to *circa* 800 BC, means that Chalcolithic Culture was flourishing in the area of Kosal region during *circa* 2000 – 800 B.C.

References

1. Singh, P. (1990), *op.cit.*, Varanasi.
2. Singh, Purushottam, *et al.*, (1991-92), *op.cit.*, pp. 55-60.
3. *I.A.R.* 1961-62, p. 56; I.A.R. 1974-75, pp. 46-47 and pp. 76-77.
4. Singh, P. (1992-93), *op.cit.* pp.
5. Tiwari, Rakesh, *et al.*, (2001-02), *op.cit.*, pp. 38-68.
   Tiwari, Rakesh, *et. al.*, (2005-06), *op.cit.*, pp. 69-75.
6. Tripathi, Vibha (2007-08), *op.cit.*, pp. 205-209.
7. Singh, P.N., *et al.*, *Bharati* No. 33, pp. 6-8.
8. Tewari, Rakesh, *et al.* (1995-96), *op.cit.*, pp. 95-133.
9. Tewari, R., *et al* (2002-03), *op.cit.*, pp. 99-114.
10. I.A.R., 1978-79, pp. 59-59, I.A.R. 1983-84, pp. 84-85.
    Tiwari, Rakesh *et al.* (1995-96), *op.cit.*, pp. 67-73.
11. Lal, B.B. & K.N. Dikshit (1982), "Pariyar—An Eastern Outpost of the Painted Grey Ware," *Puratattva*, No. 11, pp. 26-31.
12. Singh, P. (1994), *op.cit.*, p.9.

13. Tiwari, Rakesh (2005-06), *op.cit.* p. 70.
14. *Ibid.*, p. 72.
15. Saraswat, K.S., N.K. Sharma and D.C. Pant, "Plant Economy at Ancient Narhan (Ca. 1300 B.C. - 300/400 A.D.)," in Singh, P. (1994), *op.cit.*, pp. 255-342.
16. *Ibid.*
17. Tiwari, Rakesh, *et al.* (1995-96), *op.cit., p. 125.*
18. Chattopadhyaya, V.C. "A Preliminary Report on the Faunal Remains from Narhan, Gorakhpur (U.P.)," in Singh, P. (1994), *op.cit.*, pp. 246-254.
19. Singh, Purushottam (1991-92), *op.cit.*, p. 32.
20. Tiwari, Rakesh *et al.* (1992-93), *op.cit.*, p. 46.
21. Singh, P. (1994), *op.cit.*, p. 15.
22. Tiwari, Rakesh *et al.* (1992-93), *op.cit.*, p. 50.
23. Singh, P. (1993), *op.cit*, p. 30.
24. Verma, R.K. (1992), "Some Aspects of the Mesolithic of the Ganga Valley" in *Archaeological Perspective of Uttar Pradesh and Future Prospects* (ed. Tewari), U.P. State Archaeological Organisation, Lucknow, p. 53.

    Pal, J.N. (1994), "Mesolithic Settlements in the Ganga Plain," *Man and Environment*, XIX (1-2), p. 99.
25. Tiwari, Rakesh *et al.* (2002) *op.cit.*, p. 109.
26. Singh, P. (1994), *op.cit.*, pp. 38-92.
27. Singh, P. (1993)), *op.cit.*, pp. 31-32.
28. *Ibid.*
29. Tiwari, Rakesh *et al.* (1992-93), *op.cit.*, p. 72.
30. *Ibid.*, pp. 47-49.
31. Chaturvedi, S.N. (1985), "Advance of Vindhyan Neolithic and Chalcolithic Cultures to the Himalayan Tarai: Excavation and Explorations in Saryupar Region of Uttar Pradesh," *Man and Environment*, IX: 101-108.
32. Singh, P. (1993), *op.cit.*, 1994b, *op.cit.*
33. Singh, P. (1994), *op.cit.*

34. Tiwari, Rakesh *et al.* (1991-92), *op.cit.*, pp. 47-48.
35. Mishra, A. (2003), "The First Farming Community of South-Eastern Rajasthan," *Pragdhara*, No. 13, pp. 1-37.

    Personal observation of Dr. Rakesh Tiwari of Director, Dept. of State Archaeology, Lucknow
36. *I.A.R.* (1974-75), p. 47.
37. *Ibid.*
38. *Ibid.*
39. Singh, P. (1994), *op.cit.*, p. 158.
40. Tewari, R. *et al.* (2005-06), p. 72.
41. Singh, P. (1992), *op.cit.*, p. 32.
42. *I.A.R.* (1974-75) *op.cit.*, p. 47.
43. Singh, P. *et al.* (1991-92), *op.cit.*, p. 58.
44. Singh, P. (1994), *op.cit.*, p. 174.
45. Tewari, Rakesh *et al.* (2001-02), *op.cit.*, p 109.
46. Singh, P. (1994), *op.cit.*, p.222.
47. Singh, P. (1992), *op.cit*, p. 32.
48. Tewari, Rakesh *et al.* (2005-06), *op.cit.*, p. 72.
49. Singh, P. (1994), *op.cit.*, p. 223.

7

The Pre-Northern Black Polished Ware in Kosal Region

Settlements Pattern

The pre-NBPW settlements in the Kosal region are less in number and the minimum distance from one pre-NBPW settlement to another is 10 km. and maximum is 60 km. Pre-Northern Black Polished Ware Culture are represented at Narhan (Period II), Ganwaria (Period I), Siswania (Period I), Sravasti (Period I), Hariharpur (Period I), Saripur (Period I), Charda (Period I), Hulaskhera (Period IA) and Dadupur (Period I). The thickness of the pre-NBPW strata at Narhan, Siswania, Hariharpur, Hulaskhera, Dadupur is 90 cm, 15 cm, 80 cm, and 50 cm respectively. The 15 cm thick culture deposit of Siswania I can be assigned a time span of probably less than 50 years. Except Hariharpur, Saripur, Hulaskhera, and Dadupur all the settlements are located in the trans-Ghaghara region.

Subsistence Pattern

The agricultural practices developed by the authors of Narhan Culture[1] were followed in Period II as well. The discovery of carbonized grains of rice (*Oriza sativa*), barley (*Hordeum vulgare*), pea (*Pisum sativum*), and green grain (*Vigna radiata*) in Period II at Narhan confirm this assumption. The discovery of safflower seed (*Carthamus tinctorious*) already known to us from Maharashtra (about 1000 B.C.) is an important and new find in protohistoric north India. The wood charcoals of Mahua (*Madhuca indica*), Anwala (*Emblica officinalis*), Imli (*Tamarindus indica*), Jamun (*Syzygium cumini*) and Mango (*Mangifera indica*) also found from Period II at Narhan.

Although the main economy of the pre-NBPW culture was the agriculture but it was also supplemented by meat and other aquatic fauna. At Siswania[2] more than four thousand animal remains were reported. The animal taxa identified include Zebu, i.e. humped Indian cattle (*Bos indicus*), buffalo (*Bubalu bubalis*), horse (*Equus caballus*), sheep, goat (*Oris/Capra*), spotted deer (*Axis axis*), antelope (*Antelope* sp.), wild boar (*Sus scrofa sorofa*), domestic pig (*Sus scrofa cristatus*), pigmy hog (*Sus silvanius*), dog (canis familiaris), cat (*Felis* sp), hare (*Lepus* sp.), common rat (*Rattas rattus*), bandicta-rat (*Bandicota bengalensis*), tortoise (at least two species—*Chitra indicus* and *Trionyx gangeticus*) and fish of large, medium and small size and Aves including fowl

(*Gallus galliformes*). The overall picture from the lowest to the uppermost levels at the site suggests a predominantly domesticated economy in which cattle have the largest representation. Other domesticated animals include sheep/goat, pig, dog and cat. At the same time aquatic animals like tortoise and fish constitute an important source of human diet of the settlers who had the proximity of the river at the site. The remains of bandicoot-rat and common rat suggest well settled life, associated with staring grains. A few wild animals were also haunted including wild boar, pigmy hog, deer and antelope. The fact that most of these species (excluding perhaps dog and cat) constituted items of human diet as is shown by the characteristic cut and chop marks observed on the bones. Another important feature of faunal assemblage is the occurrence of worked bones. A number of pieces from cattle metatarsus (compact tissue) were flaked to give shape of bone tools.

Structural Activity

The inhabitants of this period lived in the wattle and daub houses. At Ganwaria[3] the houses of Period I have mud walls with roofs supported on wooden post, a post being found in position. As a safeguard against inundation the ground level was raised by piling up yellow compact clay for subsequent occupation. At Siswania[4] no structural remains of pre-NBPW period could be located though reed marks on clay lumps suggested structures of wattle and daub during the pre-NBPW period.

Material Culture

During Pre-NBPW material remains yielded pottery, terracotta figurines, bone beads, metal and bone objects, etc.

Pottery – At Narhan[5] Period II is marked by total absence of Black-and-Red Ware either plain or painted, but the frequency of black slipped ware increases in this period. The principal shapes in black-slipped ware are bowls and dishes. Convex sided dishes, deep bowls with straight/tapering sides, miniature vessels and flanged bowls are new types which were added in the Black Slipped Ware of Period II. This type of dishes (carinated and convex) appear in this ware in early levels at Rajghat and Praladpur in Varanasi in a date range of about 700 B.C. which is perfectly in accord with the evidence coming from Narhan where such dishes occur only in Period II. The only evidence of the occurrence of dish in BSW comes from the Chalcolithic levels of Koldihwa[6] .Thus, it is clear that dish is a new addition in this ware as far as Narhan is concerned. At Narhan both wares have their distinct shapes, a fact pointing towards the early dating of BSW at this site. Convex-sided dishes of BSW are significantly absent in Period I of Narhan Culture (a feature common to BRW of this period) while the shape is quite frequent in Period II. This indicates a distinct change in the food habit of the people from the first to the second period. The Red Slipped Ware continues in limited quantity, plain red ware is the dominant ceramic industry at Narhan. The main shapes of the Red Ware is basins, bowls, vases.[7]

The pre-NBPW deposits at Siswania[8] is characterized by the presence of black-slipped ware, a couple of these sherds being white painted, black-and-red ware (plain) and associated red ware. The shapes include bowls, dishes, vases, miniature vases, perforated footed bowls and jars having cord impressions on the exterior parts of the body. In some quadrents, NBPW is also present in the earliest level suggesting a small duration of pre-NBPW occupation at the site. It was thus observed that the early settlements of the site were located closer to the river Kuwano on its left bank and with the increase of population during NBPW period, the settlement spread towards east, particularly during later periods where it occupied a very large. The Period I of Ganwaria[9] (*circa* 800 B.C. to *circa* 600 B.C.) is marked by black-slipped ware, fine grey ware, red ware vases and dishes with red rim and grayish bottom associated elsewhere with the PGW, red ware bowls and dishes with the mirror-like polish occasionally painted in black dots and circles. At Hariharpur, the main ceramic industries of this period are Red Ware, Black Slipped Ware and Black-and-Red Ware. Black-and-red ware without any surface treatment has been recovered in good number. In Black slipped ware bowls, beakers and dishes are the main types. Such shapes are commonly found at sites in the Gomati-Ganga plain. In red ware bowls, dishes and vases are the principal types. The pre-NBPW culture of Hariharpur continued from *Circa* 1000 B.C. to 700-600 B.C.[10]

Hulaskhera[11] Period IA yielded Black Slipped Ware, Black & Red Ware, Red Ware and Grey Ware. The Black slipped Ware is well levigated and well baked. It is treated with a smooth, often shining, slip on both the surfaces. Burnishing is also noticed on a few sherds. The fabric is usuallyfine. The shapes include bowl, dish and large to small vessels with medium to thick core. The bowl consist straight, convex, concave and globular body with flat or sagger base. Their external surface generally bears grooves or ridges below the rim or at the waist. Dishes comprise convex sides and usually flat base. The external surface of the dishes also consist grooves or ridges quite often.

Black and Red Ware is of two types—handmade and wheel turned: handmade sherds comprise coarse fabric, thick section and gritty core. I bears rustication and straw marks on outer surface. Wheel turned sherds consist fine fabric. Generally the clay used is well levigated. The external surface is occasionally treated with red slip. The main shapes are bowls and water vessels. It may be noted that most of the sherds are externally red and internally black while internally grey surface is also evident. The upper exterior of an example is also black. Burnishing on both the surfaces of a few is notable. Red ware is the predominant pottery of phase IA. It consists handmade and wheel turned varieties. The handmade sherds are of coarse fabric and thick and gritty core. Their exterior is usually rusticated and bear straw marks and ripples. Husk marks are also found on one or both the surfaces. An example shows cord impression on external surface. Well baked wheel turned sherds made of well levigated clay comprise fine to medium fabric and are often treated with a fine slip of different shades of red colour over one or both the surfaces. The metallic sound of a few of them is notable. Burnishing is occasionally noticed. Two sherds bear painted linear strokes in black pigment over exterior surface. Two sherds bear painted linear strokes in black pigment over exterior surface, while an example og grey stroke is also evident. The shapes include dish, bowl and water vessel. Dishes are convex sided and flat based. Bowls are of various types, such as conves sided, straight sided, lipped or channeled, perforated and legged with externally folded rim, deep bowls with nail headed rim. Quite many examples bear grooves and ridges over the exterior surface. Water vessels comprise concave neck and folded rim. Grey ware sherds are of a fine variety, well levigated and well baked having fine fabric and smooth finish. Their shapes are however beyond recognition. Number of such example is less.

The aforesaid description of the wares of the Narhan Culture indicate homogeneity in the pottery of the Saryupar region during 1300 B.C. to 800 B.C. But the sites of the eastern part of Upper Ganga Plain show some distinction between the Saryupar plain sites. The excavation of the Dadupur[14] revealed that the Red Ware is the dominant pottery during this period. Other associated are the Black-Slipped ware, and Black-and-Red ware. The percentage of the Red Ware is 73.29%. Some of the Red Ware potsherds have a tendency of peel off. Hndmade and wheel turned, both the types are common amongst them. These potsherds are made of well-levigated clay and are well baked. Their core is grey and most of them are treated with red wash. Some of them bear either red or chocolate colour slip and a few cord impressions on their surface. Rustication is also observed over the exterior surface of some of the sherds. Main shapes in this ware are bowl, dish, water vessel and large sized basin. One shapeless sherd of coarse red ware is found decorated with paralleled painted bands in black pigment. Black slipped ware forms about 25% of the total pottery assemblage. This pottery comprises a fine variety. Both the surfaces of the potsherds are treated with a fine and smooth black slip. Main shapes in this ware are bowl and dish. The Black-and-Red ware represents only 1.77% potsherds of the total pottery assemblage. Most of them are of coarse variety. Their core is thick. Though all the sherds are shapeless, they appear to be broken parts of medium sized pots. Some of the sherds are of fine variety. Their internal surface is treated with a fine and smooth black slip. A few of them bear red slip on their outer surface.

Terracotta Human and Animal Figurines

At Narhan[13] stratigraphically the earliest representations in human form are two archaic figures from Period II. These are the fish star shaped statuettes generally 3 to 5 cm in height. These are crudely modeled by hand and roughly pinched in clay to the desired shape to represent minikin or stylized human shape. They are shaped like fish-star, flattened on the back and front with four points marking the ends of the arms and legs, and the whole topped with rounded outline, which forms the head. The face is pinched so that nose ridge results. A majority of them have no eyes at all. Most of these are devoid of any sex indication like breast etc. Although their religious connotation is not proven but for want of any better name the excavater given the nomenclature "mother goddess" to these star shaped figurines.

The earliest occurrence of terracotta animal figurines is in Period II which yielded three bull / nilgai (*Boselaphus tragocamelus* or Indian antelope) figures, two dogs and one indeterminate object. The bull /Nilgai figures are very small in size but well made and fired biscuit-red. The miniature figure of bull/Nilgai with raised, elongated neck. The hump and tail are made by fixing additional clay. The grotesque figure of a dog with bulky hind portion, stumpy legs and pointed face is reported from an upper level of period II.[14]

Beads & Ornments

At Narhan[15] the stone and glass were employed for bead making in Period II onwards. Out of 13 agate beads, 11 come from Period II alone. There are two specimens of agate beads in the Narhan collection which are unfinished (the boring has not been done) which indicates that they were locally made. The number of carnelian beads are 6, chert 1, Faience 1, Glass 5, Jasper 4, Quartz 1. Terracotta beads of arecanut shaped are six in number in which two are flat based and twelve are arecanut shaped with incised line and striation marks on the body and two concave based. Ten terracotta beads are in elongated Ghata shaped with concave base, five with flat base and twelve in annular Ghata shaped and ten in standard Ghata shaped. Other terracotta beads are one in collared spherical with incised check pattern on the body and one in Amalaka shaped.

Apart from beads, one ivory made pendant is also reported from Narhan II.[16] The pendant has horizontal bands on the body. The pre-NBPW phase of Hariharpur yielded terracotta beads. Drop pendant of bone which has a shining in outer surface and transverse cut on the top and a crudely made fragment of bone bangle is also reported from Narhan in Pd. II. Not only bone bangles are reported from Narhan but twenty glass bangles[17] and four copper bangles are also reported from its Period II.

Bone Objects

Period II of Narhan has yielded a large number of points and arrowheads.[18] The number of points and arrowheads are 91 and 103 respectively. Greater variety of tanged arrowheads (91) and others are socketed (1), barbed and socketed (1), barbed and tanged (10). Period I of Hariharpur[19] also yielded bone points.

Terracotta Discs

At Narhan[20] the circular discs are in bright red colour with incised lines on the edges are reported in Period II. Some of the terracotta discs are of smoky grey colour with rope pattern impressed on both sides. The rope pattern is deeply impressed on the edges is also reported from Sravasti.[21]

Pottery Discs or Hop Scotch

The pottery discs have been reported from Narhan[22] and Hariharpur.[23] At Narhan the pottery discs occur in sizeable number in period II. They are invariably made of broken potsherds, by cutting and grinding and giving them a round, flat shape. The parts of the utensils from which these discs were usually cut are the bases and the sides. Period II yielded as many as seventy pieces of which fourteen have single perforation in the centre. The discs of this period are made out of broken pieces of Black Slipped Ware, Grey Ware and Red Ware. It is generally believed that those without perforation were used as play objects of gaming counters and others with perforation in the centre might have been used either as wheels of toy cart or as spindle whorls.

Gamesman

Terracotta gamesman[24] which have a flat base and a conspicuous neck of red colour occur at Narhan. Some of them bear bright red slip. Others are smoky grey in colour and are crudely made. Twenty nine pieces of terracotta gamesman are reported from period II. The biggest specimen measures 2.75 cm at the flat base and has a maximum height of 2.20cm. However, some of these are smaller in size measuring 1.5 cm and 1.4 cm only.

Metal Objects

At Narhan one copper antimony rod, one nail parer, one fish hooks have been reported from period II.[25] Forty two iron objects in which Arrowhead (5), Spearhead (3), Chisel (12), Nail (9), Sickle (1), Lump (slag) (8) and 4 indeterminate occur in Period II at Narhan. Copper and iron objects also reported from Pre-NBPW at Hariharpur[26].

All the material remains which was used by the pre-NBPW folk indicate their rural background.

Chronology

Stratigraphically and culturally Pre-NBPW phase in the Kosal region is a buffer stage in which NBPW is absent, but it lacks the salient chalcolithic feature of the area. It is predominated by Black Slipped ware along with less frequency of Black-and-Red Ware and Red Ware. By this very fact its stratigraphical thickness is very less than its earlier chalcolithic and later NBPW strata.

Since Period I of Dadupur have only 0.85% PGW, in contrast to 24.93% Black Slipped Ware, and other remains, it can be safely placed under Pre-NBPW phase. The 2.00 – 2.50 cm thick deposit of Period I at Dadupur have following Radiocarbon dates:

Laboratory No.	**C^{14} date based on**	**C^{14} date based on**	**Calibrated**
	5568 ± 30 years	5730 ± 40 years	age on Sigma
	half life		**half life**
BV – 1822	3270 ± 80 BP 1320 ± 80 BC	3368 ± 80 BCP 1420 ± 80 BC	1679 - 1422 BC
BS – 1759	3380 ± 60 BP 1430 ± 160 BC	3480 ± 160 BP 1530 ± 160 BC	1685 - 1465 BC
BS – 1829	6150 ± 120 BP 5200 ± 120 BC	6334 ± 120 BP 4380 ± 120 BC	5284 - 4851 BC
BS – 1825	3430 ± 90 BP 1480 ± 90 BC	3532 ± 90 BP 1580 ± 90 BC	1739 - 1695 BC

Here sample No. BS-1829 have irrelevant due to its very early date by contaminated charcoal sample. On the basis of other dates the lower limit of pre-NBPW phase at Dadupur may safely be placed in *circa* 1600 BC and upper limit in any case it might be roughly later than 1400 / 1300 BC.

Albeit at Hulaskhera, no C^{14} and thermoluminiscence date is reported from its pre-NBPW phase of Period IA and IB, but by comparing its cultural material from Pariyar and Sringverpur, it may tentatively be placed between *Circa* 1000 to 700 B.C. At Siswania[27] in Basti district, only 15 cm thick deposit of pre-NBPW is present, which was compared by its excavator with 1.40 meter thick deposit of Sringverpur Period I. By this comparison, he postulated the beginning of pre-NBPW phase at Siswania is about 8th Century B.C. Albeit four C^{14} dates is reported from pre-NBPW level of Siswania in which one is much earlier (3616, 3591, 3525 B.C.), while three are absolutely recent (1025-1290 CE; 1651 CE; and 1300 C.E.). Like Siswania, the pre-NBPW phase of Narhan in Period II is only 90 cm thick cultural deposit present above to Period I of Narhan culture is dominated by Black Slipped Ware with the total disappearance of Black-and-Red Ware. By this fact the pre-NBPW phase at Narhan can be dated from *Circa* 800 – 600 B.C.

References

1. Singh, P. (1994), *op.cit.*, pp. 301-302.
2. Mani, B.R. (2003-04), *op. cit.*, p. 104.
3. Ghosh, A. (1989), *An Encyclopaedia of Indian Archaeology*, p. 143.
4. Mani, B.R. (2003-2004), *op.cit.*, p. 104.

5. Singh, P. (1994), *op.cit.*, pp. 93-95.
6. Pal, J.N. (1986), *Archaeology of Southern Uttar Pradesh*, Allahabad, p. 139.
7. Singh, P. (1994), *op.cit.*, p. 94.
8. Mani, B.R. (2003-04), *op.cit.*, p. 102.
9. Ghosh, A. (1989), *op.cit.*, p. 143.
10. Tripathi, Vibha. (2007), *op.cit.*, p. 208.
11. Tewari, Rakesh *et al.* (1995-96), *op. cit.*, pp. 97-98.
12. Tewari, Rakesh *et al.* (2001-02), pp. 105-106.
13. Singh, P. (1994), *op.cit.*, p. 141.
14. *Ibid.*, p. 153.
15. *Ibid.*, p. 158.
16. *Ibid.*, pp. 163-164.
17. *Ibid.*, p. 205.
18. *Ibid.*, p. 178.
19. Tripathi, Vibha. (2007-08), *op.cit.*, p. 208.
20. Singh, P. (1994), *op.cit.*, pp. 183-184.
21. Sinha, K.K. (1967), *op.*cit, Pl. XVIII, No. 7.
22. Singh, P. (1994), *op.cit.*, p. 201-202.
23. Tripathi, Vibha (2007-2008), *op.cit.*, p. 208.
24. Singh, P. (1994), *op.cit.*, p. 198.
25. *Ibid.*, pp.222-223.
26. Tripathi, Vibha. (2007-08), *op.cit.*
27. Mani, B.R., 'Excavations at Siswania (District Basti, U.P.): 1995-1997' in *Puratattva*, No. 34, p. 101.

8

Northern Black Polished Ware Culture in Kosal Region

Settlement Pattern

Geographically Kosal region is a part of middle Ganga plain where a large number of Northern Black Polished Ware Culture settlements are located on the bank of rivers, lakes or ponds. During this period, not only the number of settlements were increased but the size of settlements were also expanded. In the Kosal region approximately 200 Northern Black Polished Ware settlements have been explored in the districts of Jaunpur 53, Lucknow 49, Gonda 25, Basti 20, Gorakhpur 10, Sravasti 14, Barabanki Siddharthnagar 07, Balrampur 05, Pratapgarh 01, Sultanpur 12, and Bahraich 4. During NBPW period, minimum distance from one site to another site is 3 km and maximum is 40 km in the Saryupar plain of Kosal region. It shows the expansion of habitation is being increased in the area. Those sites which is situated between Ghaghara and Rapti Doab are situated about 10-15 km far away from the Ghaghara River. Because the current of Ghaghara is very high, so there is no possibility of habitation along with river Ghaghara during those days. Even present days the flood of river devastated many villages which are inhabited in its neighbouring areas. The explorations in the areas covering Basti and Siddharthnagar not only nature of the settlements were studied, but a number of mounds with their name or their village names were identified with ancient cities or with townships having corporate guilds (nagara and nigama). Such identification of modern names of places with nagaras and nigamas, like Siswania with Sitavya, Ukada with Ukkattha, Ama with Abuma, Nagara with Nagaraka, Mehdawal with Medatalumpa, Saltauwa (along with Sevaidih) with Sadavatika or Salavati and Behil with Vehalinga—all going back to the time of Buddha as also proved from the antiquarian remains found from these sites; Saketa, Sravasti, Kapilvastu, Setavya were the important cities of Kosal during Buddha times. The cities were located on the main east-west route, Uttarapatha. The constant cultural interaction with north India and north-west India was one of the most influential factors to the development of the cities like Sravasti etc., that is, the impetus of the urbanization was originated from the cultural interaction with other parts of Gangetic plains. This cultural contact can be attested in every aspect of material culture.

In relation to the cultural contact and interaction outside the NBPW zone, it is much interesting to noe that there was a cultural amalgamation between the PGW distribution zone and the NBPW distribution zone. This phenomenon can be corroborated by the discoveries of PGW in the NBPW distribution zone. Although some of the sites are much dubious for their identification as PGW was imported into this site. Besides, what would be interesting is that some specimens of imitation of PGW are discovered from Sravasti. They are slight different from genuine PGW in terms of shape, surface treatment and firing, but have black painting on the surface. Since it is highly probable that whether they were made by local people, it can be suggested that some demand for the PGW or imitated PGW insisted even in the NBPW distribution zone. This fact indicates the existence of an information exchange and a cultural interaction between the PGW and NBPW distribution zones. It becomes clear that the whole north India became linked of information-exchange and trade, with subdivisions based on various aspects of material culture.

Sravasti which was one of the important city occupied a unique position in this exchange and interaction system. It is located on the border between the PGW and NBPW distribution zones and on the significant route towards the Himalayan region. In this term, Sravasti was a place to which various information and commodities were brought from various regions. It is strongly suggested that the cause for the beginning of the formation of the city should be found in this point. At the present condition of our knowledge, the cultural interaction with Himalayan region is yet to be clear, but reaching upto the site of Kapilvastu, settlement in Ganga basins built up a stronghold for its cultural contracts with distant regions. Sravasti stood on a high road, which connected the most important places of Buddhist India including Rajagriha in the east, Taxila in the north-west and Pratisthana in the south. The road from Sravasti to Rajgriha passed through Setavya, Kapilvastu, Kushinagar, Bhognagara and Vaishali. Another highway connected it to Pratisthana through Saketa, Kausambi Vidisha and Ujjain. Yet another road connected that city with Varanasi. Another important city of Kapilvastu was the capital of Sakyas. The city of Kapilvastu was also connected by road the Vaishali and other cities. Kusinagara was the capital of Mallas identified with the modern town of Kushinagar in Padrauna district whereas the Pava was the capital town of the second branch of Mallas. Pava is most likely the modern town of Fazilnagar or Chetiyanwa i.e. Chaitya-gahwa, ten miles to the south-east of the ruins of Kusinagar in Padrauna district of Uttar Pradesh. But the exact identification of other Gana states of Kosal like Ramagrama, Pipphalivana and Pawa which was ruled by Koliyas, Mallas and Moriyas extending towards east and north-east is a matter of controversy amongst the archaeologists and historians.

The excavated settlements of the NBPW Culture in the Kosal region are Narhan (Period III), Imlidih-Khurd (Period III), Dhuriapar (Period II), Sohagaura (Period III), Lahuradeva (Period III), Sravasti (Period I & II), Piprahwa (Period I), Ganwaria (Period II), Siswania (Period II), Charda (Period IIA & IIB), Pirvitanisarif-Trilokpur (Period I), Ayodhya (Period I), Hariharpur (Period II), Saripur (Period II), Hulaskhera (Period II), Dadupur (Period III), Kalli-Pachchhim (Period I). The thickness of the NBPW strata is 1.20 m at Lahuradeva, 1.80 m at Hariharpur, 1.00 m at

Hulaskhera, 1.60 m at Dadupur and 1.40 m at Siswania shows that the culture existed very long span of time in comparison to earlier Chalcolithic Culture in the same region.

Subsistence Pattern

The life of the NBPW people were more sedentary based on agriculture which was indicated by the excavations of Narhan and other sites. At Narhan[1] charred of this period include rice (*Oryza sativa*), barley (*Hordeum vulgare*), wheat (*Triticum aestivum* and *Triticum sphaerococcum*), Kodon millet (*Paspalum scrobiculatum*), black gram (*Vigna mungo*), green gram (*Vigna radiate*), pea (*Pisum sativum*), Khesari (*Lathyrus sativus*) and sesame (*Sesame indicum*). Fruit stone of jujube (*Zizyphus maurtiana*) and endocarp pieces of anwala (*Phyllanthus emblica* Linn) and Sandal wood (Santalum album L.) have also been recovered. The discovery of anwala throws fresh light on the knowledge of herbal drugs used by the ancient settlers of the Ghaghara valley. At Hulaskhera[2] the botanical remains yielded wheat (*Triticum aestivum*), barley (*Hordeum vulgare*). The plant remains of Pirvitani Sarif[3] provided enough evidence that the ecological conditions of the Rapti-Ghaghara doab (*Himalayan tarai*) was suitable for the agriculture based subsistence economy. The early settlers of Rapti-Ghagara Doab may have exploited the useful plant species in their riverine environment. The ancient agricultural economy comprises of the starch rich cereals, barley (*Hordeum vulgare*), Rice (*Oryza sativa*), Bread wheat (*Triticum aestivum*) supplemented by the protein requirement obtained from leguminous seeds of pulses iz. Khesari/Grass pea (*Lathyrus sativus*), Field pea (*Pisum rivense*), Lentin (*lens culinaris*), Green gram (*Vigna radiata*), Black gram (*Vigna mungo*), Pigeon pea (*Cajanus cajan*), Aconite bean (*Vigna aconitifolia*). Other cereals are Kodon millet (*Paspalum scrobi culatum*) and Sawan millet (*Echinochloa colonum*). Oil seeds comprised Field Brassica (*Brassica junacea*), Linseed (*Linum usitatissimum*), Sesame (*Sesamum indicum*).

The palaeobotanical remains of Pirvitanisarif-Trilokpur suggested a highly advanced agricultural economy was enjoyed by ancient settlers. Barley and wheat are main cereals of West Asian origin. Both six row hulled and naked barleys appeared in West Asia by 6000 B.C. It was most profitable crop, cultivated throughout the Indus region from Early Food Producing Era (7000-5500 BC) to Late Harappan Culture (1900-1300 B.C.). Being tolerant of alkaliinity, frost and drought this crop is less exacting in its nutritive requirement. In light of occurrence of barley from many sites in northern India dating back from 2nd millennium B.C to 1000 B.C., the cultivation of this crop at Pirvitani Sarif is well understood and self-explanatory. The wheat grains of Pirvitani Sarif belong to two forms of highly evolved hexaploid species viz. dwarf wheat (*Triticum sphaeorococcum*) and bread wheat (*Triticum aestivum*). The ancient settlers of Indian cultivated dwarf wheat (*Triticum spaeorococcum*) which was wide spread and is highly drought-resistant species. The evidence of Kodon millet (*Paspalum scrobiculatum*) and Sawan millet (*Echinochloa colonum*) from Pirvitani-Sarif indicated that in the plains or tarai region of Uttar Pradesh, these crops were cultivated during ancient times. These millets are drought resistant and adopted for cultivation under adverse climatic conditions of soil and also less exacting in their nutritive requirements than other crops of wheat, barley, lentil, pea, etc. These millets are grown as summer crops. At this site field pea (*Pisum arvense*), grass pea (*Lathyrus sativus*) and lentil are of west Asian and European origin but Green gram (*Vigna radiata*), horse gram (*Dolichos biflorus*), black gram (*Vigna mungo*) and moth bean (*Vigna aconitifolia*) are of indigenous origin; also Pigeon-pea/Arhar (Cajanus cajan). Field pea is grown as a winter crop which was an important source of protein in the part. Lentil and field pea is seen from early phase of NBPW (ca 800-600 B.C.) onwards. Grass pea or Khesari and Moth bean was grown by the ancient settlers at Pirvitani Sarif since the commencement of NBPW (*C* 800 B.C.). Pigeon pea/Arhar (Cajanus cajan) is an extremely rich in protein extensively grown in the area since middle phase of NBPW (*ca* 600-300 B.C.). It is sown at the commencement of the rainy season and ripens by March-April. It is a native of tropical Africa or it may be indigenous in S.E. Asia. Horse gram (*Dolichos-biflorous*) can sustain on poor soils and is drought-resistant. Usually horse gram is cultivated as a dry crop. It is recovered at the site from he overlapping phase of Shunga-Kushan i.e. 200 B.C. onwards. The plant as grown on Himalayas is more robust, the pods are larger and broader, their stem and leaves are much valued all over India. It is also a good fodder for cattle.

Pulse crops are well known for their ability to fix Nitrogen from atmosphere and thereby improving fertility of soil. Agricultural economist and soil scientists recommend the cultivation of pulse crop alternately with other cereal crops, with a view to improve the quality of Nitrogen starved soil. In this context, it may be pointed that at Pirvitani-Sarif, the ancient settlers have got the knowhow about relation of crops. From the point of view of economy, cultivation of black gram, geeen gram, horse gram and moth bean is certainly advancement over that of lentil, chick pea, field pea and grass pea.

Oileferous crops of the site are Linseed (*linum usitattissimum*), Sesamum indicum (*Sesame*, til) and Brssica juncea (*field brassica*). Linseed is also reported from Narhan from Black-and-Red Ware phase dating 1000-800 B.C.. At the site its appearance from middle phase of NBPW (ca. 600-300 B.C.) is an additional palaeobotanical record in the Rapti-Ghaghara Doab. Whereas the cultivation of sesamum commenced from 300-200 B.C. i.e. late phase of NBPW at Pirvitanisarif. More or less contemporaneous fird of sesame from Narhan district Gorakhpur has also provided evidence of its cultivation in Ghaghara valley, eastern Uttar Pradesh. Although around 800 B.C. its earlier records are from Charda, district Bahraich in Rapti Valley. The cultivation of Field Brassica, a very important oil-seed crop of now-a-days, is record is 1000 B.C. old in the Ghaghara Valley, whereas at Pirvitanisarif it is recovered from the early and middle phase of NBPW i.e. 800-600 B.C. and in the later phases too.

Apart from the evidence for the cultivation of crops, the finds of some fruit remains[4] have given an interesting insight into the subsistence pattern of early settlers at ancient site of Pirvitanisarif. Seeds and remains of cultivated as well as wild jujube (*Ziziphus mauritiana* and *nummularia*), phalsa (*Grewia asiatica*) have been recovered. Jujube fruits appear to have been eaten by ancient settlers during the Chalcolithic period in India. It is an erect branched tree, grown in orchards in fleshy and large sized fruits. Seeds of Phalsa have been recovered from early phase of NBPW at Pirvitanisarif around 700/800 B.C.

Charda[5] is another important site of the Ghaghra region have yielded palaeobotanical remains which throw light on the subsistence pattern of the ancient settlers of the region. Period II (IIA 8th Cent B.C. to 2nd cent. B.C. and IIB 2nd cent. B.C. to 1st cent. A.D.) of Charda yielded cereals of Barley (*Hordeum vulgare*), Rice (*Oryza sativa*), Bread wheat (*Triticum aestivum*), Dwarf wheat (*Triticum aestivum*), Kodon millet (*Paspalum scrobiculatum*) and Ragi millet (*Eleusine coracana*). Pulses of Charda as same as Pirvitanisarif i.e. Field Pea (*Pisum arvense*), Green gram (*Vigna radiata*), Blck gram (*Vigna mungo*), Horse gram (*Dalichos biflorous*), Cow-pea (*Vigna unguiculato*), Lentil (*Lense culinaris*), Khesari / Grass pea (*Lathyrus sativus*), Pigeon Pea (*Cajanus cajan*), Sesame (*Sesamum indicum*) and Linseed (*Linum usitatissimum*) are also found at Charda. Fruit remains yielded jujube (*Ziziphus nummularia*) and Watermelon (*Citrullus lanatus*).

The aforesaid palaeobotanical remains indicate that the cultivated rice was the staple food grain of ancient proto-historic and early historical communities in northern India. Basically, the site like Charda, Pirvitanisarif, Lahuradeva etc. lies in the rice growing zone. Now Charda in Gangetic plain of eastern Uttar Pradesh has emerged as a new site in India where rice cultivation was in continuation from 800 B.C. to 1100 A.D. The site of Charda included the remains of Lobia / Cowpea (*Vigna unguiculata*) is a plant of great antiquity and has been in cultivation for thousands of years, in the tropics of old world. In India, it has been known since Vedic times and it is possible that India and China are the other two secondary centres of origin, the former of the Caljang cowpea and the latter probably of the Asparagus or yardlong beans. Lobia is extensively cultivated throughout the area for its grain during the rainy season and it usually grown along with millets and other crops. The evidence of watermelon (*Citrullus lanatus*) at Charda is another important palaeobotanical remains because its first record from Senuwar (ca. 1200-600 B.C.) in district Rohtas, Bihar, from the Chalcolithic phase; in Indian sub-continent is the first one. Now the Charda find is the additional contemporaneous record in the Upper Gangetic Plain. It grows in hot and dry situations on any ordinary soil provided there is sufficient moisture; but it thrives best on deep, rich well-drained, sandy loam, fully exposed to the sun. It is often cultivated on moist sandy river beds after the water has receded. Watermelon is a large sweet and juicy fruit.

Not only the cereals and fruit plants throw ample light on the subsistence pattern and palaeoenvironment of the area but weeds and wild taxas which is recovered from the excavations also of a great consideration from the palaeoenvironmental and subsistence pattern point of view. A large number of weeds and wild taxa have been reported from the Narhan, Pirvitanisarif and Charda which may give enough indication of the agro-ecosystem and point out how the crops fit in this system. The meaning of term "weed" is not clerly definable but it may be used about any plant growing among pure crop. More generally the weeds grow obtrusively in cultivated fields. The environmental requirements of specific weed are not fixed or static. Weed are naturally the components of the native and naturalized flora. The remains of wild taxa were found mixed with the crop produce in a number of archaeological samples.

In ancient period, man was dependent on wild plants for food, medicine, ceremonial and other requirements; in fact these are still in use. Presently, young shoots of weeds and wild taxa viz. *Amranthus* sp., *Chenopdium album*, *Commelina bengralensis*, *Medicago sativa*, *Portulaca* sp., *Rumex dentatus* and *Triauthema portulacastrum* are used as vegetable (pot herb). Grains of wild grass e.g. *Panicum* sp. is eaten in times of scarcity. The aforementioned weeds are reported from Narhan, Charda, Pirvitanisarif and other sites of this region which comprised the food economy at the site of ancient settlement.

There is a sudden decrease in the number and types of bone points and arrowheads in this period at Narhan indicating a more sedentary life based on agriculture. Five tanged arrowheads and two points have been also reported in this period.[6] This is perhaps because of the fact that with the advent of metal tools the bone points and arrowheads became ineffective and useless. But as mentioned above the subsistence pattern was mainly based on agriculture instead of hunting and gathering. However, occurrence of large number of bones, both charred or uncharred are also indicative of domestication of animals and practice of their meat-eating. A good proportion of bone pieces with cut marks, and charred bones recovered from Lahuradeva, Hulaskhera, Charda, Pirvitanisarif-Trilokpur indicate that the meat was an important component of the dietary system.

At Charda[7] in Period IIA about 2% and in IIB about 5% were charred bones indicating that these were roasted.

Bone tools were reported from Narhan, Lahuradeva, Charda, Pirvitanisarif Trilokpur, Kalli Pachchim, Hulaskhera, etc. Bone arrowheads and points were reported from Lahuradeva, Charda, Narhan.

Structural Activity

Settlers of this period lived in mud, mud brick and burnt brick houses. At Narhan[8] the structural remains of this period comprised mud brick houses with associated mud floors and wattle-and-daub constructions. Burnt lumps of clay with reed marks were met with. A noteworthy feature is the discovery of a storage jar buried under a house floor and a copper vessel placed in inverted position against it. The mid levels of the deposit of Period III of Lahuradeva[9] have revealed two successive floors. These, about 6-7 cm thick floors were made of mud and ash and rammed with tiny potsherds. Post holes were also marked on the floors.; Burnt-clay nodules are the other structural components. It appears on the basis of above evidence that the houses of this period were in form of circular or oval huts and their walls would have been erected by reed like material, which were being plastered by clay. Upper levels of this period also revealed some of the broken kiln burnt bricks showing that limited brick structures were also being built. Rammed floors with post holes and reed impressions on clay lumps besides brickbats, occasionally found in heaps of debris from the level of Period II of Siswania[10] indicate that normal constructions of wattle and daub, timber and mud were in vogue and mixed structural features might have also been in use in rich constructions where brick masonry was also added in the traditionally accepted forms of construction. Evidence of hearths were noticed on the working levels of the habitational deposits of this period. At Sravasti in Period I, the use of a large number of decorative tiles of terracotta was common but not any remains of structure could be located but absence could be due to the limited area under excavation. But in the succeeding (Period II) houses were built of burnt bricks laid in mud mortar. Ring wells were provided as part of the civic amenity to the township.[11]

At Sohgaura the latest level of Period III is represented by fallen debris of a structure which was destroyed by a conflagration. The collapsed material indicates that the walls of the houses were constructed of bricks and the ceiling of wooden beams and batons over which kneaded clay mixed with husk was spread.[12] Thirty structural remains were encountered at Pirvitanisarif-Trilokpur, which constitute nine phases. Earliest four phases are associated with Period I. The study of structural activities of Period I are based on the floors exposed in this period. Half of these were made of rammed of brick-jelly, while rest of the floors were of rammed clay mud floors. Wattle and daub was found with reed and bamboo impressions which indicate that people used huts as well as houses, thatched with wooden and grass roofs. In Period I of Phase I in floor 3 is the earliest evidence of structural activity at the site. Built on natural soil of rammed earth, measuring 0.50 m (north-south x 1.75 m. (east-west) with 10 cm. thickness. A 'V' shaped hearth is built over it. In Phase III of Pd. I, there was a part of wall made of burnt bricks, retaining seventeen courses. Its seven courses were laid in the foundation. Brick measuring 52x24x7 cm, 50x24x7 cm, 48x24x7 cm and 31x24x7 cm. were used in this structure. The bricks were laid in mud mortar. It was oriented east-west. Its extent length the wall was 4.0 m and its width was 0.24 m. The structure-1A indicate three walls which was the part of the structure making two rooms with a partition wall. Brick measuring 52x24x7 cm are used in this structure.[13] The burnt brick structures also reported from Ganwaria Period II.[14] The site of Kalli Pachchhim have the evidence of structural evidences in the form of mud rammed floor, Post holes.[15] Evidence of a hearth with burnt patches. In Period I floor is made of mud mixed with potsherds and rammed.[16]

Pottery

At Lahuradeva in the Pd IV is characterized by the presence of NBPW ceramic industries of the preceding periods also continued to occur. Normally the ceramic of this period are made of well-levigated clay and comprise fine to medium fabric. Sherds of coarse variety of black-and-red ware and red ware, however, are comparatively in a small proportion. Potsherds found in lower level show continuity in decorative patterns. Quality of NBPW is very fine having golden, silvery and bi-chrome varieties. Some sherds are also decorated with painted patterns generally executed in black colour. Convex sided dishes in NBPW, black slipped ware, and red ware are represented in a larger proportion.

Interestingly, a few red ware sherds with perforated body, continue to occur even in this period.[17]

The ceramic industries of the Period III of Narhan[18] comprises red ware, thick grey ware, black slipped ware, a few sherds of NBP Ware and a kind of cord impressed pottery, the last one hitherto unrecorded from the sites of middle Ganga Plains, except in the Neolithic context at sites like Mahagara and Koldihwa in the Vindhyan ranges which, however, belongs to an altogether different tradition. Red ware is the principle ceramic industry and is divisible into three fabrics, viz. fine, medium and coarse. The fine fabric comprises the characteristic bowls with incurved or vertical featurelss rim and a flat base, carinated handis with almost rounded base, reported from the middle of this period. Basins with nail headed externally collared rim, lipped basins, jars with splayed out rim and pear-shaped vase with collared rim were reported in the medium fabric. Cooking vessels were the principal type in coarse fabric. The grey ware is generally of coarse fabric with such types as medium sized dishes with pronounced incurved sides.

The NBP Ware sherds are limited in number and include dishes and bowls. Some of the dishes of black slipped ware have concentric circles in the centre. Similar decorations are seen in coarse grey ware and coarse NBPW at Rajghat. The Period II represented by NBPW was rich at the site of Siswania with a wide range of ceramics including continuation of early shapes of Period I. However, black slipped ware without any painting, black-and-red ware and associated red ware were also present. Black-and-Red Ware sherds of vase, dish and deep bowls have been found which were well fired and have medium fabric. Coarse black-and-red ware sherds have also been found. The black-slipped ware included mainly convex-sided dishes and bowls, besides deep bowls and slightly inturned rim or having mild depression in the exterior part of the rim. They were well-fired and were medium to coarse in fabric. Red ware of both hand-made and wheel turned varieties were the predominant ceramic types represented by jars with externally flared rim having cord impressions on the exterior part of the body, deep bowls with sharp inturned rim, bowls of medium size with incurved rim, channeled bowls, perforated bowls, footed bowls, vases, convex-sided dishes, miniature lids or stoppers, basins including channeled or lipped basins, miniature pots, black painted red ware etc. Vases of Ahichhatra 10A type were present in the second period along with carinated handi. NBPW of both monochrome as well as polychrome varieties having silver golden black, red and grayish shades have been found comprising mainly the convex-sided dishes and bowls with sharp rim, sometimes having mild depression on the exterior part, ranging from medium to fine fabric, occasionally Painted Grey Ware sherds of conves sided incurved dishes and well fired were found from the levels of this period.[19] The other sites of Saryupar region is the Dhuriapar, Imlidih Khurd, Ganwaria and Sohgaura where NBPW and other associated wares were reported. The Period III of Sohgaura is characterized by the presence of NBPW. However, the ceramic traditions of the preceding period such as the red, black-and-red, black slipped and grey wares continue to occur. The frequency of occurrence of the NBPW is markedly less. The commonest shape in this ware is the dish with incurved rim. The red ware predominates with shapes like bowls, dishes, vases with incurved splayed, collared, featureless and everted rims.[20]

The NBPW of Ayodhya is a very fine quality and in a variety of shades—steel grey, blue, silvery and golden. Alongside the NBPW, grey ware with simple linear decorations in fugitive black colour—evidently a developed form of the PGW was also in use.[21]

On the basis of Sravasti excavations Sinha has suggested two phases of NBPW, one earlier (*c* 500 B.C. to *c* 300 B.C.) termed as (a) the Early phase of NBPW and other decidedly later (*c* 300 B.C. to *c* 50 B.C.) termed as (b) the Late Phase of NBPW.[22]

The Early Phase of NBPW

The NBPW of early phase is hard, dense having fine body fabric with thin sections. The sherds have a glossy surface with highly lustrous sheen and when struck, give a sharp metallic sound. They are characterized by following features—

(1) The nature of clay uses is well levigated and does not show any sign of tampering material.

(2) The core is always grey. Below a thin slip of shining black or any other colour, a grey surface (both outer and inner) is seen. This shows that all the pots were fired under reducing condition.

(3) The paste is fine and the pots were invariably potted on a fast wheel.

Mostly NBPW is monochrome but few painted specimens are also reported in this phase. In monochrome NBPW, the surface colour is about 90% of the sherds is jet black or brownish black or bluish black. The remaining 10% are either steel blue, pinkish, silvery, golden, brown, chocolaty, violet and deep red. Mostly painted NBPW are reported in eastern U.P. and Bihar. The surface colour in the monochrome group of NBPW is always one although there is a wide range of colour variations. In this variety a design in one colour is set off against the other, so that there may not be any overlap between two colours. It is in these sherds that we have some designs which appear to have been copied from the painted designs of the PGW. The common pattern of producing thick and thin horiozontal bands, vertical strokes, vertical strokes coming out from a horizontal rim band, transverse band or stroke and simple circular bands or aches common in the PGW are also found in the painted variety of NBPW of Sravasti.

In painted variety of NBPW, we also get some sherds in which the horizontal division of the two grades of colour is very clear. The upper portion of the body has the better quality of lusture and colour while the lower portion is less superior finish and different colour. Such sherds have also been reported at Sravasti. But the technique of producing these painted specimens of NBPW totally differs from that of the PGW in which the unfired pots are painted with a colour-dipped brush. This results in the production of a separate layer of painted designs superimposed over the plain grey surface. So on PGW the designs are pigment colour-oriented. But in painted NBPW it is slip colour oriented in which one colour is set off against the other. Although a few designs have been copied from the PGW, but the technique of painting totally differs. The common specimens in this group are the sherds in which a design in black is set off against the red or a design in red is set off against the black in both cases, there was no overlap between the red and black areas. The other combination of colour are dark steel blue set off against red, grey set off against light red, black set off against dark-brown, black set off against brown, and black set off against ash-grey.[23]

(1) At Sravasti, early phase NBPW includes corrugated bowls, bowls with internally incurved thickened rim, deep bowl with a featureless rim, dish with an overted externally grooved rim and incurved sides, necked vase having an out-turned rim and externally thickened rim and different types of basins.

The Late Phase of NBPW

The NBPW in this phase suffered decline not only in the quality of the clay, shaping surface treatment but also in firing. On contrast to the preceding early phase of NBPW, the specimens from this phase clearly display lack of sophistication.

Though the people of this phase had not altogether given up the use of highly lustrous sherds of NBPW. The need for this deluxe variety had become considerably less due perhaps to the increasing use of metallic wares. The NBPW of this phase in contrast to the preceding early phase is thicker in thicker in section, having darkened unoxidized smoky core and fired at a lower temperature. The surface colour of the vessels ranges from black to dull grey. The surface dressing is either a self slip or wash. The fabric too is of an inferior quality. Although it is much thicker and coarser in section than its predecessor but it is definitely a continuation of the earlier tradition in shape as well as jewel fabric including surface finish. The variety of shapes is almost restricted stereotyped to bowls and dishes while in the preceding phase a great variety of vases, bowls and lids. The tradition of painting is nearly absent in this NBPW.

Another site of Saryupar region is the Pirvitanisarif-Trilokpur[24] wherein Period I NBPW, PGW, Orange-red slipped ware, grey ware, black slipped ware and red ware are reported. The Northern Black Polished Ware found was in fine and thin fabric, polished on both the surfaces in black golden, chocolate, red steel blue and silver grey colours. Sometimes the polish was applied on the exterior only and the interior remained grey. The black patches were also noticed on those sherds, which were polished with golden colour just vice versa the golden patches were found on the blackish outer surface. These pots were occasionally decorated with grooves, vermilion strokes, chord and corrugated. In some of the potsherds these polish being had peeled off. Dishes, bowls and channeled bowls occurred in this ware. Although the quantity of PGW shapes were limited even it was dark grey on the exterior and light grey inside the rim was painted with black colour, horizontal lines. Another specimen of dish was also found with vertical lines of black on exterior. Others sherds were found shapeless.

The grey ware sherds were also in fine fabric with thin profile made of well levigated clay. Dishes and bowls occurred mainly in this group. We found a good number of potsherds in orange-red slipped ware in medium to fine fabric; fine orange reddish slip was applied over it on exterior surfaces. Sometimes the interior was plain red and grey. These were decorated with black smearing on the exterior; finger ripple marks were also noticed. Dishes, bowls, basins channeled bowls occurred in this group.

The black slipped ware occurred in fine and thin fabric comprising bowls, basins, dishes and a piece of handi. These pots were very simple and devoid of decoration. Red ware found at the site of Pirvitanisarif-Trilokpur can be divided in two groups: (1) fine red ware which was fine and thin in fabric. It was treated with fine red slip and appeared in the shapes of dishes, bowls and channeled bowls. Sometimes black smearing was found on the exterior of these pots. Some other pots were decorated with rim bands on exterior. (2) Dull red ware which appeared in huge quantity, represented jars, storage jars, vases, miniature vases, handis and basins.

The site of Charda has yielded NBPW ware in its period IIA. The rimless handis, pear-shaped vases, channel spouted bowls are interesting types of this period.[25] Period II of Hariharpur was marked by the NBPW in which the steel blue, black and silvery shades of NBPW are very common with occasional pieces of chocolate and red coloured sherds. The other ceramic assemblage of this period consists of Black Slkpped Ware, Grey Ware and Red Ware. Straight sided corrugated bowls, dishes with incurved rim are the principal types in BSW, GW and NBPW. Bowls, lipped basins and vases are the main type in red ware. Among the characteristic pottery shapes, special mention may be made of bowls with flanged and corrugated sides, sharpened nail headed, out turned and featureless rims in BSW, NBPW and RW. Other types of this period are dishes, vases, basins and storage jars of Red Ware. Dishes and Bowls are common in BSW, GW and NBPW.[26]

At the site of Hulaskhera the NBPW comprises fine and crude varieties both. The main shapes are bowl with vertical side and slightly out-curved rim, bowl with corrugated side, bowl with rounded body and slightly out-curved bewelled rim and convex sided dishes. The sherds are well-baked and made of well levigated clay comprising fine finish. Monochrome and bychrome varieties are equally represented. The slip is shining and smooth. Shade is generally silvery and sound is metallic. The surface of the sherds with peeled off slip shows red spots. Monochrome sherds comprise shiny coat on interior surface while the exterior is treated with red or brown slip. The core is red, smoky or grey. A few examples show dotted decoration painted in black pigment. The number of this deluxe ware sherds is not much, but it is sufficiently represented.

Beads & Ornaments

At Narhan[27] in Period III ear studs of red jasper and bangles of terracotta, glass and agate were found. Three carnelian, two glass, one jasper and twenty terracotta beads were also reported in this period at Narhan. The carnelian beads are in a shape of plano-convex and triangular spacer. Terracotta are of flat based arecanut shaped. Elongated ghata shaped with concave base, ghata shaped annular, short ghata shaped annular and standard ghata shaped. Therracotta ghat shaped beads, arecanut shaped beads, spherical beads, glass beads, stone beads found from the excavations of Pirvitanisarif-Trilokpur. Beads of semi-precious stone and pear shaped terracotta beads are reported from Lahuradeva Period IV. The beads of carnelian, agate, crystal and terracotta have been found in Period III of Sohagaura.

The other site of the Kosal region is Siswania where different types of beads were reported. At Siswania[28] a bull shaped pendant with gold foil was reported. The site of Kalli-Pachhim yielded fragments of a bracelet which have a plano-convex section and bangles made of stone ivory and glass bangles. The stone bangles were made of chalcedony. Copper bangles were also reported from its period I. Fragments of a lac bangles is also found in Kalli Pachhim.[29] Pendents of terracotta which have a shape of nib shaped and violin shaped are reported here. Glass bangles, ghat shaped beads have also been recovered from Charda of period IIA.[30] Beads of stone, bone and ivory is also reported from Charda IIA.[31] A crystalbead, quartz-rock crystal medium hexagonal, upper and lower surface is flat, length 1.8 cm, width 1.4 cm and an agate-onyx bead, diamond shaped, stauting perforation and flat surfaces, length 1.6 cm, width1.7 cm were reported from Charda excavation. Greenish glass bangles were also reported at Charda in Period IIA. Terracotta bangles were also reported from Charda IIA.[32]

At Sravasti, the excavation yielded a total number of 169 beads including eighty five of terracotta.[33] Of the rest, glass account for twenty two beads which number includes seven of stratified glass showing colour combinations. The glass beads were evenly distributed in both the periods i.e. Early Phase of NBPW and late phase of NBPW. Of the semi-precious stones, carnelian and agate were most popular accounting for 19 and 11 beads respectively. Banded agate was commonly employed in both the periods I and II and often the raw stone was skillfully cut so that the bands got arranged variously as chevrons, eyes and zones. Crystal and amethyst were the material for nine and three beads, respectively and these came mostly from period II. Jasper and lapislazuli were the other semi-precious stones used for making beads, with three and one specimens respectively. Copper, bone and shell were also variously employed for making beads. The most interesting specimens are three exquisite eye beads of stratified glass, two of which were recovered from the lowermost levels of Period I and the third was a surface find. This type of bead is not reported from other sites in northern India except Taxila[34] (Bhir mound) where occurrence of identical specimens is recorded.

The suggested date for Taxila specimens on the basis of findspot is between 6th – 3rd Century B.C. but Beck[35] would prefer the earlier limit on grounds of their supposed affinity with beads found on Mediterranean sites. According to him these beads were either actually made in Mediterranean region and imported in India or were made by craftsmen who came from that area. If this assumption is correct, it must be true of Sravasti specimens as well. It has to be admitted that Taxila and Sravasti specimens have come to us in a highly finished stage indicating the perfect, though complicated technique of manufacture and in view of the reportedly rare occurrence of the specimens on the Indian sites, it is difficult to controvert Beck's assumption regarding their possible origin. There is another class of 'eye' beads found at Sravasti and they are of banded agate wherein the stone was cut in a manner that the natural bands formed themselves into 'eyes'. This type is not common on Indian sites but is reported from early Mauryan and pre-Mauryan levels of Bhir mound at Taxila. There is a good number of rare non-geometric shapes mainly from Period I, e.g. leech-bead of agate, axe-amulet of Carnelian and dagger pendants of carnelian and shell. Identical specimens are available from Taxila from comparable levels. A cylinder bead of lapis-lazuli from lower levels of Period I is of considerable interest as the stone is not available in India and either the raw material or the finished product itself must have been imported. A near identical specimen is available from pre-Mauryan levels of Bhir mound, Taxila.

In the entire collection at Sravasti, there is a solitary etched specimen in stone. This is an unfinished zone bead of agate from an early level of Period II and similar to the one found at Taxila.

Of the faceted beads which is made of double pentagon of crystal, a specimen of exquisite workmanship and was recorded from the deposits of Period II. An elliptical amethyst-bead from Period II is worth noting. Roughly specimens have been reported from many north Indian sites e.g. Taxila, Sirkap, Hastinapur, Ahichhatra and other sites.

Of the many glass beads, an interesting example is a spiral bead of stratified glass from Period II, wherein a thread of white glass was wound round the black. This type also is available from the sites mentioned above. Mention also may be made of vase beads of opaque glass from Period I at Sravati. The arecanut or vase shaped beads of terracotta ware found in large numbers from Period I. These beads occur at many sites in northern India, mainly from Mauryan and pre-Mauryan levels. An interesting variety in terracotta is a moulded cylinder bead showing an impressed design found by double row of chevrons and is ascribed to Period II.

An ear-ring with open knobbed ends. The copper wire has been twisted cable-wise is a piece of exquisite workmanship from Pd. I and copper bangles found from period II at Sravasti. The excavations of Sravasti yielded bangles made of glass, agate and terracotta reported from its Period I & II. The glass bangles are mainly of sea blue and light green glass and include occasional specimens with thick section which must have been used as bracelets. Bangles made of terracotta and agate were generally recovered from the level of Period II. Some of the specimens in terracotta bear stamped patterns. In Period II the bangle of black glass recovered at Sravasti. A ring of flattened copper wire reported from a lower level of Period II of Sravasti.[36]

Bone Objects

At Narhan out of seven bone objects, two bone points and five are tanged arrowheads.[37] At Siswania[38] bone points and arrowhead are reported from Period II. The excavation of Sohagaura[39] yielded only bone styli whereas the site of Lahuradeva include bone arrowheads, awls and points in Period IV. The excavations of Pirvitanisarif-Trilokpur[40] yielded bone points, bone arrowhead from Pd. I. Pd. IIA of Charda yielded bone points.[41] At Sravasti in early phase of NBPW (Pd. I) and late phase of NBPW (Pd II) four types of bone and ivory arrowheads have been reported—

Type (a) 1. Bone arrowhead, sides tapering to a fine circular point and a socket-hole behind for shaft tanon (Pd.I).

2. Ivory arrowhead, similar to above but showing a polished surface (Pd. II).

3. Bone arrowhead of a smaller size and a wider lower end, otherwise similar to above (Pd.I).

Type (b) 1. Bone arrowhead with a well defined tang, a sharp point and has a polished surface (Pd. I).

2. Ivory arrowhead similar to above but of a longer size (Pd. I).

3. Bone arrowhead with a less defined tang and not very evenly shaped (Pd. I).

Type (c) 1. Bone arrowhead sharpened at both ends and roughly shaped (Pd. II).

2. Bone arrowhead, sharpened at both the ends, unevenly shaped and having a flat section in the middle portion (Pd. II).

Type (d) Bone arrowhead with a trilateral point and a tang.

Period I of Kalli-Pachchim yielded bone arrowheads, bone points and bone stylus. The excavation of Hulaskhera recovered tanged bone arrowheads bone awls and bone stylus. Bone points were also reported of Hariharpur Period II and Musanagar Pd. III B.

Metal Objects

The excavations of Narhan yielded copper objects in which one antimony rod from Period III.[42] Apart from copper object two iron chisels and four nails have been reported from Narhan (Pd. III). At Sravasti (Pd I & II) copper object[43] include bangles, ear ornaments, antimony rods, nail pairers, bell pendants, borers, needles. The nail pairer and the borer from Pd. I deserve special notice as roughly similar objects have been reported from Period III of Hastinapur.[44] Iron objects include nail, an arrowhead. An elephant goad from upper levels of Period I is an interesting find. Roughly similar specimens have been earlier reported from the early Mauryan levels of Taxila.[45] This metal (iron) was comparatively scarce in Pd I and most of the objects were recovered from the upper levels. But this phenomenon may not be of much consequence in view of the limited area of excavation. In Period II of Sravasti a knife blade with a single cutting edge and a sharpened upper end with a tng for the handle, leaf shaped spear head, nail, arrowheads, chisel of iron have been reported. A socket fragment possibly belonging to a spade has been reported from an upper level of Period II. At Charda a few iron pieces including nails, spear heads, blades, iron slags and other unidentified pieces were found from the excavation from Period I. Iron slags were also reported from Sravasti. The presence of iron slags[46] in the excavated material of Pd. IV shows the smelting activity at the site of Lahuradeva during Period IV. Apart from iron slags, iron and copper artefacts were also reported at this site from Period IV. Iron and copper objects have also been also reported from Hariharpur (Pd II), Sohagaura (Pd. III), Siswania (Pd. II). At Sohagaura copper objects such as hooks, rods, nails, arrowheads of iron were reported. The site of Kalli Pachchim (Pd I) yielded a good quantity of iron slags as well as a few iron implements. In Period I of Kalli-Pachchim include thirteen iron objects. The most of the objects are in a bad state of preservation and fragmentary. At Kalli-Pachchhim in Period I iron spear heads, iron scraper (Khurpi), nails were reported.[47] The site of Hulaskhera also comprised of iron and copper artifacts from Period II.

Terrcotta Figurines

At Sravasti[48], the excavation yielded a total number of thirty three human figures have been reported but no human figures were recovered from Pd. I. The images recovered from Pd. II which fall under four different types—

(a) Mother Goddess types—Only a solitary hand modeled specimen is available from an early pit of Period II, cut into levels of Period I. The characteristic feature of the type is an exaggerated hip-portion, adorned with an ornament and a disproportionately thin waist.

(b) Naga Figure – In this category, as well, there is a solitary specimen which has come from a middle level of Period II. Naga worship was a popular cult in the centuries immediately preceding the Christian era, as is evidenced by a wide distribution of Naga figures on other sites. In the earlier stages, perhaps the entire body was that of a serpent and at a later stage, the serpent and the female figure combined in one. The Sravasti specimen falls under the latter category. Kramrisch[49] assigns these figures to Shunga-Kushan Period (C. 100 B.C. – 100 A.D.). The stratigraphic evidence from Sravasti, though pointing to a slightly earlier date, is not at variance with the date proposed by Kramrisch.

(c) Moulded plaques of Mithunas and allied figures - About half a dozen specimens under this category were recovered. All of these came from middle and upper levels of Pd. II. Exactly similar mithuna plaques were recovered from excavation at Ahichchhatra[50] mainly from the stratum preceding the strata which yielded Panchala coins. In some of these plaques an important feature is the presence of sacred symbols on the head-dress. These symbols have been found in plaques from Ahichhatra and are also seen in the Kosam terracotta figure at Oxford. The description of the moulded plaque of Mithuna is given below—

"Moulded plaque showing a standing female holding perhaps a flower in her right hand and the left resting on the belly. The facial features e.g. lonzenge shaped eyes, nose and mouth have been indicated later on after the plaque has been taken out of the mould. The elaborate head dress, among other things, consisted of a turban with central floral pattern and streamers, falling from the floral knots. The image is shown wearing a longish necklace which comes as far as the hip portion. This and also the folds of the lower garment are different from the specimens described above. The image also lacks the soft and graceful moulding of the ones mentioned above and which are stratigraphically somewhat later than the image under consideration. From a late level of Pd. II)."

In all these moulding, one notices the faithful transmission of contemporary sculptural idiom to the terracottas, the common man's medium of religious and artistic expression.

The terracotta human figure are also reported from Lahuradeva (Pd IV). The excavations at Pirvitanisarif-Trilokpur[51] yielded a terracotta human figurine, archaic type, it is hand-made and the face is made with pinching fingers. Two small hands are spread in both the sides. Legs are broken. Rest of the body including bust is cylindrical in Period I.

Terracotta Animal Figurines

Terracotta animal figurines were reported from several sites of the region. The terracotta animal figurines of Sravasti[52] Period I were modeled by hand. The specimens from Period I, though limited in number, closely recall similar figures from comparable levels of Rajgir[53] and Vaisali[54]. A characteristic feature of these terracottas is the presence of incised lines on the body. The type did not continue in the succeeding period of Sravasti. Slag and other animals remains occurred from Sravasti Period I.[55]

1. In Period II of Sravasti[56], the elephant figures are by far the largest in number and in many cases the body is shown with decoration. It may be noted that the elephant figures including the specimens with decoration occur commonly at early historical sites in north India, chiefly from Mauryan levels. In view of their wide distribution the presence of decorative and often symbolic motif on the body portion, it may be assumed that the elephant was regarded in the period as an animal of some importance and an object of respect. Of the other animal figures in Period II, mention may be made of a figure of a humped animal with wings. In Period II, the evidence of animal terracotta figures of fish, dog, horse, humped bull, winged humped lion were reported.

At Narhan[57] in Pd III there is an evidence of animal terracotta figurines of bull, horse, dog, duck and bird. The evidence of terracotta animal figurines are also reported from Pirvitanisarif-Trilokpur[58]. The animal figurines are ill-baked and hand modeled. The evidence of these figurines are badly damaged so it is not possible to recognize these animals. A terracotta hollow head of a bird, size 5.3 cm x 3.1 cm is reported from Pd I.

The site of Kalli Pachchim[59] include in Pd I, the fragmentary, grey snake hood the front decorted with incised circles and oblique notches on the upper part. The middle has a horizontal row of circlets with in two horizontal lines below, long oblique lines, the space in between notched from the opposite direction, thus making a check pattern.

Terracotta Objects

Pottery Discs

Terracotta discs have been reported at Narhan[60] in Pd III which have biscuit red colour with incised designs on both sides and a disc of smoky grey colour with black slip and rope pattern on the edges. Crude human figure incised on one side is reported from Period III of Narhan. A large number of terracotta discs have been reported from Period I at Sravasti[61] which bearing symbolic decorations. They are totally absent in Period II. These are two categories of discs—the plain ones in which the decoration is around the circumference and the others in which both the sides show representation mainly of sun, and sometimes of Svastika. The symbol depicted, particularly, the sun, closely recalls similar symbols on punch-marked coins. The Period II of Sravasti comprised Plano-convex disc showing a wheel like design with spokes, ends of which are pierced. The Pottery Hop scotch and terracotta discs have also been reported from the excavations of Pirivtanisarif-Trilokpur in Pd. I. At Charda[62] two terracotta discs in which one terracotta red disc, one surface is incised with nail impression on the edge encompassing a nail impressed scroll. The other surface has nail impression on the edge and a nail impressed circle and other terracotta disc is blackish and plain. Hop scotchs made of potsherds have also been reported from Charda in

Pd IIA. The Pottery discs are also found from the excavation of Hariharpur[63] (Pd II), Hulaskhera [64] (Pd. II), Dadupur[65] (Pd. III).

Terracotta Wheels

Among the playthings found from excavation, terracotta wheels are very common. The site of Narhan (Pd III) yielded terracotta wheels of grey colour.[66] Sravasti Pd. III include toy cart's wheel.[67] A terracotta tiny wheel, which have a diameter of 2.1 cm, thickness 0.6 cm reported from Pirvitanisarif-Trilokpur[68]. At Kalli Pachchhim[69] terracotta toy cart and terracotta wheel, made of medium grained clay mixed with rice husk tampering material having a central perforation for the axil is reported from its period I. The terracotta wheels having a red slip on both sides, the upper surface is concave with a central perforation and a diameter is 6.0 cm and thickness 1.0 cm from Pd I. Wheels are also reported from the excavation of Hariharpur (Pd. II).[70]

Gamesman

A class of antiquities of terracotta known as gamesman have been reported from a number of sites. At Kalli-Pachchhim the terracotta gamesmen are reported from Pd. I in which length varies from 2.1 to 2.3 cm and cylindrical tapering sized or conical with a hole.[71] Gamesmans are also reported from Pd I at Pirvitanisarif-Trilokpur (Pd. I) and Dadupur (Pd. III).

Sling balls & Marbles

A class of antiquities commonly met on sites of early historical periods are terracotta balls, variously described as marbles, pellets, sling balls etc. They are solid, handmade well rounded and baked mostly in oxidizing condition with resultant red colour. In Pd. III at Narhan[72] there is an evidence of four sling balls whereas from Pd IIA at Charda a terracotta, red, sling ball of large size which have a diameter 8.0 cm has been reported.[73]

A few terracotta marbles in red colour, almost fine and round in shape were recovered from Kalli-Pachchhim (in Pd. I).[74]

Other Terracotta and Stone Objects

The excavations of Narhan yielded one terracotta pestle.[75] The terracotta pestle of Pd. III in a broken piece in which maximum extant length of 8.7 cm and diameter is 5.5 cm. The Pestle with triangular notches for grinding is reported from Sravasti in Pd. II. Some stone pestles and mullers were also found from the Charda (Pd IIA). These mullers were made of red sandstone and grey sandstone.[76] Terracotta dabbers are reported from Lahuradeva[77] (Pd. IV) , Hariharpur[78] (Pd III), Sravasti[79] (Pd. I), and Kalli-Pachchhim[80] (Pd. I). The terracotta dabbers of Kalli Pachchhim are of red concave sides, rounded but ends and height varied from 5.5 to 8.5 cm. and diameter varied from 3.2 to 7.5 cm. At Stavasti, a potter stamp has been reported for impressing a lattice design.[81] The site of Hariharpur[82] yielded a skin rubber. Fragments of terracotta crucibles are reported from the site of Kalli Pachchhim.[83] The crucible are handmade height varied from 2.1 cm to 2.7 cm and diameter varied from 2.9 to 4.0 cm. A terracotta net sinker which have a length of 4.2 cm and width 3.6 cm and a terracotta head scratcher is reported from Pirvitanisarif-Trilokpur in Pd. I. The length of a terracotta net sinker is 4.9 cm and witdh is 3.1 cm.

The material remains of NBPW period reflect that they were skilled in pottery making, metal technology. The quantity and variety of terracotta figurine increased. The antiquities suggest that they seems to be objects of daily use.

Chronology

The major cultural tradition that follows the Black Slipped Ware / Black-and-Red Ware in the area of Kosal is generally referred to as the Northern Black Polished Ware Culture, previously it was thought that it appears around 700 to 500 B.C. in the core region of northern India i.e. in middle Ganga plain is now seriously challenged by recent discoveries. In its periphery region like Pakistan, recent excavations in the Bantu district at the sites of Akra (900-790 B.C.) and Terkala Dheri (1000-400 B.C.) have provided more accurate radiocarbon dates that would push the chronology for NBPW at Taxila and Charsadda to early as 900 B.C.[87] Even at Sringverpur, south to the Kosala, the C^{14} and TL dates from early occurrence of NBPW at Period II are 960, 840, 820, 819, 793, 740 and 710 B.C. confirm its full fleged occurrence in Period III which has been inscribed to *circa* 700-200 B.C. The C^{14} dates of NBPW at Noh[88] in Rajasthan is 685 ± 150 B.C. and 660 ± 100 B.C. and recently at Jhusi, not far away from Sringverpur is 640 ± 90 B.C. confirm its beginning in the periphery region of Kosala in about 8th century B.C. By this background the early date of NBPW at Ayodhya, which is aocre place in the region of Kosala, is well justified and relied.

References

1. Singh, P. (1994), *op.cit.*, p. 265.
2. Tewari, Rakesh *et al.* (1995-96), *op.cit.*, p. 126.
3. Tewari, D.P. (2006), *op.cit.*, pp. 182-183.
4. *Ibid.*, p. 203.
5. Tewari, D.P. (2002), *op.cit.*, pp. 186-187.
6. Singh, P. (1994), *op.cit.*, p. 178.
7. Tewari, D.P. (2006), *op.cit.*, p. 141.
8. Singh, P. (1994), *op.cit.*, p. 22.
9. Tewari, Rakesh, *et al.* (2002-03), *op.cit.*, p. 51.
10. Mani, B.R. (2003-04), *op.cit.*, p. 103.
11. Sinha, K.K. (1967), *op.cit.*, p. 18.
12. *I.A.R.*, (1974-75), p. 47.
13. Tewari, D.P. (2006), *op.cit.*, pp. 23-27.
14. Ghosh, A. (1989), *An Encyclopaedia of Indian Archaeology*, New Delhi, p. 143.
15. Tewari, D.P. (1999), *op.cit.*, p. 21.
16. *Ibid.*
17. Tewari, Rakesh *et al.* (2002-03), *op.cit.*, pp. 38-40.
18. Singh, P. (1994), *op.cit.*, pp. 22-23.
19. Mani, B.R. (2003-04), *op.cit.*, p. 102.
20. *I.A.R.*, (1974-75), p. 47.
21. Ghosh, A. (1989), *op.cit.*, p. 32.

22. Sinha, K.K. (1967), *op.cit.*, pp. 27-30.
23. Mishra, A.K. (1989), *The Indian Black Wares (First Millennium B.C.)*, Delhi, p. 94.
24. Tewari, D.P. (2006), *op.cit.*
25. Tewari, D.P. (2002), *op.cit.*, p. 47.
26. Tripathi, Vibha (2007-08), *op.cit.*, p. 206.
27. Singh, P. (1994), *op.cit.*, p. 158.
28. Mani, B.R. (2003-04), *op.cit.*, p. 103.
29. Tewari, D.P. (1999), *op.cit.*, p. 109.
30. Tewari, D.P. (2002), *op.cit.*, p. 105.
31. *Ibid.*, p. 133.
32. *Ibid.*
33. Sinha, K.K. (1967), *op.cit.*, pp. 60-61.
34. Beck, H.C. "Beads from Taxila", *Memoirs of Archaeological Survey of India*, No. 65, pp. 23-24.
35. *Ibid.*, pp. 11-13.
36. Sinha, K.K. (1967), *op.cit.*, p. 67.
37. Singh, P. (1994), *op.cit.*, p. 178.
38. Mani, B.R. (2003-04), *op.cit.*, p. 103.
39. *I.A.R.*, (1974-75), p. 47.
40. Tewari, D.P. (2006), *op.cit.*, p. 123.
41. Tewari, D.P. (2002), *op.cit.*, p. 127.
42. Singh, P. (1994), *op.cit.*, p. 222.
43. Sinha, K.K. (1967), *op.cit.*, p. 66.
44. Lal, B.B. (1954-55), "Excavation at Hastinapur and other Explorations in the Upper Ganga and Satluj Basins, 1950-1952," *Ancient India*, Nos. 10 & 11, p. 95.
45. Marshall, J., *Taxila II*, p. 575.
46. Tewari, D.P. (2002), *op.cit.*
47. Tewari, Rakesh (2001-02), *op.cit.*, p.52.
48. Tewari, D.P. (1999), *op.cit.*, p. 132.
49. Sinha, K.K. (1967), *op.cit.*, pp. 52-54.

50. Stella Kramrisch (1939), "Indian Terracottas," *Journal of the Indian Society of Oriental Art*, VII, p. 96.
51. Agrawal, V.S. (1947-48), "Terracotta Figurines of Ahichchhatra, District Bareilly," *Ancient India*, No. 4, p. 109-110.
52. Tewari, D.P. (2006), *op.cit.*, p. 117.
53. Sinha, K.K. (1967), *op.cit.*, pp. 55-57.
54. *I.A.R.*, 1953-54, p. 9; 1954-55, p. 16; 1957-58, p. 16; 1958-59, p. 13.
55. *I.A.R.*, 1958-59, p. 12.
56. Sinha, K.K. (1967), *op.cit.*, p. 56-57.
57. Singh, P. (1994), *op.cit.*, p. 153.
58. Tewari, D.P. (2006), *op.cit.*, p. 115.
59. Tewari, D.P. (1999), *op.cit.*, p. 85.
60. Singh, P. (1994), *op.cit.*, pp. 184-186.
61. Sinha, K.K. (1967), *op.cit.*, pp. 58-59.
62. Tewari, D.P. (2002), *op.cit.*, p. 111.
63. Tripathi, Vibha (2007-08), *op.cit.*, p. 206.
64. Tewari, Rakesh, *et al.* (1995-96), *op.cit.*, p. 126.
65. Tewari, Rakesh, *et al.* (1995-96), *op.cit.*, p. 72.
66. Singh, P. (1994), *op.cit.*, p. 193.
67. Sinha, K.K. (1967), *op.cit.*, p. 58.
68. Tewari, D.P. (2006), *op.cit.*, p. 117.
69. Tewari, D.P. (1999), *op.cit.*, p. 123.
70. Tripathi, Vibha (2007-08), *op.cit.*, p. 206.
71. Tewari, D.P. (1999), *op.cit.*, p. 111.
72. Singh, P. (1994), *op.cit.*, p. 208.
73. Tewari, D.P. (1999), *op.cit.*, p. 111.
74. Tewari, D.P. (1999), *op.cit.*, p. 115.
75. Singh, P. (1994), *op.cit.*, p. 188.
76. Tewari, D.P. (2002), *op.cit.*, p. 131.
77. Tewari, Rakesh, *et al.* (2005-06), *op.cit.*, p. 73.
78. Tripathi, Vihha (2007-08), *op.cit.*, p. 206.
79. Sinha, K.K. (1967), *op.cit.*, p. 58.

80. Tewari, D.P. (1999), *op.cit.*, p. 123.
81. Sinha, K.K. (1967), *op.cit.*, p. 58.
82. Tripathi, Vibha (2007-08), *op.cit.*
83. Tewari, D.P. (1999), *op.cit.*, p. 127.
84. Singh, P. (1994), *op.cit.*, p. 23.
85. Kanungo, A.K., *et al.* (2006), *op.cit.*, p. 121.
86. Mani, B.R. (2003-05), *op.cit.*, p. 103.
87. Khan, F., J.R. Knox, P. Magee & K.D. Thomas (2000), "Akra: The Ancient Capital of Bannu North West Frontier Pakistan," *Journal of Asian Civilization*, XXIII, 1 July, p. 1-202.
88. *I.A.R.*, 1971-72, p. 86.

9

Kosal Region During Shunga-Kushan Culture

Settlements Pattern

Although the Kosal region was not the central zone, it was the peripheral region of the Kushana empire which were connected with trade and commerce by the operation of the forces of supply and demand by the way in which and the extent to which these peripheral regions provide goods and service to the central region. Being a peripheral region where a large number of Shunga-Kushan settlements were located. Out of 353 Shung-Kushan settlements 81, 50, 47 settlements are located in the districts of Basti[1], Siddharthnagar[2], Gonda[3] respectively. Other districts which yielded Shunga-Kushan Culture are Jaunpur, Sravasti, Lucknow, Bahraich, Barabanki, Pratapgarh and Sultanpur. 87 settlements lie in the district of Jaunpur, 29 in Sravasti, 21 in Lucknow, 17 in Bahraich , 08 in Barabanki, 08 in Pratapgarh, and 05 in Sultanpur. The increased number of settlements indicate burgeoning of population during Shunga-Kushan period in the region. The district of Lucknow yielded 21, Pratapgarh 08, Sultanpur 05, Bahraich 04, Sravasti 29 and Barabanki 08 of Shunga-Kushan culture sites.

Kushan settlements were not only located on the bank of river but also near ponds and lakes. In the Gonda district only three settlements were on the major rivers of Ghaghara and rest of the 30 were located on the tributaries for the protection of the inundation of the flood. Likewise Gonda, the explored settlements of Basti and Siddharthnagar in the Saryupar plain of Kosal region shows three categories of locational pattern[4] viz.

(a) Settlement situated along the rivers including small ones which are of both perennial and non-perennial nature,
(b) Settlement situated along the lake/Tals,
(c) Settlements situated far away from present river bed.

Of these, 15 settlements are found under (a), under (b) and 11 under (c). Regarding the size of these, the river side settlements ranged on an average approximately from 5000 sq. m to 1,20,000 sq. m in area, save for a single settlement which is about 22,50,000 sq. m. in diameter having a deposit of 6 to 7m. The cultural deposits on an average ranged between 1 and 4 m.

Settlements located on lakes, show a sharp increase in their number, size and duration of occupation in comparison to the river side settlements, which approximately ranged in size between 15,000 sq.m. to 22,50,000 sq. m. and 2 to 8 m. thick cultural deposit. This clearly suggests that the lakes were much more attractive for the human settlements than the rivers during Kushan period. The location of settlements on such lakes might have been due to the availability of water round the year, sufficient aquatic food from the lakes might have been due to the vast alluvial soil around them and above all, to avoid the devastating effect of the floods, a salient feature of the region.

Settlements which are found located without any water course ranged in size on an average between 5,000 sq. m. to 1,00,000 sq. m with a cultural deposit ranging between 0.5 m to 5 m. A single settlement is found extended in an area of about 2,00,000 sq. m. It has been observed that settlements belonging to Shunga-Kushan phase were large in comparison to single culture settlement of Kushan period. Some of these were occupied for a very short duration.

Another interesting feature which also came into light that Kushan settlements were not only located along the river bank and on the tributaries but also found in the hinterlands so well because the Kushanas built so many tanks and dug up wells which fulfilled their needs for potable water and for irrigation. The various tanks and wells show their technological innovation during Kushan period.

It has also been observed that rivers and lakes were occupied from pre-NBPW to the Kushan period whereas the settlements situated without any nearby water source were inhabited during the Shunga-Kushan phase. The results confirm a continuity in the explored area right from pre-NBPW phase to Kushan period.

Explorations in district Basti and Siddharthnagar in the Saryupar plain of Kosal region have brought into light that out of 58 explored sites, 52 settlements have Kushan occupation, 23 starts from the late-NBP and continued up to Kushan period and 25 having single culture Kushan settlements. It is candid from the above that the explored area abounds in Kushan occupation suggesting a sudden increase in the population during this cultural phase. It needs to be pointed out that the northern portion of the explored area is rich in Kushan occupation in comparison to the southern portions of the region, where several single Kushan culture settlements period came into existence. Most of these settlements are found within a distance of 25 to 30 km from famous Buddhist stupa site of Piprahwa. It is likely that these settlements emerged possibly due to the nearness of the great Buddhist pilgrimage.

The another factor which is responsible for the concentration of the settlements in the said region is probable of the availability of the gold in the sand. Some of the nalas (tributaries) of river Rapti in the tarai area on the border of Siddharthnagar and Gonda districts have gold contents in their sand. Some people have made experiments of heating the sand at high temperature and smelting process has brought to light gold ingots. A large number of Kushan coins reported from the number of settlements such as Dasaen, Banda, Chordahi, Bhiladih, Sarghat, Bharat Bharti, Kadirabad Ganje, Kathela Kothi, Bharvalia and Kakraha which included

Ayodhya coins, coins of Kadphise II, Kanishka and Huishka, etc.[5]

Subsistence Pattern

Only few sites have yielded palaeobotanical remains which could throw ample light on agriculture base of subsistence economy of ancient settlers of this region. Period II (Shunga Period ca 200 B.C. - A.D. 100) and Period III (Kushan Period ca 100 A.D. – 300 A.D.) of Pirvitanisarif Trilokpur[6] comprises H*ordeum vulgare* (barley), *Oryza sativa* (rice), *Vigna mungo* (Black gram), *Vigna radiate* (Green gram), *Echinochloa colenum* (Sawan millet), *Dolichos biflorus* (horse gram), *Sesamum indicum* (Til), *Triticum sphaerococcum* (dwarf wheat), *Triticum aestivum* (bread wheat), *Lathyrus sativus* (Grass pea). Besides all the aforementioned cereals of the Shunga period *Lens culinaris* (Lentil), *Vigna aconitifolia* (Moth bean), and *Linum usitattisimum* (Linseed or flax) have also been reported.

Out of nine pulses recovered at Pirvitanisarif, chick pea (*Cicres arietinum*), field pea (*Pisum arvense*), grass pea (*Lathyrus sativus*) and lentil (*Lens culinaris*) are of West Asian and South European origin. Green gram (*Vigna radiate*), horse gram (*Dolichos biflorus*), black gram (*Vigna mungo*) and moth bean (*Vigna aconitifolia*) are of Indian origin, also Pigeon pea/Arhar (*Cajanus cajan*).

Except the evidence of Pigeon-pea/Arhar all the aforementioned pulses have been recorded from the Shunga-Kushan Period at Pirvitanisarif. The evidence of Pigeon pea/

Arhar (*Cajanus cajan*) has been found from the Period I (NBPW period).

Period III of Hulaskhera[7] yielded botanical remains of wheat (*Triticum aestivum*), barley (*Hordeum vulgare*), rice (*Oryza sativa*), wild rice (*Oryza rufipogon*), dwarf wheat (*Triticum spaherococcum*), finger millet (*Eleusine coracana*), green gram (*Vigna radiate*), grass pea (*Lathyrus sativus*), oat (*Avena* sp.). Jowar millet (*Sorghum* sp.), garden pea (*Pisum sativum*), Jujube ber (*Ziziphus* sp.), Bathua (*Chenopodium album*), etc.

Animal represented at the Pirvitani Sarif[8] are mostly large to medium sized herbivores, both domesticated and wild. A few of them are charred or roasted (one or two as a result of even fire), a few have cut marks, intentional or natural. In one or two cases, tooth marks are also present. A few soft and spongy ends, particularly of long bones, have been chewed and/or chopped off.

Cattle economy is the mainstay of the inhabitants food preference, followed by buffalo, pig, sheep/goat, chital etc. Bovides predominate in the assemblage, which indicates their high utility value, both living and after death in terms of primary and secondary exploitation. This provides a perfect reason for keeping them as domesticates. Generally the domesticated bones outnumber those of wild. It seems that cattle enjoyed a high status in subsistence economy at Pirvitani Sarif. They may have also been used for the yield of secondary products, which can be achieved through systematic husbandry practices. This can be a genuine reason for the predominance of cattle at this site. It is suggested that the wild fauna may have provided occasional requirements to supplement the food product from domestic stock. Period II and III include the evidence of faunal remains of *Bos indicus, Bubalus, Axis axis, Sus scraofa cristatus, turtle*, etc. which had chop and cut marks and also charred. The aquatic animals like tortoise and fish, constitute an important source of huan diet of the settlers who had the proximity of the river at Siswania.[9] The remain of bandi cool rat and common rat suggest well settled life, associated with storing grains. A few wild animals were also hunted including wild boar, pigmy hog, deer and antelope. The fact that most of these species (excluding perhaps dogs and cat) constituted items of human diet—as is shown by the characteristic cut and chop marks observed on the bones of Siswania. Another important feature of faunal assemblage is the occurrence of worked bones. A number of pieces from cattle metatarsus (compact tissue) were flaked to give shape of bone tools.

Structural Activity

At Narhan[10] the structural remains were marked by the use of burnt bricks (44 x 23 x 6 cm, 50 x 26 x 5 cm) a large room having three phases of construction. A ring well with inner diameter of 0.70 m and exposed upto 5 courses of rings in a depth of 0.60 m was found to the south-west of this room. Amongst the notable structural remains a portion of a multi-roomed house having well laid walls made of burnt bricks and a deep brick well are worth mentioning. Although a burnt brick floor which may be a part of structure is also found.

At Kopia [11] the evidence of water tank near furnace pit throw light on glass technology of the site in locality II. Excavation revealed remains of walls of regular structures in locality II (Northern deposit), but not with the quality of finish seen in the structures. The structures are of poor quality and later part they were made with fallen and broken bricks of the earlier period, indicating economic decline of the settlement. A single course brick platform at a depth of 8.28 m with some minor structures is also seen. Locality II yielded ample structural evidence to indicate that it was associated with glass making / working. All the structures were made of burnt bricks of the size of 38x37 / 36 x 23 / 22 x 6/5 cm or brickbats of various sizes. This brick size is typical of the Kushan period. Structures of the locality II area can be broadly assigned into two structural levels. However, in each structural level there are sub-phases. The lower structural level has two sub-structural phases and upper structural level has three sub-structural phases. The construction method followed in lower structural levels shows typical header and stretcher pattern. Structures in the upper level and its sub-phases are made of rubble and brickbats. Bricks are joined together with clay mortar. In locality II (structural phase I, sub phase I), a brick platform survives to a length of 1.69 m from east and 1.82 m from south. A vertically placed northeast-southwest oriented single lined brick wall emanates from west. This wall survives to a height of five courses of bricks. A horizontally placed single brick platform exists at the base of this wall. The floor is part of this wall. A parallel wall surviving upto a length of 1.25 m is present in the north. The second wall survives upto a height of two bricks.

The most prominent feature of this phase is that in between these two walls, there is a double layered large conical shape basin with flared sides and flat base, which looks more like a specific purpose container. A pit of 50 cm in diameter and full of crucible pieces and glass is exposed in this sub-phase. Taking all these evidences into consideration, the structure appears to be a house where some industrial activity like glass working or bead making was taking place.

Locality II, North-western deposit: Albeit in this area no trench was dug upto virgin soil but from the material remains recovered, it was clear that this part of the mound was related with glass making industry. This locality yielded very mixed antiquities have no structural activity but it yielded glass pieces in plenty, without any context. About 25 m west of the locality II there is an old water channel. About 25 m north and 15 m west have found a number of big storage jars in a line adjoining the water channel.

A floor with a 10 cm thick deposit of glass pieces and crucibles was found in locality II. This indicates glass working on a very large scale. There is a small squarish underground water tank right in the centre of the trench. The size of bricks used to make this tank is 35 x 22 x 5 cm. The inner side of the tank is step-like in section after first seven courses of bricks from the bottom. The width of the steps varies from 1.5 to 2 cm. The bricks are vertically placed and in single line. There are different numbers of surviving courses of bricks in different section of the tank, 29 courses in south, 18 in north, 30 each in east and west side. There are two prominent water channels after 24 courses from bottom on southern side of the tank. The upper portion is disturbed at various levels at all sides and at southern side it appears falling from water channel level. Both the channels are three brick courses high and 17 cm wide. Floor of the tank is made of 35 x 22 x 5 size bricks. The inside size of the tank at floor level is 1.22 m (east to west) x 1.25 m (north to south); at top it is 2.20 m (east to west) x 2.22 m (north to south). The depth of the tank till floor level from datum is 9.42 m. The surviving height of the walls from floor of the tank is 1.53 cm on its south, 1.63 m on its west and east and 1.02 m on its north side.

In NW quadrant there is an east-west facing three course thick brick wall. Length of the wall is 71 cm from west baulk, and width is 45 cm. The foundation of the wall is made of clay mixed with potsherds. This wall starts at a depth of 8.29 m.

At a depth of 7.71 m abundant residues of glassmaking lay on the surface and for about 5 cm below the surface. In the same level in SE quadrant there was a big circular pit in trench AWx 32. From top one could easily see a number of downward inverted bricks in an ashy context. On exposing the trench in NW and SE quadrants a floor plastered with clay was noticed at a depth of 7.78 m. This floor level seems to be located on virgin soil. In SW quadrant, there is a small pit of 65 cm diameter and 36 cm depth. The content of the pit consisted of brickbats and potsherds. This pit is placed 27 cm from west baulk and 70 cm from south section.

At a depth of 7.68 m a horizontally placed single brick wall emanates from north baulk of NE quadrant and survives to a length of 57 cm. It has a height of four courses of bricks and is placed 11 cm from east baulk. Size of the bricks is 33 x 21 x 6 cm. Foundation of the wall is made of large size single coursed bricks, which rest over a 10 cm thick base of clay mixed with potsherds.

On exposing the large pit in SE quadrant, noticed a number of *in situ* crucible pieces in which glass is melted a number of tuyeres along with a large quantity of charcoal. Probably, it was glass furnace. The excavation was done down to 28 cm from the floor level of NW-SW quadrants cutting the virgin soil and leaving the furnace area intact. The upper part of the furnace was probably doom-shaped. Diameter of the excavated furnace is 1.35 m at its outer periphery, 1.19 m at its inner periphery, and 80 cm at the bottom. Height of the surviving part of furnace is 65 cm.

Locality I: In locality I, excavation revealed that the fortification was built in several stages. In the later stage large size bricks were used whereas the earlier fortification was made of mud. In NE and SE quadrants, a part of a large rectangular four coursed brick structure was exposed. The height of the structure appeared to be intact and the whole structure looked like the boundary of a monastery. Bricks are of unusually large size, 52 x 30 x 8 cm. but excavator did not reach virgin soil in any of the trenches in locality 1.

The structural remains during Kushan period at Sohagaura[12] only yielded several ring wells only.

The cultural period of III of Pirvitanisarif-Trilokpur[13] belonging to the Kushan age which also witnessed three structural phase represented by 13 floors and other structural remains. The structural phase I of Pd. III was represented by two mud floors. A rammed mud floor was found at the depth of 187-195 cm in which was 8 cm thick. A hearth, walls of a room and a drain were found attached with this floor. Another mud floor of the Phase I was found at a depth of 92 cm from the top. It was 6 cm thick. The red ware representing generally Kushan shapes were found on this floor. A ghost-wall was also found which was made of burnt-bricks measuring 48 x ? x 7 cm. Its only three courses were remained *in situ* laid in headers in mud mortar. It was oriented east-west. The structural phase II of Pd III consisted the wall which was built of burnt bricks measuring 25 x 25 x 6 cm, which was largely damaged by the brick robbers. Its only three courses remained in situ laid in headers and stretchers in English bond with mud mortar. Another burnt brick wall measured 40 x 25 x 4 cm. was found in which mud mortar had been used. Probably thick brick-bats rammed with earth was packed in the foundation of this wall. A floor of brick bats of a single course has been reported from Phase II of Pd. III. Phase III of Pd. III was represented by walls of a structure made of burnt bricks. Its major axis running east-west, measuring 6.37 meter retaining 10 courses, was 24 cm wide and with a height of 70 cm. Its bottom most course was in offset and appeared to be in the foundation which was cut into layer 6. This complex of walls seems to be belonging to two rooms of a house. The wall on the eastern flank was oriented north-south and adjoined with the section facing south, measuring 2.42 x 0.24 x 0.50 meter. The brick used in this wall measured 26 x 21 x 7 cm. The wall in western flank seems to be a partition wall measuring 1.36 x 0.26 x 0.73 meter; oriented north-south was built by burnt brick measuring 29 x 24 x 7 cm. The portion of wall lying further west to the partition wall was totally damaged by the brick robbers. All the brick were laid in mud mortar. A mud rammed floor located in the middle of structure number 2, was exposed at the depth of 1.50 m. Three big sized jars and a few bricks measuring ... x 26 x 5 cm, along with pots like vases, basins and bowls were found laid on it. A structure containing remains of two walls of a room made of burnt bricks was built on the top of structure 2. Its extent measurement was 1.30 x 0.56 meter comprising bricks measuring 30 x 24 x 7 cm and 15 x 10 x 7 cm.

Pd. III of Charda[14] yielded the remains of structures and floors. Phase I of Pd. III have the evidence of wall of a burnt brick-bats and were two arms at right angles to each other, possibly making a room. Both the arms have retained eight courses of brick bats laid in mud mortar. The size of brick bats was 36 x 31 x 6.5 cm. Five courses were in the foundation and remaining three were part of the walls. Phase II of Pd. III consisted the remains of rammed mud floor. A circular deep oven was noticed on this floor. The oven contained charcoal pieces, charred bones and ash. Phase III, IV of Period also have the evidence of structures which is in form remains of a burnt brick bat wall. The remain of a wall of Phase IV was mainly built of burnt brick bats. A few full bricks had been noticed. The full bricks measured 25 x 21 x 6 cm and 21 x 10 x 6 cm. Whereas the brick bats were not of uniform size. The maximum width of wall was 10 cm and thickness is 6 cm. It had retained two courses only laid in mud mortar and was oriented east-west. The brick bats suggested reuse of building material. The extent length of the wall was 1.90 m, width 0.47 m and height 11 cm. As well as the Phase VII of Pd. III contained the remains of a burnt brick wall (structure 5) which was made of brick bats was oriented east-west. Its length was 4.0 m, width 40 cm and height 48 cm. It had retained six courses laid in mud mortar in headers. The bricks measured 40 x 25 x 7 cm.

At Siswania[15] the structures of Pd. III were as same as noticed in the previous period (NBPW) continued during the Shunga period also suggesting no basic change in the traditional concept of building activity which gave preference to timber and mud structures. But the building activity increased during the Kushan period (Period IV) when burnt brick structures were erected. Although burnt brick structures and rammed floors have been noticed, but no proper house plan was encountered. Terracotta tiles were also found from these deposits which gave an idea of the superstructure and roof of buildings.

Three ring wells and a brick well of Kushan period were found. Amongst the three ring wells, one was exposed in which cut through earlier levels with fifty two rings, each being 13 cm to 15 cm in height with a diameter of 80 cm. Lime was used to seal the gaps between them and they were sunk upto the water table. The brick well was exposed with fifty seven courses of wedge shaped bricks measuring 26 x 24 cm to 30 x 8 cm. These structures of Kushan period found on the eastern slope of the mound suggest existence of the residential area there. Towards north-west of this, around the highest part of the mound and to the north of the Ram Janki Temple, remains of a workshop of metal smiths was located which existed from the late levels of NBPW period to the Kushan period. Slag, complete and broken pieces of crucibles and metal pieces of iron and copper were found besides hearths of various shapes and sizes. Natural nodules having metallic contents were noticed on the surface and from various levels in excavations suggesting workshop for metal work at the site.

Period III of Hariharpur [16] (Shunga-Kushan Period) yielded the evidence of flimsy structural activities of fired bricks only.

At Kalli-Pachchhim[17] in Period II the remains of three structures and floors have been reported. A floor in square, made of brick jelly and rammed smoothly, available to an extent of 1.75 m. The thickness of floor is 12 cm. Two mortars (okhalis) were noticed on this floor. The burnt brick bats were reused to build structure whose wall is oriented north-south. The length of wall is 1.34 m and the width is 43 cm. It is also in the form of Ghost wall. The other structure is also found in the same area as above the previous one. It is also made of brick bats and superimposed on earlier structure. The bricks of the earlier structure were roused in its construction. Structure-3 was in the form of only a wall built by burnt bricks, circular east-west is available to the extent of 2m, has eight courses one of which four are in foundation. The size measures 34.0 x 25.5 x 6.5 cm. A rammed mud floor mixed with pot-sherds is available in the entire excavated area of the quadrant on which a circular over ground furnace having internal diameter 80 cm, the thickness of the wall are 30 cm and the depth of the oven is 25 cm. There are two platforms on the sides for the workmen to sit. The entire construction appears to be a workshop.

Period III of Hulaskhera[18] is characterized by the Red Ware and brick structures belonging to the Sunga and subsequent period generally known as Sunga-Kushan period.

This period comprises three structural phases. Earliest of them are built of kiln burnt bricks measuring 44 x 26 x 7 cm, 43 x 26 x 6 cm, 43 x 26 x 5-6 cm. Maximum 12 courses of the bricks in a single brick wall are encountered. Foundation is usually laid of compact earth, sometimes mixed with small pieces of pottery. Though the complete house complex could not be exposed due to the over lapping preceding structures, it seems that the aforesaid wall and another adjoining wall measuring 7.42m, belong to a large structural complex comprising many rooms. A entrance in the southern wall of this structure is also found. Its exposed width is 40 cm, rest of it is under the main baulk. It is interesting to note that the walls of this structure remained at the same place at least for three times, which is very well evident by the floor levels of the three different sub-phases. The floors were made of clay or brick jelly, plastered with mud mortar or treated with baked bricks. Besides a small portion of the floor was treated with mud bricks measuring 46 x 26 x 6 and 40 x 26 x 6 cm.

The second structural phase is represented by the house complexes built of the kiln burnt bricks measuring 38 x 24 x 6, 36.5 x 22.5 x 6, 37.x 25 x 6 cm. Lanes or by-lanes with the width of about 0.76 to 1.00 m. are provided between the two complexes. Each complex comprised two to three rooms with earthen or brick treated floors. Entrance gates, measuring 1.00 to 0.80 m in width, have their openings towards the lanes or by lanes. The tiles found in this phase provide evidence of slopy roofs covered by them.

Another structure unearthed is of considerable importance found in an open space to the south of the main complex. It has 6.90 m long and 2.90 m wide floor treated with burnt bricks measuring 37 x 23 x 5 cm. Seven to eight cm. thick plaster of clay mixed with lime is provided between over the brick floor. It would have been covered with a thatched roof of 'chappar' or tiles. Two thick wooden posts were erected at a distance of about 8 m. to support the roof, besides two smaller posts were also provided with each of them. The evidence to provide base for this surmise has come out in the form of two large and two smaller post holes on the floor level. To the eastern side of the floor was a huge pit filled with ash, which might have served as a fire place. Eastern and western portions of the floor are washed away.

The most important structure to mention herein, of this period, is the occurrence of a road across the lake. It has been unearthed upto about 200 m. in length, situated in the southern part of the mound, which use to submerge under the waters of Kerala Jheel for most of the year. This road may be divided into northern and southern parts on the basis of its construction. The southern part measuring 120 m in length is built by raising two side walls at a distance of 9.80 m from each other. These parallel walls laid in north-south direction are built with well baked kiln burnt bricks measuring 40 x 22 x 5, 39 x 23 x 65, 35 x 22 x 5 cm and so on. Another 40 cm wide wall is provided between them in the centre. Besides, cross walls are made at a distance of 2.30 to 3.00 m to make boxes measuring 4.05 x 2.5 and 3.80 x 2.5 m. on either side of the central wall.

The walls of the boxes are built in header, while the side walls are in header-strecher masonry bond. These boxes are filled with the compact blackish clay, which might have been dug from the lake. About 5.10 cm thick layer of brick bats mixed with earth was provided to make the surface smooth and even. The double rectangular boxes intended apparently to hold the dumped clay in position and prevent it from being washed away by water. Reinforcements were provided on both sides of the road by depositing the sand and brick bat with earth. Maximum 18 coarses of this structure with a depth of 1.20 m are found. It was found thinning towards south and remained only 50 cm in thickness.

The northern part of the road is made by providing a layer of about 10-20 cm of earth mixed with brick bats and brick jelly on the surface. Brick made side walls and boxes did not continue in this part, which is a clear evidence that only the southern part of the road was built on box pattern, laid in the midst of the lake, so that it may ensure the transportation throughout the year between the two settlements on either sides of the lake. While, as far as northern part is concerned, only surface treatment was enough to facilitate the movement.

It is to be noted that the habitational deposits are also found from the area across the lake. Besides, even now the passage connecting the mound with the main land lies by the side of this road. Therefore, it may be concluded that this road was constructed to connect the two settlements located on either side of the lake and to provide smooth transport specially across the lake.

In the third structural phase of period II, larger rooms of the aforementioned house complexes were converted into smaller rooms by raising a dividing wall in between to provide more accommodation. Besides, a few more rooms were added to the earlier houses and a circular structure was introduced in a corner of the rooms to accommodate the larger storage jars. Different types of cereals were found in these jars and on the floors. It is to be noted that the walls of this phase were based on tapering foundations measuring 75 and 60 cm at the base and above over which rests the 35 cm wide wall. The additions, to the earlier structure and introduction of circular structures in the corners of the rooms are indicative of population growth at the site.[19]

Material Culture

The material culture yielded the remains of pottery, terracotta figurines, bead and ornaments, bone, stone and metal objects.

Pottery

At Narhan the whole mass of ceramic[20] of this period (IV) is red ware because of firing in oxidizing condition. In comparison to the pottery of the NBPW, the ceramic industry as a whole suffered a decline not only in the choice of the clay but also in surface treatment and firing. The pots are made of coarse clay which is full of husk, straw and other impurities and some of large-sized pots are under fired resulting into a smoky grey core. The industry is essentially plain and devoid of any decoration, painting or incision. The shapes are mostly utilitarian. Large sized vases with splayed out rims and concave neck, vases with grooved shoulders, cuts pot type vessels and lids with knobbed handle, pans or karahis with beaded rim and elongated loop handle and goblets with thickened neck and pointed ware. Another noteworthy find is a jar-stand with three perforations. In the fine fabric of the Red Ware, mention may be made of several specimen of the famous sprinkles (also termed bottle necked vessel or spouted vase) of the Red Polished Ware. A complete specimen of this type has a pear shaped body with very thin sides, a spout with a strainer and a bottle neck with conical knobbed opening.

Period IV of Sohgaura[21] is marked by the absence of the NBPW, the dominant ceramic industry being the red ware represented by such shapes as bowls, dishes, vases, basins, spouted vessels, sprinklers and lids. Some of the sherds were found to be decorated with stamped and incised designs.

The excavation of Kopia[22] in locality yielded a relatively high quantity of potsherds of different wares. In locality II at the northern slope quantity of pottery is relatively low but size of the pots appears larger and thicker in section and at northwest slope potsherds are few but crucible fragments and glass pieces are in abundance. The crucibles were made in two layers; on a pot made of vitrified clay an outer layer of clay mixed with straw was applied to resist the temperature. The red slipped ware was very less in quantity in locality II and NBP was nil, micaceous pottery was scarce. Some of the best specimens of nearly intact pots of very fine quality red ware were unearthed in locality II.

The Period IV of Siswania[23] red ware including red-slipped variety was the main ceramic industry of this period and the typical Kushan shapes like sprinklers, inkpot lids and thumb-impressed incurved bowls have been found besides basins with nail headed rims, cooking pots, spouted pots, vases and handled pots and pans.

Pd. III of Charda[24] yielded bowl vase, surhahi, knobbed lid. Some of the pots were the red slipped whereas the Pirvitanisarif-Trilokpur included fragments of jars and vases of red ware.

At Hariharpur[25] the principal types of Sunga-Kushan period include various types of vases, spouted vessels, cooking vessels, sprinklers, inkpot lids, bowls and miniature pots. Period III of Hulaskhera[16] is characterized by the red ware which is the most dominant ceramic industry. Although the black slipped ware is also found but in a very restricted number. The red wares are represented by the shapes such as lipped bowl, bowl with inturned rim, dish, vase, basin, sprinkler, ink pot type lid, large storage jars and spouted vessels. Sherds bearing stamped mangalik motifs such as swastika, nandipada, leaf and pushp are noteworthy. Besides, carinated handis-treated with an additional layer of clay on the lower exterior to make it more resistant to fire, handled karahi, one stone lid and a small stone pot with a carination on outer surface are other important pottery types. Different types of water vessels also occurred.

The pottery of Kushan period of Kalli-Pachchhim[26] is represented by red ware of medium to coarse fabric. The pot-sherds in coarse fabric are made of coarse grained clay, some times mixed with straw and fired at medium to low temperature. All these are treated with red wash. The troughs, storage jars, basins and vases are main pottery types. The pot-sherds in medium fabric are made with levigated, medium grained clay, treated with well fine red slip, some times painted with black pigment on red surface on the exterior. The pot-sherds are decorated with incised liner patterns, stamped decorations and nail impressions. The mica dusting and rustications are also found. The design include a series of horizontal bands dots and star patterns. The main shapes are bowl, basin, vase and miniature pots.

Terracotta Human Figurines

From Period IV of Narhan[28] included 52 specimens of star shaped Mother Goddesses, which are described below—

(1) Hand modeled mother goddess of smoky grey colour with fan like head-dress, pinched face, stumpy arms and pronounced breasts.
(2) Crudely modeled figure, head missing, right arm drooping, left arm broken, pronounced breasts and blender waist.
(3) Hand modeled mother goddess of smoky grey colour, slit mouth and ornamented with necklace.
(4) Crudely modeled figure with pinched face, pellet-lit eyes and two necklaces.
(5) Crudely modeled figure of red colour and having bright red slip.

Three terracotta large sized human heads coming from Period IV. They are marked by large, lenticular eyes, prominent nose, open mouth, thick lips and generally plump face. The female figure is smaller in size and of smoky grey colour. While remaining male figures are baked red. This class of human head is a typical discovery from the present site as they do not bear resemblance with similar figures from other sites of the middle Ganga Plain. The only figures of this class comparable to the Narhan ones come from the early levels of Pd. III at Vaisali (200 B.C. - 200 A.D.) which compare very well with the chronology of Period IV at Narhan. Their detailed description is given below—

(1) A large, moulded head of a male figure with large, protruding eyes, prominent nose and plump, smiling face, the right ear has a disc shaped ornament but the left one is broken. There is a thick necklace made by appliqué technique and having distinct incised designs.

(2) Moulded head of a male figure, with elongated eyes, long aquiline nose and plump face, the ears are broken but there is a top knot on the head with pierced design which presumably represses a turban with a top-knot. It bears a bright red slip.

A human head with foreign ethnic features has also been found from Narhan Period IV. This human head is well modeled showing a circular head dress with pill like hair, having a knot over forehead, aquiline nose, ears missing, lenticular eyes, well baked to red colour. Six Naigamesa type of figurines have also been reported from Narhan. These are in a composite man-animal form. They consist of human body with an animal face with goat like features and large dangling ears having either pierced holes or slit mark. The mouth is indicated by a deep cut slit. Some of these figures have projecting hair creast on the head. The female figures have well modeled breasts. All the figures are generally modeled flat, having a thick neck and broad shoulders form with the arm/stumps extended obliquely. The hands are generally indicated by cup like depressions. Typologically these are comparable to those of Vaisali and Rajghat. The height of these figurines varies from 4 cm to 6 cm.

Terracotta human figurines were also reported from Siswania and Kopia. At Siswania[29] human figurines including heads with foreign ethnic features. Naiganesha and Naigamesa figures, mother goddess figurines were found. At Kopia[30] twenty nine terracotta figurines were recovered and many more were collected from the surface. Almost all belong to the Sunga-Kushan period. Most of them are fragmentary, broken at the joint, in the case of human figurine, at the junction of the head and the body. It is the same with bigger size animal figurines but smaller size are found comparatively intact and made in one mould. They are characterized by coarse modeling, and having large goblin-like bulging eyes. The head seems to have been mould made while the body is handmade, and both are then joined together. A good number of heads are found. A beautiful female face was found on fortification.

At Charda[31] terracotta fragmentary head of human figurine, the portion below the eyes and nose is damaged, wearing a head band, which has circular punched marks. The eye brows, nose and possibly the eyes are in appliqué. The long drawn fish shaped eyes have circular punched pupils. The two holes depict nostrils. Another terracotta human figure, both the hands portions below waist and head are missing. It was handmade, hollow slightly splayed base. The missing head was modeled separately and luted in the socket on the shoulder. A terracotta head of a female, split mouth, a perforation on the head through the neck was found. A terracotta, head of Naigamesh, showing eyes, nose, face and right ear was found at Charda. The nose is pointed and long, round eyes in appliqué with punched pupils, wearing a circular ear ornament. The strands of combed hair hanging on both sides and a ponytail at the back of the head, prominent thicker lips with split mouth. The length is of 5.2 cm.

The excacations of Pirvitanisarif-Trilokpur[32] Period III included very few human figurine in comparison to animal figurines. A fragmentary terracotta showing human figures in sitting posture, leg toe with fingers, heel damaged, and portion above knee is damaged was found. Another terracotta sitting human female torso left hand flexed at the elbow wearing three bangles, the figure is in round face.

At Hulaskhera[33] the terracottas comprise several human heads. Their bulging eyes, open mouth, prominent moustaches and vertical lines or punch marks on the face to show the board are notable. Almost all the examples found from the deposits of the Sunga-Kushan period are handmade. The clay used is neither well prepared nor properly baked. The human figurines are made in two parts. The upper part or head consists a conical base and the lower part comprise a hole on upper surface, so that the two may be fixed together. This technique is followed throughout in this period. Applied pattern is observed for ornamentation and decorated purposes. Stamped designs and incised lines and holes to show the ears, nose and eyes are also sometimes seen. Generally the terracottas of this period are heavy and comparatively inferior in artistic qualities. Sometimes red slip is also observed.

The site of Kalli Pachchhim[34] yielded only a female head, the face damaged, possibly of mother goddess, of large producing eyes. The hair combed back with a pig tail, wearing a decorated hair band or a teria.[35]

The terracotta human figurines were also reported from several other sites of Kosal region like Sohagaura and Hariharpur etc.

Terracotta Animal Figurines

The Period IV of Narhan[36] site comprised terracotta animal figurines of bull, elephant, dog, camel terracotta animal figurines. Grotesque figure of a bull with stumpy legs and broken hump is reported from a late level of Period IV. Stylized figure of a camel with raised neck, cut slit mouth and pronounced hump, looking like a saddle. The fore left leg and the hind right leg are missing, well baked and fired to biscuit red colour. The treatment of the legs and the neck give the impression that the animal is running. The very realistic modeling of the camel indicates that the coroplast was fully familiar with this animal. This is the solitary example at Narhan but the camel figures have also been reported from Kausambi and Kumrahar. One hand made figure of a dog is also reported from Narhan Period IV. Stylized figure of a bird sitting on a high pedestal with prominent beak. The feathers and tails are missing reported from an early level of Period IV of Narhan.

The site of Siswania Period IV included the terracotta animal figurines like horse, bull, ram, elephant etc.[37]

At Pirvitanisarif-Trilokpur[38] Period III yielded terracotta animal figurines of elephant, ram, humped bull, lion and also a terracotta Gajarohi (Elephant-rider). But these are in a badly damaged condition. In a figure of an elephant only trunk portion is available. It is decorated with five stamps. The designs include Chakra, leaf and palm patterns. It is hand made. Its palm extent measurement is 5.8 cm x 5.2 cm. Terracotta humped bull is also damaged. It has a punched eyes but the fore and hind legs are damaged. Its extent measurement is 6.6 cm x 3.6 cm. Terracotta fragmentary face of a ram indicating slit mouth, nostrils, elongated eyes and possibly ears. The size of a ram is 4.1 cm x 3.3 cm. In a terracotta Gajarohi (elephant rider) figurine fore and hind legs and trunk are broken of an elephant and made of two piece mould. Rider wearing a conical cap, long face, nose damaged, eyes defaced. Its extent measurement is 9.5 cm x 8.0 cm. A terracotta hand made figure of Ganesha is also reported and its extent measurement is 5.7 cm x 3.3 cm.

At Charda[39] terracotta horse and bull figurines were reported. A terracotta fore part of a caparisoned horse, the fore legs, ears, shout and hind portion are in a broken form, lozenge eyes with a puncture in centre. The forehead is decorated with incised ornaments, the head also has a decorative piece, and both are in appliqué. The saddle is indicated by incised horizontal lines with notches. The front edges of the saddle have leaf shaped stamped designs. In a terracotta standing bull, both horns, ears and hump are modeled. The legs are stumpy and in another terracotta bull has two incisions in the right side on the back. A terracotta, fragmentary elephant trunk with a tusk and a flying bird, the beak and tail are in a broken form, the head shows two punched eyes, the wings have grooves presenting the feathers.

At Kalli Pachchhim[40] hand made humped bulls which have a short-shout, hanging ears, joint horns, prominent hump fore legs were reported. A fragment of a craprisoned horse, only face is reported. It has slit mouth, depressed nostrils, lozenged eyes with a puncture in the middle indicating the pupils and embossed flower on fore head, but both ears and portion beyond neck is in a broken form has been reported. Manes are depicted by vertical strokes, bears bright red slip. Bull bears red slip. A hand modeled animal figurine, possibly a dog with a short tail has been reported from Kalli-Pachchhim. It is red slipped bull figurine, handmade, grayish in colour, both the horns, ears and the right foreleg is broken, short-shout and prominent hump. Height 6.6 cm, length 7.7 cm. Such type of figurines are reported from Kausambi, Rajghat and Kumrahar. Although the specimen referred is associated here with Gupta Period but the Strella Kramarisch has described this type of bull "timeless" because these have been found from every level of excavation. A flying bird, handmade, the wings and the tail shows feathers by way of notches is also reported from Kalli Pachchhim. Its height is 4.0 cm and width 3.6 cm.

Beads & Ornaments

Various types of ornaments and beads of terracotta and semi-precious stone have been reported from several sites of Kosal region like Narhan, Dhuriapar, Sohagaura, Kopia, Siswania, Charda, Pirvitani Sarif, Kalli-Pachchhim, Hulaskhera, Hariharpur, etc. during Shunga-Kushan Period. The excavation of Narhan yielded 127 beads[41] of semi precious stones and terracotta during Shunga-Kushan period. Out of 127, 73 Terracotta, 28 Steatile, 09 Carnelian, 06 quartz, 05 Glass, 03 Amethyst and 01 each of Agate, Chert, Faience. Seventy three terracotta beads of Period IV of Arecanut shaped (flat based, concave based, convex based), ghata shaped (elongated ghata shaped with concave base, ghata shaped annular, ghata shaped with flat base, short-ghata shaped annular, standard ghata shaped) long barrel circular, long bicone circular, and spherical shaped bead. The agate bead of Period IV is of 'Eye' shaped, long barrel, circular. A nine faceted bead of red carnelian coming from Period IV is an interesting specimen as such beads are not common in this material. Black glass beads of long barrel circular with three white bands on the body and long flattened hexagonal bead of transparent rock crystal of quartz have been reported from Narhan Period IV.

Ear ornaments[42] of terracotta and red jasper have also been found from Period IV of Narhan. Two well finished ear stud of red jasper with circular section and gentle concavity at the sides. The surface is well finished and it has a smooth, shining surface. It has a diameter of 1.9 cm and thickness of 1.1 cm. But the terracotta ear stud of smoky grey colour with pronounced concavity of sides as well as concave base have been reported from period IV of Narhan. Two copper rings and thirty one bangles[43] have been reported from Period IV of Narhan. Out of thirty one beads, 19 made of terracotta, 08 glass and one each of bone, agate and ivory. Terracotta bangles are by far the commonest, white glass is the next in order of frequency during Shunga Kushan Period. Most of these are generally flat on the inner side but convex on the outer side. Some of these, particularly in terracotta, bear pleasing designs mainly because of the plasticity of the material. Glass bangles occur in various shades of black, blue and green.

At Siswania[44] an ear studs, ghata shaped beads, arecanut shaped beads, decorated and plain beads, extra large beads, bangles having plain surface decorated and having circular, flat triangular section. Glass bangles, rings and other objects including studs of rings and beads. Besides beads in ivory, coral, semi-precious stones—carnelian, agate, chlorite, jasper, quartz, chert, amethyst and chalcedony were significant objects recovered from excavation. The copper bangle, wire, hairpin and bracelet have also been reported from Shunga-Kushan Period at Siswania.

Pear shaped terracotta beads have been reported from Lahuradeva Period V. A stone and terracotta beads and pendants have also been found from Sohagaura Period IV.[45] Terracotta glass and bangles and stone beads are reported from Dhuriapar[46] and Hariharpur[47] during Shunga-Kushan Period. The excavation of Kopia[48] yielded 15 terracotta beads, 17 glass beads, one glass pendant, nine glass rod, four glass tubes, one glass bead segment and four stone beads. Of the fifteen terracotta beads, four are arecanut in shape and a few are melon shaped. Out of 15 glass beads, the collar shaped and drawn Indo-Pacific beads dominate the shape. Along with the beads there were nine glass rods and four tubes, all of them produced in drawn technique. This indicates the possibility of the existence of an Indo-Pacific bead industry here. A few colouring agents of glass are also found as they are used in present day Papanaid upet. Glass beads are of blue, black, orange, green and golden yellow colours. Of the four stone beads, two carnelian, one quartz and another is made of agate. Of the 26 bangle pieces, 19 made of glass and rest are of terracotta with generally roundish and exceptionally flattish rectangular in section.

Glass was found in abundance in locality II of Kopia. The northwest slope mound seems to have been specifically associated with glass making and working because the finding of hundreds of glass chunks and debitage of glass production besides a furnace pit next to a water tank. Thus the finds in the habitational area at the northern end include a number of glass beads and bangles along with bead polishers and some basins and storage jars of very typical shape which makes us believe that the people related to the glass bead/bangles making lived here.

The excavation of Pirvitani Sarif-Trilokpur Period II yielded terracotta aricanut shaped bead, terracotta short barrel shaped, spherical grey bead, terracotta small cylindrical grey bead with dents in half of the surface, terracotta bangle, terracotta bracelet, terracotta ear stud, spherical banded agate bead, bluish glass spherical bead. The Period III (Kushan Period) include terracotta aricanut shaped bead in blackish colour, terracotta barrel shaped bead, terracotta pendent, terracotta bracelet, black glass bangles, dark green glass bangles, cylindrical bead of banded agate, one end is pointed, fiancé bead of diamond and square shaped.[49]

The excavation of Kalli Pachchhim (Period II) consist of terracotta bracelets, bangles, also a grey terracotta violin shaped pendent with a lateral perforation, terracotta ghat shaped, terracotta spacer bead, terracotta small circular, arecanut shaped, terracotta grey pendant, glass, etched, pentagonal shaped bead, stone discular black bead.[50]

Bone Objects

The number of bone object are found at a number of sites in the Kosal region during Shunga-Kushan Period. Although there is small number of bone objects in the form of arrowheads and bone points. At Narhan[51] during Kushan Period (Pd. IV) only one bone point and one tanged arrowhead have been reported. Two bone points have been recorded from Pirvitani Sarif[52] in Period II. Bone points occurred from Kopia[53] and Siswania[54] during Shunga-Kushan Period. Bone and ivory objects have also been found at Siswania, which include points along with a hoard, a hoard of one hundred and thirty five fragmentary bone points, arrowhead, with tangs at bottom with hole, with sharp edges on both sides and other types.

Metal Objects

Copper Objects

The Narhan[55] site (Period IV) include only nine objects in which five antimony rod, one ring, two fish hooks and one indeterminate. Siswania yielded copper objects in the form of antimony rods, rings (one with a figure of Lion), button, fish hooks, small bell and needle. Pirvitanisarif-Trilokpur[56] Period III consist copper objects like copper antimony rod and copper spiral ring.[57]

Iron Objects

The excavation of Narhan yielded twenty eight iron objects in which fifteen nails, three chisels, five slag, two arrowheads, two indeterminate and one spearhead.[58] At Siswania iron nails, rods, arrowheads, sickle, broken swords, rings, hooks, knives, spear heads have been reported.[59] Iron nails have been reported from Pirvitani Sarif Trilokpur. The excavation of Kalli Pachchhim include thirteen iron implements but most of the objects are in a bad state of preservation and fragmentary. Iron bar celt iron knife have been reported from Kalli Pachchhim.[60] Some iron objects have also been reported from Hariharpur, Dhuriapar and Kopia. At Kopia[61] seventeen iron pieces, most of them nails, and many slag pieces were found its Shunga-Kushan phase. Iron spearhead and plough have been found from the excavation of Hulaskhera during Shunga-Kushan period.[62]

Stone objects

At Pirvitanisarif-Trilokpur[63] stone pestle and stone pounder have been reported from its Period III. Stone grinder, muller, quern, pestles and chert weight are found from Siswania[64] Period IV. Stone weights of quartz and sand stones and pestle made of band stone is reported from Kalli Pachchhim.

Other Terracotta Objects

Terracotta Discs. The terracotta discs have been reported from a number of sites during Shunga-Kushan Period. At Narhan[65] a well made piece of grey colour with black slip discs have been reported from Kushan Period. These terracotta discs of the Period are comparatively bigger in size. At Pivitani Sarif Trilokpur[66] terracotta discs have been reported from Period II and III. The diameter of pottery discs varies from 3.3 to 3.7 cm. Discs have also been reported from Hariharpur and Dhuriapar.

Terracotta Pestles

Terracotta pestles are a very common antiquity which is very frequently found in the early historical sites of Kosal region The Narhan site yielded three pestles.[67] These pestles are flattened by long use. One fragmentary pestle of Period IV has stone chips embedded in it for increasing the efficacy of the tool. A similar specimen comes from Prahladpur from sub-period IB. These pestles are ill-fired, having triangular notches on the body. Terracotta pestles have been found from Siswania, Dhuriapar and Kopia during Kushan period.

Terracotta Wheels

Terracotta wheels have been reported from various settlements like Kopia, Pirvitani Sarif, Siswania, Narhan,

Kalli Pachchhim, etc. during Kushan Period. At Narhan[68] the diameter of the terracotta wheels varied from 6 cm to 9.6 cm. Terracotta wheels having the hub and the spokes embossed on both sides. The specimen has 24 spokes on the outer side and on the inner side, 18 spokes and the wheels bear a red slip which has peeled off at places. But another terracotta wheels of Period IV is of red colour with embossed hub, 29 spokes and a raised outer rim. At Siswania[69] double perforated wheels have been reported.

Terracotta Gamesman

Gamesman or stoppers have been reported from Siswania[70] Period IV. Period II of Kalli-Pachchhim yielded terracotta gamesman of cylindrical flat base top.

Sling balls or Marbles

Sling balls or Marbles have been reported from a number of sites in the region. At Narhan[71] Period IV consist twenty eight sling balls. The balls are made of medium to fine grained clay and baked very hard. A few specimens bear red slip which has generally peeled off at places because of constant use. The excavation of Pirvitanisarif[72] Period II and III consist the evidence of marbles. The diameter of the marbles varies from 1.2 to 2.40 cm.[73] Marbles were also reported from Hariharpur and Siswania during Kushan Period.

Stamps

A class of antiquities of indeterminate use and variously described as Potters Stamps, Moulds or Dies for stamping and even lids, have also been recovered from the Narhan.[74] The present site yielded thirteen pieces coming mainly from Period IV and V. The designs comprise radiating lines with horizontal / transverse incision within concentric rings. All of them have beautifully made handles. The stamps have central orifice. The diameter varies from 8 to 9 cm. Stamps have also been recovered from Siswania Period IV and Kalli-Pachchhim Period II. The Kalli-Pachchhim terracotta potters stamp has one side decoration with incised notches of concentric circles.[75]

Terracotta skin rubber

Skin rubbers found from Kopia and Pirvitani Sarif etc. during Shunga-Kushan Period. They generally occur in square, triangular, rectangular and circular shapes and bear incised, oblique criss-cross lines and pricked by dots. They are generally made of clay mixed with lime or sand to make the surface rough.

Terracotta Dabbers

Terracotta dabbers have been recorded from Siswania Period IV, Kalli-Pachchhim Period III. At Kalli Pachchhim dabber having concave sided and rounded but ends. The height varies from 3.6 to 7 cm. and diameter 3.2 to 7.0 cm.

Coins, Seals and Sealings

A large number of uninscribed copper cast coins and various types of copper coins of local rulers of Ayodhya dynasty such as Dhanadeva, Satyamitra, Aryamitra and Dhamadata have been found from the excavation of Siswania and also from surface which suggests that the sites was under the Shunga rulers of Ayodhya branch who separated their kingdom towards the end of second century BCE from Magadh and became part of the Kingdom of Kosala of which it formed part originally in previous periods too. Four clay sealings with the legend Idadevasa (Indradevasya) in Brahmi characters of *circa* 2nd century BCE along with Ujjaini symbol were found from the levels of Period II in which one has the letters written from right to left. One sealing of the same period has Brahmi legend Nathadevasa.[76] Several copper coins of Shunga Period were collected from the excavation of Pirvitanisarif-Trilokpur. But these were badly corroded and nothing was clearly visible. The coins of Shunga were circular, rectangular, squarish in shape. On the obverse side of the coins were depicted four or five symbols, an animal, elephant, a swastika at a corner, tree in railing, a small circle. But on the reverse side details are not available. Few coins have yielded the depiction of Tree in railing, a circle inside, four clear dots, inside circle a snake, a swastika at a corner.[77] At Narhan a copper coins were reported from the upper levels of Period III. It is a cast coin, square in shape. It bears an elephant, taurine, swastika and jayadhvaja on the obverse and tree in sailing, taurine symbol, a three arched hill and a hollow cross on the reverse. It belongs to variety of Allan's classification.[78]

Kushan copper coins have been reported from Siswania (Period IV), Kopia (surface), and Kalli-Pachchhim. The coins of Kopia (06) were of three different rulers of the Kushana dynasty, one each of Wima Kadphises and Kanishka and rest are of Huviska. These coins are in good condition and bear Kushan monogram, nandipada, portrait of the ruler on obverse and deity on reverse and have dotted border. Greek script is partially visible in some coins.[79] Several sealings with legends Shreshthi Kamalasya palaeographically assignable to the Kushana period were obtained from Narhan.[80] Kalli-Pachchhim also yielded the Kushan copper coins of Kanishka or Huvishka. Two coin hoards, one of 64 silver punch marked and the other of 37 copper coins have been found in small pots in Period IV of Ganwaria.

Chronology

On the basis of material culture like pot forms, terracotta figurines, coins, seal & sealings, structural remains a date range of *circa* 200 B.C. to 300 A.D. has been proposed for this period in the Kosal region.

References

1. *Indian Archaeology—A Review 1974-75*, p. 38, 1962-63, p. 33, 1974-75, p. 38, (1975-76), p. 19.

Tiwari, Rakesh and R.K., Srivastava (1993-94), "Explorations along the Ami river and in its nearby areas in district Siddharthnagar,

Basti & Gorakhpur," *Pragdhara*, No. 4, A Journal of the U.P. State Achaeology Department, 1993-94, pp. 1-41.

Singh, P., A.K. Singh and Indrajeet Singh (1990-91), "Explorations along the Kuwano River in Districts Gorakhpur & Basti," *Pragdhara* No. 1, pp. 70-81.

2. Tewari, R. and R.K. Srivastava (1993-94), *op.cit.*, pp. 1.44.

   Mani, B.R. (1997-98), "Two Seasons of Archaeological Investigations in Trans-Ghaghara Plains (District Basti and Siddharthnagar, U.P.)," *Pragdhara* No. 08, p. 103-135.

3. Tewari, D.P. and Durgesh Srivastava (1999-2000), "Archaeoogical Exploration in District Gonda (U.P.)," *Pragdhara*, No. 10.
4. Singh, B. and R. Kumar (1993-94), "Explorations in district Basti and Siddharthnagar in the Saryupar Plains of Eastern Uttar Pradesh," *Pragdhara*, No. 4, p. 11.
5. Mani, B.R. (1997-98), *op.cit.*, p. 108.
6. Tewari, D.P. (2006), *op.cit.*, p. 197.
7. Tewari, Rakesah *et.al* (1995-96), *op.cit.*,p. 128.
8. Tewari, D.P. (2006), *op.cit.*, p. 161.
9. Mani, B.R. *op.cit.*, p. 104.
10. Singh, P. (1994) *op.cit.*, p. 26.
11. Kanungo, A.K. *et al.*, *op.cit.*, pp. 104, 109
12. I.A.R. (1974-75) p. 47.
13. Tewari, D.P. (2006), *op.cit.*, pp. 51-59.
14. Tewari, D.P. (2002), *op.cit.*, p. 40.
15. Mani, B.R. (2003-04), *op.cit.*, pp. 103-04.
16. Tripathi, Vibha (2007-08), *op.cit*, p. 208.
17. Tewari, D.P. (1999), *op.cit.*, p. 22.
18. Tewari, Rakesh *et al.*, *op.cit.*
19. *Ibid.*
20. Singh, P. (1994), *op.cit.*, p. 23.
21. I.A.R., (1884-75), p. 47.
22. Kanungo, A.K. *et al.*(2006) , *op.cit*, p. 110.
23. Mani, B.R. (2003-04), *op.cit.*, p. 103.

24. Tewari (2002), *op.cit.*, pp. 89-91.
25. Tripathi, Vibha (2007-08), *op.cit.*, p. 208.
26. Tewari, D.P. (1999), *op.cit.*, pp. 45-68.
27. *Ibid.*
28. Singh, P. (1994), *op.cit.*, pp. 141-145.
29. Mani, B.R. (2007-08), *op.cit.*, p. 103.
30. Kanungo, A.K. *et al.* (2006), *op.cit.*, p. 110.
31. Tewari, D.P. (1999), *op.cit.*, pp. 119-123.
32. Tewari, D.P. (2006), *op.cit.*, pp. 99-103.
33. Tewari, Rakesh *et al.* (1995-96), *op.cit.*, p. 128.
34. Tewari, D.P. (1999), *op.cit.*, p. 77.
35. *Ibid.*
36. Singh, P. *op.cit.*, p. 153.
37. Mani, B.R. *op.cit.*, p. 103.
38. Tewari, D.P. (2006), *op.cit.*, p. 129.
39. Tewari, D.P. (2002), *op.cit.*, pp. 123-127.
40. Tewari , D.P. 1999, *op.cit.*, p. 85.
41. Singh, P. (1994), *op.cit.*, p. 158.
42. *Ibid.*, p. 202.
43. *Ibid.*, p 205.
44. Mani, B.R. (2003-04), *op.cit.*, p. 103.
45. I.A.R., 1974-75, *op.cit.*, p. 47.
46. Singh, Purushottam *et.al.*, (1991-92), p. 58.
47. Tripathi, Vibha (2007-08), *op.cit.*, p. 208.
48. Kanungo, A.K. *et al.*, (2006), *op.cit.*, p. 110.
49. Tiwari, D.P. (2006), *op.cit.*, p. 135.
50. Tiwari, D.P. (1999), *op.cit.*, p. 111.
51. Singh, P. (1994), *op.cit.*, p. 178.
52. Tewari, D.P. (2006), *op.cit.*, p. 121.
53. Kanungo, A.K. *et al.*, (2006), *op.cit.*
54. Mani, B.R. (2003-04), *op.cit.*, pp. 103-04.

55. Singh, P. (1994), *op.cit.*, p. 222.
56. Tewari, D.P. (2006), *op.cit.*, p. 135.
57. *Ibid.*
58. Singh, P. (1994), *op.cit.*, p. 223.
59. Mani, B.R. *(2003-04) op.cit.*, pp. 103-4.
60. Tewari, D.P. (1999), *op.cit.*, p. 132.
61. Kanungo, A.K. *et al.* (2006), *op.cit.*, p. 110.
62. Tewari, Rakesh *et al.* (1995-96), *op.cit.*, p. 128.
63. Tewari, D.P. (2006), *op.cit.*, p. 127.
64. Kanungo, A.K. *et al.* (2006), *op.cit.*, p. 110.
65. Singh, P. (1994), *op.cit.*, p. 186.
66. Tewari, D.P. (2006), *op.cit.*, p. 127.
67. Singh, P. (1994), *op.cit.*, p. 188.
68. *Ibid.*, p. 193.
69. Kanungo, A.K. *et al.* (2006), *op.cit.*, p. 110.
70. *Ibid.*
71. Singh, P. (1994), *op.cit.*, p. 198.
72. Tewari, D.P. (2006), *op.cit.*, p. 131.
73. *Ibid.*
74. Singh, P. (1994), *op.cit.*, p. 191.
75. Tewari, D.P. (1999), *op.cit.*, p. 123.
76. Mani, B.R. (2003-04), *op.cit.*, p. 103.
77. Tewari, D.P. (2006), *op.cit.*, pp. 219-224.
78. Singh, P. (1994), *op.cit.*, p. 22.
79. Kanungo, A.K. *et al.* (2006) *op.cit.*, p. 121.
80. Singh, P. (1994), *op.cit.*, p. 22.

10

Kosal Region During Gupta Period

Settlement Pattern

Out of 153 Gupta Settlements in Kosal region, 29 lie in the district of Jaunpur, 68 in Gonda, 06 in Basti, 02 in Siddharthnagar, 03 in Gorakhpur, 10 in Sravasti, 10 in Bahraich, 14 in Barabanki and 21 in Lucknow.

The excavated settlements of Gupta Period in the Kosal region are Narhan (Period V), Charda (Period III), Pirvitanisarif-Trilokpur (Period IV), Dhuriapar (Period III), Kalli-Pachchhim (Period III), and Hulaskhera (Period IV).

Subsistence Pattern

Only two sites i.e. Charda and Pirvitanisarif-Trilokpur yielded the remains of cereals and other botanical remains during Gupta Period in the Kosal region. The site of Charda yielded remains of barley (*Hordeum vulgare*), rice (*Oryza sativa*), dwarf wheat (*Triticum sphaerococcum*), ragi millet (*Eleusive coracana*), black gram (*Vigna mungo*), green gram (*Vigna radiata*), field pea (*Pisum arvense*), grass-pea (*Lathyrus sativus*), lentil (*Lens culinaris*), aconite bean (*Vigna aconitifolia*). Period III of Pirvitanisarif Trilokpur yielded barley (*Hordeum Vulgare*), rice (*Oryza sativa*), bread wheat (*Triticum aestivum*), Sawan millet (*Echinochoa colonum*), Kodon millet (*Paspalum scrobiculatum*), lentil (*Lense culinaris*), Khesari / grass pea (*Lathyrus sativus*), green gram (*Vigna radiate*), black gram (*Vigna mungo*), Field pea (*Pisum arvense*), Aconite bean (*Vigna aconitifolia*), Horse gram (*Dolichos biflorus*), Jujube (*Ziziplus* sp.), sesame (*Sesamum indicum*).[1]

The sites of Charda and Pirvitanisarif-Trilokpur yielded faunal remains during Gupta period. The faunal remains consists of sheep, goat, deer, buffalo, cattles, pig and turtle.

Structural Remains

So far as structural activities of Gupta Period is concerned in the Kosal Region, it is not very impressive. At Narhan, the structures of this period were generally found to be robbed by villagers.[2] Hence there is no structural remains have been reported here. No structural activities were found in Period IV of Pirvitanisarif Trilokpur because the deposit of this period was disturbed by brick robbers also.

Structures of Hulaskhera[3] of Period IV was made of broken bricks of earlier i.e. Kushan Period and brick bats, mud mortar were used in the costruction. Foundations are laid by mud clay mixed with brick-bats and pot sherds. The constructions are irregular. Floors are often paved with bricks and brick bats. The width of the walls of the houses range from 35-50 cm. The walls of the earlier phase were used as foundations in a few examples. Inner surface of the walls was smoother than the exterior and the rooms are comparatively smaller. A rectangular underground structure (soak pit) measures 1.20 x .08 x 1.32 m. A structure of cubical bricks is unearthed. Besides, carved bricks with different motifs such as padma patra and tada patra etc. have also been revealed in the deposit of this period. These bricks might have been used in some type of religious structures but unfortunately not a single structure of this kind is encountered in the excavations. Some of them definitely of a decorated pillar and bhumi or sikhara amalaka. Probably due to the silting and other natural causes,water level of Karla jheel raised in this period and the road made in Period III submerged. Hence a 6.80 cm wide and 50 cm high road, built in this period, is encountered in the excavations, while the rest of the portion is washed away. The remaining portion is made of broken bricks of the earlier period and filled with earth mixed with brick bats. Its construction is irregular and wavy, like other structural wall of this period.

At Kalli-Pachchhim[4] three rammed mud floors are reported in Period III. The thickness of rammed mud floor in trench No. 3, square A-3 Qdt-3 could not be determined. A red ware storage jar and two other jars are associated with this floor. A single coarse burnt brick alignment is resting in the floor. It is 2.85 cm long, oriented east-west in the excavated area. The complete brick measures 31.5 x 19.5 x 6 cm. One of the rammed mud floor was 1.4 cm thick. A storage jar was placed on the floor. The burnt patches and a small pit besides pot-sherds were found on the floor. Another floor was 10 cm thick and the pot sherds occurred on the top of the floor.

Material Culture

Pottery

At Narhan[5] the general decline in the art of pot making in Period V and there is a predilection for large-sized vessels made of coarse clay. Save for stray hand made pots, the entire pottery is wheel made as witnessed by striations on the body as also in the marks of the cutting thread at the base and the fabric ranges from medium to coarse. The use of husk and straw is commonly noticed in the body of the clay.

The shapes are avowedly utilitarian in purpose and the industry for the most part comprises large-sized vases with out turned, thickened rim or internally pressed rim and expanding sides and globular body. Besides some vessels of this class have narrow / high neck with thickened, splayed out rim. Among the smaller vessels mention may be made of deep bowl with featureless, internally sharpened rim, then tapering sides and a flat base. Lid with cylindrical central knob, and lid with inkpot like central cup and a rounded base are the other diagnostic types. Dishes and narrow bowls were the other vessels of daily use. A large sized hand made lipped basin is a noteworthy find of this period.

The excavation of Pirvitanisarif Trilokpur[6] Period IV yielded only fragment of a knobbed lid in a dull red ware.

Knobbed lid has raised sides and flat base, thick, medium fabric, reddish, blackish core. Fragment of bowls, storage jar, miniature bowl, basin, miniature vase, handi found at Kalli-Pachchhim Period III. The pottery[7] of Period III is red ware. Bowls and basins having red slip on both surfaces whereas in a vase and handi red slip on the exterior and rim inside. Bowls have thickened and internally beaked rim, a groove on the exterior and a bowl with reddish grey slip on the interior, globular sides, ring base, the exterior is decorated with two horizontal rows of punctured triangular, notches, the same pattern is repeated on the ring. Miniature bowls have flaring sides either bluntly beveled rim and foot base. The storage jar possibly hand made, vertical rim, constricted neck and coarse grayish section has been reported at the site. Basins were with externally thickened rim, flaring sides, a ridge on the exterior and the vase have averted rim, vertical neck, splayed shoulders. A fragment of vase having flaring mouth, two grooves and a ridge on the exterior, depression inside, oblique neck and bulging shoulders was reported at Kalli-Pachchhim.

The pottery of Kalli-Pachchhim bears post firing incised pattern comprising criss-cross lines vertical strokes. Fragment of a bowl bears moulded design comprising a horizontal frieze of bosses enclosed between two horizontal bands below a vertical frieze with bosses on the side is a panel having a criss-cross with bosses at interior section. A sherd having red slip on the exterior, post firing incisions comprising concentric circle filled with square, the outer most circle has radiating strokes on the side or three triangles horizontally hatched. A sherd also bearing red slip on the upper sides and buff slip on the lower sides, decorated with intersecting two horizontal rows of loops.[8]

At Hulaskhera[9] Period IV include red ware ranging medium to coarse fabric. The main pottery types yielded large storage jars, plain and decorated bowls, short and high necked water vessels, spouted vessels, vases, dishes and surahis. Decorated bowls of this period deserve special mention which bear flower, circle, wavy lines, and other designs on their exterior. Button knobbed, bell shaped and cylindrical lids, bowls with straight or rounded sides, incense burner and carinated handi are also found in this period.[10] The handis have a separate coat of clay on its lower half, on exterior, to make it more resistant to fire. One complete miniature sprinkler found in this period is of considerable significance.

Terracotta Figurines

Human and animal terracotta figurines are reported from Narhan, Pirvitanisarif Trilokpur, Hulaskhera, Kalli-Pachchhim of the Kosal Region.

Human Terracotta Figurines

The excavation of Narhan[11] Period V yielded fifty nine Human Terracotta figurines. Out of fifty nine terracotta human figurines, eighteen belonging to star shaped Mother goddess, nineteen standing female figures, sixteen Gupta and post-Gupta plaques, two each large sized human heads, human heads with foreign ethnic features and one each of female figures with hollow cylindrical body, sitting human figure.

Star shaped mother goddess of this period were crudely modeled figure with pinched face and hollow eye sockets with incipient arms and legs. One of the mother goddess was elongated crudely made figure of red colour with stylized head. These star shaped figurines having bright red slip. Two specimens of female figures with hollow cylindrical body were recorded from the excavations and in both cases the head is missing. In one specimen the body is completely hollow upto the neck where it has become solid. The other specimen has a flat base but it is not clear whether the lower part contains a cavity. In both the cases the breasts are heavy and made by appliqué technique. Both the arms are also missing. The treatment is rough and the firing is not uniform. These pieces bear traces of a deep red / chocolate slip. Large sized human heads of Period V is made by mould. The human head is marked by large, lenticular eyes, prominent nose, open mouth, thick lips and plump face. It has a bright red slip which is now peeled off at places. The human heads with foreign ethnic features were reported from Period V of Narhan which is fan shaped head dress, large protruding eyes and eye-brows marked with rope like incised pattern. Another human head of this period having pinched nose and elongated, slanting eyes made by appliqué technique extremely thin lips giving appearance of a slit mouth. There was a tenon below the neck which is now broken.

Several sites of the Ganga Plain have yielded a large number of terracotta male and female heads and plaques from Gupta levels showing lovely hair styles. The moulded plaques are made of single mould in moderate relief while the back is left flat and plain. These are made of finely levigated clay with no admixture of degressant and are well baked. A majority of them represent standardized figures—models of fashionable male and female—wearing a variety of gorgeous coiffures. The most favourite form of coiffures was the wig-like arrangement of the hair. A sizeable collection of male figures and heads with lovely hair styles, rich coiffure and wig like arrangement of the hair have been reported from the Narhan Period V. At times the hair crowns the head as a semi-circular parasol with spiral locks arranged like ribs close to each other, all radiating from a top-kot. This was sometimes marked by a central parting, sometimes this is arranged into two side masses with or without parting simanta backed by a crest. In the Narhan collection there are eleven specimens where only the head is preserved but the body and lower portions are missing. In all the cases these figures have an oval, smiling face with large eyes, aquiline nose, full lips and plump cheeks. In each case, the hair style varies from the other one.

Standing female figure discovered from Gupta levels of Narhan (Period V) may be grouped under this category. On the basis of the state of preservation and their hair style, these can further be sub-divided into four categories:-

1. *Complete standing female figures*

Four specimens of this class have been reported from Period V. These figures are not well preserved but all of them are plaques made by single mould, the underside being flat.

2. *Female head and bust*

In this class the figures are broken just below the breasts. In all, six figurines can be placed in this sub-type. Two of these figures show the Bhramaraka style of hair dressing while two figures have top knot on the head and three plaits of hair flow on either side upto the neck.

3. *Female busts with prominent breasts*

In sub-type III can be included seven female busts with prominent breasts. In these cases the upper and lower portions are missing with the result that details regarding human anatomy, dress, ornaments and hair styles cannot be reconstructed.

4. *Standing human figures with only legs preserved*

These include plaques (8 in number) where the lower portions of the body below the waist are preserved. In three cases even the feet are missing.

A solitary specimen of sitting human figure occurs from Period V ascribable to the Gupta Period. The figure is broken and the head is missing. It has been depicted in sitting posture and its both hands are holding an indistinct object near the chest. The specimen is well baked and has a bright red colour.

The excavations of Pirvitanisarif-Trilokpur[12] (Period IV) yielded terracotta human female figurines, terracotta male and female heads. Narhan like the heads with lovely hair styles have also been reported here in Gupta period. Terracotta human figurines prepared out of a single mould.

One of the male head, covered with locks of hair with form of a parasol at the top and frizzled locks falling on both the sides in parallel rows, prominent cheeks and nose, bow shaped eye brows and broad eyes. Another terracotta human head in which face completely damaged trefoil coiffeur prepared out of single mould. Fragment of a terracotta human female figurine, ankadhatri, upper part showing head up to belly and one specimen of female head with crest jewel in the parting of the hair, locks falling on the back and sides, wearing wheel like kundalam in both ears has been reported from the site.

The terracotta human figurines of Hulaskhera[13] Period IV include Dampati (husband-wife), mithun (couple), mata-putra (mother-child), anka dhatri, Krida dhatri and abhisarika, Naigamesh figures with three tier head dress, female figurines with beautiful head gears such as honey comb, etc. and decorated with simanta chatula, dwarpala figurines bearing a dagger and mrchhakatika are the main types. Besides, numerous male and female heads with different hair styles are notable. Naigmesh type terracottas include male and female both types. Their face is like a goat with long dangling pierced ears and hooked nose. The fan shaped projecting top knot on the head has one or two holes. These figures are associated with the god Harinaigamesh. Similar terracottas have also been found in the excavations at other sites such as Narhan, Ahichchhatra, Rajghat and Kausambi, etc. The terracottas of this period appear to be moulded from a shallow mould and look stampy. A few hand made examples are also represented. Such terracottas are with parallel limbs without fingers and other features.

Period III of Kalli-Pachchhim[14] female heads having round face, bow shaped eye brows, combed hair hanging on forehead, long goat like ears, slit mouth, possibly hand made. The red slip all over it. Another specimen yielded head of a female figurine, round face, slit mouth, nose slightly damaged, long drawn eyes, bindi on the forehead, hair pasted in middle. The head and neck have been made separately, goat like ears are in appliqué lulled over the head on the sides. Two plaques have also been found from Period III. These plaques are made of single mould, showing a haloed human face, slightly elongated round chin, heavy lower lip, broad nose, elongated eyes, heavy eye lids, prominent eye brows. The hair arranged in frizzled locks falling on the sides. Five plaques which is prepared by single mould, standing male human figures. The arms stretched down, a punch on the stomach indicate navel, the feet are marked with toes indicated by strokes. The left arm is a kimbo. A unique standing female (Aankadhatri) figurine has been reported here. The standing female figurine, holding a child in the left arm, the child touches the breasts with the left hand. The right hand of the lady is flexed and resting on the belly. The trefoil hair has a crest jewel. The face has been rubbed off only the nose and the slit mouth are seen. Two female heads with trefoil hair with a simant, frizzled hair falling on both sides, face showing broad nose, slit mouth, round chin have been noticed at Kalli Pachchhim. A male head, single mould made, the radiating locks of hair in the form of a parasol, ushnisha on the top and frizzled locks falling on both sides. The extended ear labs have ornaments. The face depicts eye brows, eye lids and long drawn eyes, broad nose, the lower one is thicker and round chin occur at the site and a female bust with head also have been reported. The nose is damaged, the facial features have been rubbed off. Both the arms broken, the hair parted in the middle with a bun on the top tied with a ribbon, frizzled locks falling on both sides. The right ear lobe has a ring, grayish and ill-fired. Two specimens of terracotta figurines one is elephant rider (*Gajarohi*) and another a horse rider (*Ashvarohi*) are also noticed at Kalli-Pachchhim. The elephant-rider, made of two piece mould, only the front part depicting the trunk, the back with the rider are available. The elephant's legs are broken. The rider has a pointed nose, slit mouth, round eyes and a crest over the head. The horse rider also made of double mould, holding the reins. The rider has pointed nose, broad slit mouth with a head dress. The horse has joint fore and hind legs, mounted on a short-pedestal.

Animal Terracotta Figurines

Period V of Narhan[15] yielded fifteen animal figurines. Out of fifteen, four are of bull, two elephant, one each of ram, nandi, bird and six indeterminate. A solitary figure of Nandi coming from this period has been made by mould and displays exquisite workmanship. Miniature figure of a Nandi sitting on a pedestal in crounching position. This figure seems to have been made by double mould, and well baked and broken figure of a ram, eyes and nostrils shown by incised holes and mouth by cut slit. This figure has bright red slip on the body and is badly damaged. Elephant with realistic treatment of forehead, tusks and the trunk which is broken found from Period V of Narhan. The body of elephant is comparatively thin and the legs are missing. The broken part made by appliqué technique at the neck may indicate the rider (*Mahavat*). Well modeled stylized figure of a bull with pronounced hump, horns elongated mouth shown with cut slit but legs are broken have been noticed from Narhan. One of the well modeled stylized figure of a bull with pronounced hump. Both fore legs, left hind leg and face are broken. The treatment of the hind leg gives the impression that the animal is running.

At Pirvitanisarif-Trilokpur[16] in Period IV only a terracotta bird with two perforations across for the axil to fasten wheels, two perforations below the neck to string it for pulling. But the rear side is damaged.

The excavation of Kalli-Pachchhim[17] Period III include two Nandi, one lion, one dancing peacock, a perched bird and an elephant terracotta figurines. The couchant bull (*Nandi*) made from a two piece mould (double mould). The snout is slit for mouth. Depressions indicate the nostrils, round eye balls, the horns and ears are combined. The hump at the back of the head is damaged, tail at the back. The folds of the skin are seen on the front. It is mounted on a low pedestal. The face of a lion made of single mould, showing round protruding eyes, nostrils damged, slit mouth, short round ears, manes on the fore head. The upper lip of lion has moustaches engraved. The tail fragment of a dancing peacock has been noticed from the site. The circles represent the decorated feathers and a perched bird which is hand made, grayish, pointed beak and concave base. The trunk of an elephant made by double mould, damaged. Only one side is available, showing lozenge eyes has been reported from Kalli-Pachchhim during Gupta Period.

Ornaments

At Narhan[18] large number of beads of semi-precious stones and terracotta were noticed from its Period V. Out of 141 beads, 139 is of terracotta, 5 is carnelian, 2 each of chert and faience and one each is of glass, agate, quartz. A broken specimen of banded agate, long convex circular has been noticed from Narhan period V. One specimen of blackish chert bead of Period V is long bicone circular. The faience beads are standard faceted cornerless cubes in worn out condition. While the spherical glass bead is of black colour with white lines. Terracotta beads are arecanut shaped, ghata shaped, long barrel circular, long bicone circular, long tubular and spherical shaped. Out of eighty arecanut shaped twenty eight are flat based, twenty three concave based and one convex based. Out of thirty ghata shaped beads, eight are ghata shaped annular, two ghata shaped with flat base, three short ghata shaped, nine short ghata shaped annular and eight standard ghata shaped. Besides these, two long barrel circular, eleven long bicone circular, four spherical bead, one long tubular circular and three irregular shaped beads have been noticed at Narhan in Period V.

The excavation of Narhan Period V yielded two drop pendant[19] of red carnelian with mid rib in the centre on one face and one ear ornament of terracotta. One copper[20] bead, the two copper rings and thirty three bangles have been reported from Narhan. Out of thirty three twenty six[21] are made of terracotta, eight glass and three bone. Fragment of terracotta bracelet with four ridges on the outside presumably made by a mould is also reported from Narhan Period V.

Period IV of Pirvitanisarif-Trilokpur[22] yielded a terracotta pendant, cylindrical in shape and having a perforation across on the top, reddish in colour, fragrant of ivory, terracotta glass bangles and terracotta arecanut shaped beads. The site of Dhuriapar Period III yielded stone beads and bangles of terracotta and glass.

Hulaskhera[23] Period IV consists of bangles made of terracotta, ivory and shell. The site of Kalli-Pachchhim include fragment of terracotta bangles, bracelet and copper bangles.

Other Terracotta Objects

Terracotta Discs

At Narhan[24] Period V include terracotta discs having sun symbol in the centre and rope pattern on the edges. The same designs are reported on the reverse as well. A partly broken piece of red colour having red slip and sun symbol incised on both sides has been found here. Similar pieces came from Rajghat, Sravasti and Prahladpur. Terracotta discs having circular, plain on both the sides, reddish in colour reported from Pirvitanisarif-Trilokpur.[25] Disc / Spindle wheel possible used as a wheel with a central perforation, red slip or grayish slip on both sides were reported from Kalli-Pachchhim Period III.

Terracotta Pestles

Fifteen terracotta pestles[26] have been reported from Narhan during Gupta Period. The broken pestles with deep incised notches have been rubbed off by use have been noticed from the site of Narhan. Some of the broken pestle with plain surface and traces of bright red slip visible on the body. A terracotta pestles have also been reported from Dhuriapar[27] of Period III.

Terracotta Stamps

Terracotta stamps have been noticed from Narhan, Hulaskhera and Kalli-Pachchhim. Seven Terracotta stamps[28] with red slip and without slip have been noticed at Narhan during Gupta period. A broken piece with radiating lines engraved on the almost flat surface with three circles. The diameter of the face is 9.5 cm which is comparable to that of the specimen from Kumarhar. The extant height of the Narhan specimen is 2.2 cm. Traces of red slip partly visible on both sides. Another specimen is slightly bigger in size and it has a central orifice and diameter 11 cm, and extant height is 3 cm. A broken piece with linear designs engraved on the flat surface has been reported at the site of Narhan. The terracotta potter's stamp of Kalli-Pachchhim bearing nandipada symbol[29] and the height of the stamp is 3.6 and diameter 4.0 cm.

Terracotta skin rubber

Terracotta skin rubbers have been reported only from Pirvitanisarif Trilokpur and Hulaskhera during Gupta Period. The terracotta rubber[30] of Pirvitanisarif-Trilokpur having cylindrical in shape with red slip and dents on the outer surface and diameter is 5.1 cm and height 13.5 cm. Another fragmentary terracotta sin rubber with horizontal ribs all over the cylindrical body. The ribs are so rough that seemingly it is not possible for human use. It might have been used for animals. The diameter is 5.2 cm and height is 9.7 cm.

Terracotta Wheels

The excavation at Narhan only yielded terracotta wheels[31] in the Kosal region during Gupta Period. A well made specimen with hub and 15 spokes embossed on the outer side, the underside being flat. It bears a bright red slip. The diameter of wheel is 10 cm.

Gamesman

Gamesman[32] have been recorded only from Hulaskhera in the Kosal region during Gupta Period.

Terracotta balls

Terracotta balls[33] occur only from Narhan and Hulaskhera during Gupta Period in the Kosal region. At Narhan Period V yielded thirty three terracotta balls. The balls are made of medium to fine grained clay and baked very hard. A few specimens bear red slip which has generally peeled off at places because of constant use. The biggest one has diameter of 6.2 cm. While the smallest one is only 1.6 cm in diameter. But on an average their diameter ranges between 2.0 cm to 2.8 cm. At least one specimen bears incised designs. Another piece had two deep grooves presumably for fastening a rope. It is likely that this specimen was used as a net sinker. Identical pieces have been reported from Niponia (District Bhairahwa) and Kadzahawa (District Taulihawa) in the Nepalese Terai and have been described as net sinkers or loom weights.[34]

Pomegranate Shaped Rattles

Three pieces of the upper portions of pomegranate shaped rattles comes from Narhan Period V. This class of antiquities are generally found in broken condition because the hollow, bulbous body has a tendency of breaking from the neck. This game object had two parts. Evidently, the upper portion (handle) was modelled separately and was lulled to the hollow body after putting Kankar nodules in it, hence it had a tendency of breaking from this junction. These are well baked to red colour.[35]

Terracotta Crucible and Ritualistic Pots

Terracotta crucible and ritualistic pots only comes from Narhan Period V of Kosal region. These miniature pots are all hand made with small to deep depressions in them. They are fired red and are devoid of any surface treatment. Some of these might have been used as crucibles while others had perhaps a ritualistic use.[36]

Metal Objects :

A large number of metal objects made of copper and iron objects have been found at a number of sites in the Kosal region.

Copper Objects

Five copper antimony rods, one bead, one ring have been reported from Narhan Period V.[37] Copper antimony rods have also been noticed at Charda and Hulaskhera during Gupta Period.

Iron Objects

At Narhan twenty three iron objects[38] such as eighteen nails, two chisel, two arrow heads have been reported. Iron nails have also been reported from Pirvitanisarif-Trilokpur[39] during Gupta Period. Iron spear and arrowheads, nails, rings, hooks have been noticed at Hulaskhera Period IV.[40] The site of Dhuriapar[41] also consist iron objects in Period III. Kalli-Pachchhim yielded only three iron implements.

Bone Objects

Bone objects only reported from Hulaskhera Period IV in the Kosal region which consist only bone arrow heads and awls.

Shell Objects

The conch shell has been reported from Narhan during Gupta Period. A conch shell[42] measuring about 10 cm long and has a deep cut on its upper portion suggesting that it had been for some special purpose.

Kauri

Few species of Kauries[43] almost bean shaped, off white in colour were recovered from the excavation of Kalli-Pachchhim Period III. Bean shaped Kuries varies from 1.4 x 0.4 cm to 1.8 x 1.3 cm.

Coins, Seals and Sealings

Only Pirvitanisarif (Period IV), and Hulaskhera (Pd. IV) yielded coins, seal and sealings. At Pirvitanisarif one copper coin, circular in shape but this coin is badly incrusted nothing clear on obverse or reverse. At Hulaskhera one of the silver coins belong to the Gupta King Kumargupta. Some of the inscribed legends in Sanskrit language found on the sealing are 'Rudrah', 'Ravibhadrasya', 'Kavibhadrasya' and 'Putrasya Maharajas Kashikao putrasyagaja'. These sealings provide ample evidence of outside contacts of the inhabitants of Hulaskhera at that time.[44]

On the basis of the archaeological findings it can be said that as early as 4th cent. A.D. almost all settlements of the Kosal region started to decline. The description of Fa-hien who traveled in North India in the beginning of the 5th century A.D. that the whole part of the region of the foothills of the Himalaya, like Kapilvastu, Kushinagar as well as Sravasti, had already devastated. On the basis of this fact, it can be supposed that the foothills region of the Himalaya started to decline in general, as early as the 4th century A.D.. This observation is reinforced by the archaeological evidence as well.

Chronology

A time bracket of *circa* 300 A.D. to 600 A.D. has been suggested on the basis of pottery forms, terracotta figurines, coins, seals and sealings.

References

1. Tewari, D.P. (2006), *op.cit.*, p. 197.
2. Singh, P. (1994), *op.cit.*, p. 27.
3. Tewari, Rakesh *et al.* (1995-96), *op.cit.*, pp. 128-129.
4. Tewari, D.P. (1999), *op.cit.*, pp. 23-24.
5. Singh, P. (1994), *op.cit.*, p. 130.
6. Tewari, D.P. (2006), *op.cit.*, p. 115.
7. Tewari, D.P. (1999), *op.cit.*, pp. 67-68.
8. *Ibid.*, pp. 69-70.
9. Tewari, Rakesh *et al.* (1995-96), *op.cit.*, p. 128.

10. *Ibid.*
11. Singh, P. (1994), *op.cit.*, pp. 141-150.
12. Tewari, D.P. (2006), *op.cit.*, p. 129.
13. Tewari, Rakesh *et al.* (1995-96), *op.cit.*, p. 129.
14. Tewari, D.P. (1999), *op.cit.*, p. 77.
15. Singh, P. (1994), *op.cit.*, p. 153.
16. Tewari, D.P. (2006), *op.cit*, p. 129.
17. Tewari, D.P. (1999), *op.cit.*, pp. 87-89.
18. Singh, P. (1994), *op.cit.*, p. 158.
19. *Ibid.*, p 163.
20. *Ibid.*, p. 205.
21. *Ibid.*
22. Tewari, D.P. (2006), *op.cit.*, p. 133.
23. Tewari, Rakesh *et al.* (1995-96), p. 129.
24. Singh, P. (1994), *op.cit.*, p. 186.
25. D.P. Tiwari (2006), *op.cit.*, p. 127.
26. Singh, P. (1994) *op.cit.*, p. 188.
27. Singh, Purushottam *op.cit.*, *Pragdhara*, No. 6, p. 58.
28. Singh, P. (1994), *op.cit.*, p. 194.
29. Tewari, D.P. (1999), *op.cit.*, p. 123.
30. Tewari, P. (2006), *op.cit.*, p. 127.
31. Singh, P. (1994), *op.cit.*, pp. 193-194.
32. Tewari, Rakesh *et al.* (1995-96), *op.cit.*, p. 129.
33. Singh, P. (1994), *op.cit.*, p. 208.
34. D. Mitra, *Excavations at Tilaurakot and Kodan* (Kathmandu, 1972), Pl. CXXXII.5 & CXXXVI-4.
35. Singh, P. (1994), *op.cit.*, p. 201.
36. *Ibid.*, p. 129.
37. *Ibid.*, p. 222.
38. *Ibid.*, p. 223.
39. Tewari, D.P. (2006), *op.cit.*, p. 129.
40. Tewari, Rakesh *et al.* (1995-96), *op.cit.*, p. 129.

41. Singh, P. (1991-92), *op.cit.*
42. Singh, P. (1994), *op.cit.*, p. 200.
43. Tiwari, D.P. (1999), *op.cit.*, p. 129.
44. Tewari, Rakesh (1995-96), *op.cit.*, p. 129.

11

Conclusion

Geographically, the Kosal region (Latitude 25°10' – 27°52'N; Longitude 80°12' – 84°16'E) extends from eastern part of western Ganga plain and western part of median Ganga plain. Currently it comprises the districts of Faizabad, Bahraich, Gonda, Basti, Deoria, Padrouna, Gorakhpur, Sant Kabirnagar, Balrampur, Sravasti, Siddharthnagar, Rai Bareilly, Lucknow, Barabanki, Unnao, Sitapur, Pratapgarh, Sultanpur and Jaunpur of Uttar Pradesh.

There is no reference of Kosal in the *Rigveda*, though two of its great conqueror kings, Iksvaku (X.60.4) and Mandhata (VIII.39.9) find mention in it. In the later Vedic age, there is a mention in the *Satapatha Brahmana* ((1.4.1,14-17) of the river Sadanira, i.e. the great Gandaki as forming the boundary between the two Janapadas, Kosal and Videha. The *Atharvaveda* (X.2.32) describes the construction, wealth and greatness of Ayodhya, the first capital of Kosal, and it may be presumed that by the time of its composition Kosal had become fairly popular. Panini in his *Astadhyayi* (4.1.17) makes a mention of Kosal referred as one of the sixteen Mahajanapadas for the first time in the Buddhist Pali canonical *Anguttar Nikaya* (I, 213; V. 252)

Archaeological explorations and excavations have brought to light a number of settlements in the Kosal region ranging from Mesolithic period to Medieval period. Important excavated sites of the region are Narhan, Imlidih Khurd, Dhuriapar, Sohgaura, Lahuradeva, Sravasti, Ayodhya, Piprahwa, Ganwaria, Siswania, Charda, Pirvitanisarif-Trilokpur, Sarai-Nahar Rai, Mahadaha, Damdama, Hulaskhera, Hariharpur, Dadupur, Pariyar, Kopia, Kalli-Pachchim, etc.

During Mesolithic period which coincides on the onset of the Holocene (10,000 years BP), the area attained its present form and more fertile zones with better living conditions became available for habitation. On account of better climatic conditions there was a tendency of both inter and intra-regional movement of men and animal. The population of *Homo sapiens sepiens*, too, increased considerably in this period. In order to cope with the changing ecological and environmental conditions man also changed the pattern of his life in contrast to its past. The Mesolithic people of the southern Uttar Pradesh seasonally migrating from the Vindhyan region due to adverse hot climatic condition. The migrating Mesolithic people from the Vindhyas made their settlements on the bank of oxbow lakes full of aquatic life formed by abandoned meander of changing river courses in the southern part of Kosal. Here the settlers had ample food supplies from the lakes as well as the dense primeval forest of the fertile alluvial plains. The people came during the summer, when there was acute scarcity of food and water in the Vindhyas, a recurrent phenomena even now. These temporary sites are found scattered in Pratapgarh, Sultanpur and Jaunpur. Maximum number of settlements are located in Pratapgarh district, where the trio of such sites i.e. Sarai-Nahar Rai, Mahadaha and Damdama have been excavated. All the three settlements are located on the bank of horse shoe lakes. Mesolithic people selected these sites because of not only the availability of food, but the consideration of ecological security was also a controlling factor. These two sites are surrounded on all sides by lakes, the access to them being controlled by a narrow strip of land. Since raw material was brought from a distance, it has been used here with great economy, and as a result, we have the smallest microliths in this region. The absence of raw material was a deterrent for the spread of Mesolithic culture in the northern portion of Kosal. The migration appears to be a seasonal in character and the sites were never occupied continuously for a long time confirmed by the fact that occupational debris being very thin. But the thickness of cultural deposit at Damdama would clearly indicate that in contrast to Sarai-Nahar-Rai and Mahadaha it might have been occupied for a much longer span of time. The Mesolithic habitational strata at Sarai-Nahar-Rai, Mahadaha and Damdama is 6 cm, 60 cm, and 1.5 cm. respectively. But the situation of these sites were so alluring that the migrating people came again and again and selected the same spot. Excavations have also offered conclusive evidence that the new-comers were not aware of the existence of earlier settlement. The migrating people brought the raw material from the Kaimur range of Vindhyas and manufactured the microliths is fully documented in each site. Cores in different stages of manufacture, debitage, rejected flakes and tools, though heavily patinated, have been discovered in very well preserved and fresh form with all the corners and angle intact. Since the stone material is not available in, north of the the Ganga plain, these people were actually conscious of the scarcity of the material, so vital for their survival and also of the need for extreme economy in its use. The consequence of this was a reduction in tool size and the use of cores for tool making till they became core-rest or non-functional. The subsistence economy of the Mesolithic folk depended on hunting and gathering as it was attested by the evidence of floral, faunal, lithic and bone implements of Sarai-Nahar Rai, Mahadaha and Damdama. At Damdama, 90% of the animal bones obtained are charred or semi-charred suggesting their use in dietary item. Large number of hearths at Sarai-Nahar-Rai, Mahadaha and Damdama, full of buried clay lumps, ash and charred animal bones demonstrate that the animal flesh was roasted in these hearths. The occurrence of the fragments in the form of food processing equipments of a large number of querns, mullers, saddle at microlithic sites of Pratapgarh would indicate the gathering of wild grains and other edible had started playing some role in the life of the Mesolithic people at the sites. At Mahadaha the structural activity indicated by only a community hearth enclosed by four post holes and subsequently covered by a circular floor paved with burnt-clay lump. The evidence of post holes around an oblong community hearth found at Sarai-Nahar

Rai seems to reflect the memory of huts constructed by these people in the Vindhyan area. This indicated that the area of settlement was used both for manufacturing tools and preparing food.

There is no typical Neolithic implements have been reported in the Kosal region. Although the settlements yielded mostly handmade coarse variety of red ware bearing cord impressions on their exterior surface and cultivation of crops. Hence, the nomenclature of Early Farming Culture is much suitable instead of Neolithic Culture which begin at least around middle of the seventh millennium BC as it was attested by the evidence of cultivation of rice at Lahuradeva in district Sant Kabir Nagar. Other excavated settlements of the early farming culture in the Kosal region is Imlidih Khurd (Pd I), and Sohgaura (Pd I). These settlements were located either on river banks or on lake sides which provide water and aquatic fauna to the early settlers. The wide alluvial flood plain was available for the cultivation of crops to the early settlers also. Their subsistence was mainly based on agriculture which is corroborated by the abundant occurrence of the remains of cereals and pulses at sites of the early farming culture i.e. Lahuradeva, and Imlidkh-Khurd. Carbonised material of Lahuradeva Period IA contains grains of cultivated rice (*Oryza sativa*) and wild rice (*Oryza rufipogon*) which corroborates the beginning of rice based agriculture at the site at least around middle of the seventh millennium BC Another site i.e. Imlidih-Khurd also confirms that rice was major crop cultivated throughout the occupational Period I. Next to rice grains is wheat (*Triticum aestivum, Triticum sphaerococcum*) and barley (*Hordeum vulgare*) from the period I furnish clear indication of their relative importance at Imlidih Khurd along with Jowar millet (*Serghum bicolor*), pearl- millet-bajra (*Pennisetum typhoides*), Lentil (*Lense culnaris*), field peas (*Pisum arvense*), grass pea or *Khesari* (*Lathyrus sativus*), green gram or *mung* (*Vigna radiate*). The settlers of early farming culture of Kosal region also exploited fruits like wild Jujube (*Xiziphus rummularia*), *anwala* (*Emblica officinalis*) and grape (*Vitis vinifera*). At Lahuradeva and Imlidih Khurd yielded charred and uncharred bones, turtle shell, mollusca found in a broken condition which were also a part of their subsistence. The structural remains of Lahuradeva and Imlidih Khurd are found in the form of burnt clay lumps and nodules bearing reed and straw mark which indicate that the houses of this period were made of wattle and daub. Several floors made of mud, ovens and chulah marked the other structural activity. At Imlidih Khurd circular structures have been reported which were used as grain silo or bin by the early farming settlers. Material remains yielded various types of potteries, beads as ornaments, bone, stone and terracotta objects. At Sohagaura, Imlidkh Khurd and Lahuradeva potteries mainly consisting of red ware and black and red ware which include both hand made and slow wheel turned. Some of the black-and-red ware and red ware potsherds bear black and red slip respectively on their interior and exterior surface Burnishing is also evident. Generally the pottery is ill-fired having coarse and porous surface and uneven, sometimes sand particles in their core. The clay used for pottery making exhibits husk and straw marks and is not well levigated. A good number of potsherds are decorated with cord impressions on the exterior surface. Applied decoration showing primitive type of rope pattern is also found. The main shapes include convex-sided bowl, pedestal bowl, knobbed vessel, miniature bowl, vase globular vases. The high proportion of coarse variety of black-and-red ware is significant. Most of the pots are made in two stages, the lower and rim portions are prepared separately, thereafter the rim portion is pinched with the lower one. Beads made of steatite, carnelian, agate, faience and terracotta have been reported from Lahuradeva and Imlidih Khurd. The presence of wafer thick micro disc beads of steatite is important finding. Bone arrowheads and points of Lahuradeva and Imlidkh Khurd indicate their hunting economy.

A number of chalcolithic settlements have been reported from the districts of Jaunpur, Pratapgarh, Sultanpur, Gonda, Bahraich, Sravasti, Siddharthnagar, Sant Kabir Nagar, Gorakhpur, and Basti in the Kosal region. The settlements are either located on the bank of Ghaghara, Gomati and its tributaries or on lake sides. The favourable ecological conditions including thick alluvial soil, climate, accessibility of natural resources were largely responsible for the growth, maturity and expansion of chalcolithic culture in the region. They are all rural settlements characterized by mud architecture, plain and painted pottery, stone and bone tools with restricted use of copper. But Narhan culture in the exception having no lithic assemblage. The chalcolithic settlements of Kosal region are Narhan, Dhuriapar, Imlidkh Khurd, Sohagaura, Lahuradeva, Hulaskhera etc. whose thickness of the strata shows that in comparison to the Early

Farming Culture, it was survived for a very long span of time.

Their mixed economy was based on agriculture stock raising and hunting-fishing. A good quantity of archaeobotanical remains obtained from Narhan, Imlidkh Khurd, Lahuradeva and Hulaskhera confirm their subsistence economy. Cereal grains of hulled and six row barley (*Horedum vulgare*), Club wheat (*Triticum compactum*), bread wheat (*Triticum aestivum*), dwarf wheat (*Triticum sphaerococcum*), *bajra* (*Pennisetum typhoides*), *kondon* millet (*Pasphalum scrobi culatum*), cultivated rice (*Oryza sativa*), field pea (*Pisum sativum*), green gram mung (*Vigna radiate*), gram/ chick pea (*Cicer arietinum*), *Khesari* or grass pea (*Lathyrus sativus*), Lentil (*Lens culinaris*), linseed (*Linum usitatissium*) are reported from Chalcolithic strata of the region. The find of mustard from Narhan is the first record of this oilseed in the Indian subcontinent. Carbonised seeds and cotyledons of jack fruit or *Katahal* (*Artocarpus helerophyllus*) is also an important discovery at Narhan. The people of Narhan culture at Imlidkh Khurd exploited local fruits like wild jujube (*Ziziphus nummularia*) and anwala (*Emblica officinalis*). The Black-and-Red Ware culture of Narhan and Imlidih Khurd seems to have shared much the same kind of crop economy and enjoyed mutual contacts. The introduction of the crops of wheat, barley, lentil, fied pea etc. has also been evidenced to form an established double cropping system in this region of settlement. Rice, bajra, *kondon*-millet, horse gram, green gram, moth bean are usually grown in warm-rainy season while wheat, barley, gram, khesari, lentil and field pea are winter crops. The seeds and leaves of Amranthus (locally known as *chaulai*) also reported from Imlidih Khurd and Narhan. The above plant species are eaten as vegetables.

Although the settlers of the chalcolithic culture of Kosal practiced agriculture but the meat was an important component of their diet as is evident from the presence of a large number of charred animal bones and antlers are present at the sites. But at Narhan only 15% of animal bones were collected from the excavation of Period I. The animal bones of humped Indian cattle (*Bos indicus*) sheep/goat (*Ovis / copra*), deer of antelope (*Axis* sp.), Buffalo (*Bubalus bubalis*) recovered from the excavation of chalcolithic site in the Kosal region. The aquatic resources at the same site comprise two species of fresh water turtle, fish of small and medium size.

The Chalcolithic structural activities of the chalcolithic period of Kosal region are mainly represented by post-holes, rammed earthen floors, mud wall, burnt clay nodules often bearing reed marks, hearths and bins in the Kosal region. Post holes appear to form circular alignment. Their mud plastered screens made of reeds or similar material are represented by the burnt clay chunks bearing reed impression. Material remains consisted of potteries, beads, bone, metal and terracotta objects like preceding Early Farming culture. The main ceramic industries of the Narhan culture is white painted Black-and-Red Ware, Black Slipped Ware with occasional painting in white, Red Slipped Ware, and plain Red Ware. The principal pottery types in Black and Red Ware are bowls, basins and vases. The principal types in the Black Slipped Ware consist of bowls, dishes, vases. The quantity of basins and vases is extremely limited. In the red slipped ware the dominant category is that of bowls, basins, vases and dishes.

The red ware has bowls, vases, basins and dishes. The colours used are mostly white to creamy white. Their workmanship is apparently improved. The decorative patterns of chalcolith is continued and show some innovations. The painting include dotted, circular and linear designs. Some of which are very artistically executed. Incised and appliqué decorations continued in small proportion. It may be emphasized here that the white painted Black Slipped Wares have been found from other Chalcolithic sites of the Kosal such as Sohagaura, Imlidkh-Khurd, Narhan, etc. which shows that this pottery is the hallmark of the developed farming phase of the area. Corded pattern of decoration of the preceding phase also continued. Its proportion in comparison to other ceramic and that of Period I, however, is reduced. Quantity of slipped and burnished pottery, besides certain shapes such as dish-on-stand, bowl on stand, pedestal bowl, perforated bowl, button based lids and spouts ehanced in good proportion. Negligible occurrence of convex sided dish to be noted. Some sherds of bearing mat impression on their exterior surface are notable. The black-and-red ware is of two types—handmade and wheel turned. Handmade sherds comprise coarse fabric, thick section and gritty core. It bears rustication and straw marks on outer surface. Wheel turned sherds consist of fine fabric. Made by well-levigated clay.

The chalcolithic settlers of the Kosal region used beads of semi-precious stones and terracotta. Steatite beads have been recovered from the excavation of Sohagaura, Lahuradeva, and Imlidkh Khurd. The beads were also made of copper, ivory and bone. Apart from beads, broken bangle of bone or anteler obtained from Dhuriapar. Terraoctta glass, copper bangles, bone tools included points, arrowheads are also reported from the sites.. Some of the very well-made ground, polished and decorated bone arrowheads of tanged, barbed and socketed varieties, often bearing punctured arclets are worth mentioning for their quality workmanship. A copper arrowhead is reported from the excavation of Imlidih Khurd. At Lahuradeva a copper arrowhead made of sheet metal and a fishing hook have been reported from lower levels of Period I. These finds may be placed in early 3rd millennium BC and represent the earliest known copper artifacts in the Ganga plain.

The Period I of Ganwaria, Siswania, Hariharpur, Saripur and Charda and Period II of Narahan belonging to pre-NBPW phase. The inhabitants of this period lived in the wattle and daub houses. Although main economy of the pre-NBPW culture was the agriculture, but it was also supplemented by meat and other aquatic fresh water fauna. The material remains yielded pottery, terracotta human and animal figurines, bead and ornaments, bone and metal objects. The pre-NBPW is characterized by the presence of black slipped ware (plain and painted), few sherds of plain black-and-red ware. The principal shapes in black slipped ware is bowl, dishes, vases, miniature vases, perforated footed bowls, jars. In red ware bowls dishes and vases are the important types. Terracotta human figurines are in the fish star shaped which have been reported from Narhan Pd II. These are crudely modeled by hand and roughly pinched in clay to desired shape to represent mink or stylized human shape. Most of these are devoid of any sex indication. Although their religious connotation is not proven but for want of any better name the excavator given nomenclature "mother goddess" to these star shaped figurines. The earliest occurrence of terracotta animal figurine of bull/nilgai, dogs in Period II of Narhan is reported. At Narhan the stone and glass were employed for bead making in pre-NBPW and onwards. Out of 13 agate beads, 11 came from Period II alone. There are two specimen of agate beads in the Narhan collection which are unfinished (the boring has not been done) which indicates that they were locally made. Other beads were made of carnelian, chert, faience, glass, Jasper, quartz and terracotta. Bone objects in the form of points, arrowheads and metal objects of copper fish hooks, arrowhead, spearhead indicate that hunting and fishing was also a part of their subsistence.

In course of Northern Black Polished Ware not only the number of settlements were increased but the size of settlements were also expanded. In the Kosal region not only the settlements were studied but a number of mounds with their names or their village names were identified with ancient cities or with townships having corporate guilds (*nagara* and *nigam*). Such identification of modern names of place with *nagaras* and *nigamas*, like *Siswania* with *Setavya*, *Ukada* with *Ukkattha*, *Ama* with *Atuma*, *Nagara* with *Nagaraka*, *Mehdawal* with *Medata lumpa*, *Saltauwa* with *Salavatika* or *Salavati* and *Behil* with *Vehalinge*—all going back to the time of Buddha as also proved from the material remains found from these sites. The thickness of NBPW strata shows that the culture existed very long span of time in comparison to earlier preceding cultures in the Kosal region. The life of the NBPW people were more sedentary based on agriculture which was indicated by the cereal and other palaeobotanical remains which were recovered from the excavation of the sites of Narhan, Privitani-Sarif, Hulaskhera, and Charda. The palaecbotanical remains include rice (*oryza sativa*), barley (*Hordeum vulgari*), wheat (*Triticu aestivum, Triticum sphaerococcum*), *Kodon* millet (*Paspalum scrobiculatum*), black gram (*Vigna mung*), green gram (*Vigna radiate*), pea (*Pisum sativum*), *Khesari* (*Lathyrus sativus*), sesame (*Sesam indicum*), Linseed (*Lunum usitatissimum*), field brassica (*Brassica junacea*). The plant remains of Pirvitani Sarif, Charda, and Narhan provided enough evidence that the ecological conditions of the Rapti-Ghaghara doab was suitable for the agriculture based subsistence economy. The early settlers of Rapti-Ghaghara doab may have exploited the useful plant species in their riverine environment. Fruit remains include jujube (*Zizyphus maurtiana*), *anwala* (*Phyllanthas emblica*), *phalsa* (*Grewia asiatica*) and watermelon (*Citrullus lanatus*). There is a sudden decrease in the number and types of bone points and arrowheads in this period indicating a more sedentary life based on agriculture. The settlers of this period lived in mud, mud brick and burnt brick houses. Use of burnt bricks have been evidenced from Narhan, Siswania, Sravasti, Sohgaura, Ganwaria, Pirvitanisarif-Trilolpur, etc. At Sravasti, the use of a large number of decorative tiles was common in NBPW phase.

At Pirvitanisarif the structures were made of burnt brick measuring 52 x 24 x 7 cm, 50 x 24 x 7 cm, 48 x 24 x 7 cm and 31 x 24 x 7 cm. The material remains of this period indicates rich and improved quality in contrast to earlier. This period is characterized by the presence of NBPW ceramic industries. The ceramic of this period are made of well-levigated clay and do not show any tampering comprise fine to medium fabric. Sherds of coarse variety of black-and-red ware, black slipped ware and red ware, however, are comparatively in a small proportion. Quality of NBPW is very fine having golden, silvery and bi-chrome varieties. Some sherds are also decorated with painted patterns generally executed in black colour. The sherds have a glossy surface with highly lustrous sheen and when struck give a sharp metallic sound. Pots were invariably potted on a fast wheel. Shapes included corrugated bowls, bowls with internally incurved thickened rim, deep bowl with a featureless rim, dish with an averted externally grooved rim and incurved sides, necked vase having an out turned rim and externally thickened rim and different types of basin. Among other material remains beads of semi-precious i.e. agate, carnelian, chalcedony, jasper etc. beads of glass, terracotta and ivory have also been reported from this period. Ornaments yielded bangles, ear studs, pendant. At Siswania a bull shaped pendant with gold foil, a nib shaped, violin shaped terracotta pendants are reported. Of the semi-precious stones, carnelian and agate were most popular. Banded agate was commonly employed in Sravasti and often the raw stone was skillfully cut so that this bands got arranged variously as cherrous, eyes and zones. At Sravasti, a cylinder bead of lapis-lazuli from lower levels of NBPW (Period I) is of considerable interest as the stone is not available in India and either the raw material or the finished product itself must have been imported. A near identical specimen is available from pre-Mauryan levels of Bhir mound at Taxila in Pakistan. In the entire collection at Sravasti, there is a solitary etched specimen in stone. This is an unfinished zone bead of agate from an early level of Period II and similar to the one found at Taxila. Of the faceted beads which is made of double pentagon of crystal, a specimen of exquisite workmanship and was recorded from the deposits of Period II at Sravasti. The terracotta human figurines were recovered from NBPW level of Sravasti (Pd II), Pirvitanisarif-Trilokpur and Lahuradeva. At Sravasti mother goddess types, Naga figurines, meethunas and allied figurines were recovered. The excavation of Privitanisarif-Trilokpur yielded a terracotta human figurine of archaic types. All these figurines indicate common man's medium of religious and artistic expression.Animal figurines like elephant, fish, dog, horse, humped bull have been found from Sravati, Narhan, Pirvitanisarif-Trilokpur, Kalli-Pachchim, etc. A caprisioned horse, elephant head with a shortish forehead decorated with stamped rosettes on the forehead shows artistic skill. The elephant figures are by far the largest in number and in many cases the body shown with decoration is the characteristic of this period. At Sravasti a fragment of a winged and humped lion, a theriomorphic representation a monster is a unique find.

Typologically and numerically, the metal objects found in increased number during this period which indicate their technological skill. In the Kosal region, a large number of pottery discs, terracotta wheels, gamesman were recorded from various settlements which were used as playthings. The sites also yielded punch marked coins, seals and sealings which indicate their trade and commercial activities.

Although Kosal region was not the central zone of Kushan empire but it was peripheral region which were well connected with trade and commerce. Being a peripheral region where large number of Shunga-Kushan settlements were located which shows burgeoning of population during this period. Kushan settlements were not located only on the bank of river but also near ponds and lakes. Settlements located on lakes show a sharp increase in their frequency, area, and thickness of occupation in comparison to the river side settlements. This suggests that the lakes were more attractive for the human settlements than the rivers during Kushan period. The location of settlement on such lakes might have been due to the availability of perennial water, sufficient aquatic food from the lakes and vast alluvial soil around them and above all, to avoid the devastating effect of the flood, a salient feature of the region. Another interesting feature which also came to light that Kushan settlement were not only located along the river bank and on the tributaries but also found in the hinterlands so well because the Kushanas built so many tanks and dug up wells which fulfilled their needs for potable water and for irrigation. The various tanks and wells show their technological innovations during Kushan period. It has been observed that rivers and lakes were occupied from pre-NBPW to the Kushan period whereas the settlements situated without any nearby water source were inhabited during the Shunga-Kushan phase. The results confirm a continuity in the explored area of Kosal region right from Pre-NBPW phase to Kushan period.

During Kushan period the structural remains were marked by the use of burnt bricks of standard size measuring 38 x 37/36 x 23/22/6/5, 44 x 23 x 6 cm, 50 x 26 x 5 cm. Terracotta tiles were used for the roofing. Ring wells were found in an adequate number. At Siswania and Kalli-Pachchim remains of a workshop of metalsmiths is indicated by the evidence of slag, complete and broken pieces of crucibles and metal pieces of iron and copper. Hearths of various shapes and sizes confirm the elevation of pyrometallurgy. Natural nodules having metallic contents were noticed on the surface of site. The floors were made of clay or brick jelly, plastered with mud mortar or treated with baked bricks. At Hulaskhera each complex comprised two to three rooms with earthan or brick treated floors. Lanes or by lanes with the width of about 0.76 to 1.00 m. are provided between two complexes. Entrance gates, measuring 1.00 to 0.80 m in width have their openings towards the lanes or by lanes. The most fascinating structure is the occurrence of a road of about 200 m. in length.

Pirvitanisarif-Trilokpur and Hulaskhera throw ample light on agriculture base of subsistence economy. The palaeobotanical remains comprises *Hordeum vulgare, Oryza sativa, Vigna mungo, Vigna radiate, Salichos biflerus, Sesamum indicum, Triticum sphaerocoum, Triticum aestivum, Lathyrus sativus, Cicres arietinum, Pisum arveure, Lathyrus sativus, Lens culinaris,* etc. Material remains yielded pottery, terracotta animal and human figurines, beads and oranaments, bone, metal stone objects. The dominant ceramic industry are the red ware represented by bowls, dishes, vases, basins, spouted vessels, sprinklers, lids, lids with knobbed handles. Some of the sherds were found to be decorated with stamped and incised designs. Terracotta human figurines in the form of star shaped mother goddesses were continued from earlier period to Kushan period at Narhan. Human head with foreign ethnic features were found at Narhan, Siswania,

Kopia, Charda, etc. Terracotta figurines of *Naigamesha* were found at Narhan, Siswania, Charda. The human figurines are made in two parts. The upper part or head consists a conical base and the lower part comprise a hole on upper surface, so that the two may be fixed together. This technique is followed throughout Kushan period. Applied pattern is observed for ornamentation and decorated purposes. Stamped designs and incised lines and holes to show the ears, nose and eyes are seldom seen. Generally the terracottas of this period are heavy and comparatively inferior in artistic qualities. Terracotta animal figurines included bull, elephant, dog, camel, birds, ram, lion, humped bull, horse, elephant, rider etc. Elephant is decorated with five stamps like chakra, leaf, palm etc. Beads of semi precious stone have been reported from Narhan, Dhuriapar, Sohagaura, Kopia, Siswania, Charda, Pirvitanisarif, Kalli-Pachchim, Hulaskhera, Hariharpur, etc. during Shunga-Kushan period. Ear stud of red jasper, copper rings, glass bangles, pendants were also found. At Kopia the habitational area at the northern end include a number of glass beads, bangles along with bead polishers, some basins, and storage jars of very typical shape which makes us believe that the people related to the glass head/bangles making lived here. Metal objects in the form of copper antimony rod, ring, fish hooks, button, bell, needle etc. and a large number of iron objects like nails, chisels, arrowheads, sickle, rings, hooks, knives, spear heads have been reported from Narhan, Kopia, Kalli Pachchim, Pirvitanisarif- Trilokpur, Hulaskhera, Dhuriapar etc. Stone grinder, muller, quern, pestles shows cereal based economy. Terracotta gamesman, wheels, discs, sling balls, marbles, stamps, skin rubber have also been found.

In this region a large number of Kushan coins of Kadphise II, Kanishka and Huishka were reported.

So far as Gupta settlements are concerned, there is approximately 140 sites have been explored. The excavated Gupta sites are Narhan, Charda, Pirvitanisarif-Trilokpur, Dhuriapar, Kalli-Pachchim, Hulaskhera. Only two sites i.e. Charda and Pirvitanisarif-Trilokpur yielded the remains of cereals and other botanical remains like barley (*Hordeum vulgare*), rice (*Oryza sativa*), dwarf-wheat (*Triticum sphaerococcum*), ragi millet (*Eleusive coracana*), black gram (*Vigna mungo*), green gram (*Vigna radiate*), field pea (*Pisum arveuse*), grass pea (*Lathyrus sativus*), Lentil (*Lens culanaris*), Sawan millet (*Echinochoa calonum*), sesame (*Sesamum indicum*). The Gupta structural remains were not very impressive. Generally the structures of this period were found to be robbed. However the remaining structures indicate that they were made of broken bricks of earlier period i.e. Kushan. Brick bats, mud mortar were used in the construction. The constructions are irregular as it was seen in the excavation of Hulaskhera. The walls of the earlier phase were used as foundation of the later phase in a few cases. Inner surface of the walls was smoother than the exterior and the rooms are comparatively smaller.

The pottery of this period is mainly red ware some having red slip on both surface. The red ware ranging medium to coarse fabric. The pottery bears post firing incised pattern comprising criss-cross lines, vertical strokes, concenting a circles filled with square etc. The main pottery types yielded large storage jars, plain and decorated bowls, short and high necked water vessels, spouted vessels, vases, dishes, *surahis*, button knobbed, bell shaped and cylindrical lids, lipped bowls, carinated handi, etc. Human and animal terracotta figurines have also been reported from Narhan, Pirvitanisarif-Trilokpur, Hulaskhera, Kalli-Pachchhim of the Kosal region which expressed their artistic expressions. The human terracotta figurines include star shaped mother goddess, large sized human head, human heads with foreign ethnic feature, female figures with hollow cylindrical body, sitting human figure. The human head is marked by large, lenticular eyes, prominent nose, open mouth, thick lips and plump face. It has a bright red slip. The human heads with foreign ethnic feature is fan shaped head dress, large protruding eyes and eye brows marked with rope like incised pattern. Several moulded plaques with lovely hair styles were obtained from the Kosal region. These are made of finely levigated clay with no admixture of degressant and are well-baked. A majority of degressant and standardized figures—models of fashionable male and female wearing a variety of gorgeous coiffures. The most favourite form of coiffures was the wig like arrangement of the hair. At Hulaskhera the terracotta human figurines include *Dampati, Mithun, mata-putra, ankdhatri, Krisa dhatri* and *abhisarika, Naigamesh* etc. Animal terracotta figurines yielded bull, elephant, ram, bird, etc. Household and hunting metal objects have been reported from a number of sites like Charda, Hulaskhera, Kalli-Pachhim, etc. which yielded antimony copper rods, rings, arrowheads, spear heads, nails, chisels, hooks of iron. But bone objects only confined to the arrowheads.

The palaeo-ecology is a sensitive and challengeable subject in the field of modern archaeology. In scientific term ecology is the study of the inter-relationships between living organism and the environment (including the other living organisms present) in which they live. But in the case of archaeology it has been categorized as Human ecology means the inter-relationship between people and place/area or region in which they lived. Thus settlement archaeology is the synonymous with human ecology.

The present climate of the Kosal region is subtropical where it is controlled mainly by the south-west monsoon. Its southern part (south of Ghaghara) receives low rainfall, while its northern part (north of Ghaghara) have high rainfall which forms the *terai* belt. The geomorphic surface of the region which is a depositional surface formed during Late Pleistocene-Holocene climate cycles (12800 BP – present time), influenced also by neotectonics and base level changes, all having a Holocene sediment cover. The neotectonic activity in the basement structure of the Kosal have controlled the thickness of the alluvial deposit and have guided the direction of the behaviour of the river channel on the surface. By this neotectonic activity in the area of Himalaya, north of the Kosal developed a type of activity known as Himalayan Frontal Thrust (HFT) which results in the uplift of Faizabad ridge and Vindhyan ridge. By the development of these ridges in the basement area of Kosal, its northern part have thicker alluvial deposit in the form of megafan in contrast to its southern part. Geologically during 20,000 BP, megafan making deposit started in the northern portion of the Kosal region. By the time of middle Holocene (8000 – 5000 BP) the tectonic activity along with Himalayan-Frontal Thrust (HFT) boards north developed an open fructure on the earth surface fully disruption of river channels, upwarping of the surface and formation of lakes in the area of Kosal. The southern part of the Kosal shows evidence of upliftment during the late phase of Holocene by which soil become alkaline from *Circa* 3000 BP onwards *reh* (heavy alkaline soil) was developed in the area of Pratapgarh-Allahabad-Raibarelly belt. In contrast its northern portion have megafan of Ghaghara and Rapti having less alkaline soil.

Reconstruction of the post-Pleistocene climate of the Kosal region was based on pollen analysis of Somai lake (Rai Bareilly district), Basaha lake (Unnao district), Misa Tal (lake) (Lucknow district), Lahuradeva lake (Sant Kabir Nagar district), Khoalan Jhil (lake) near Sarai-Nahar-Rai (Pratapgarh district) and teeth enamel studies of Charda (Bahraich district), Dadupur and Kali Pachchhim (Lucknow district). The following changes in the palaeo-environment of Kosal region which effect its cultural personality is as:

(1) Before onset of the Holocene or in the last phase of Pleistocene (13000 – 11500 BP), there was a period of high rainfall in the area by which expansion of lakes and wetlands with a few alluvial ridges developed indicated by the early phase of pollen zone III of Sanai Tal (13000 – 11500 BP) which have high frequency of aquatic plants, while marshy plants and grasses are in declining frequency. Archae-zoological studies confirm the result of pollen analysis, because at this time the population of the various species of deer increased in the region of Kosal. Albeit there is no archaeological remains found in the area of Kosal region, but south of it i.e. in the area of Vindhya, this phase was full of archaeological

remains represented as a transitional phase in between Upper Palaeolithic Culture to Early Phase of Mesolithic Culture.

(2) From *Circa* 11500 - 10500 BP, was a period of reduced rainfall when we compare to earlier one (13000 - 11500 BP). During the middle phase of pollen zone III of Sanai Tal (11500 - 10500 BP), there is a sharp decrease in all plant remains, except increase in grasses type of flora. Kosal region wetlands are reduced and it corresponds to the earliest dry spell in the area which was for the first time saw the day of the light in the area since from 80,000 BP. But the area of Kosal was not so arid, which unfavoured to human settlement.

(3) From *Circa* 10500 - 5000 BP the south portion of Kosal had experienced high rainfall and enlargement of lakes, wetlands and aquatic plants was confirmed by last phase of pollen zone III (10500 - 5000 BP) of Sanai Tal and pollen zone I (8300 - 7700 BP) and II (1700 - 6600 BP) of Misa Tal. In this phase there is an increase in frequency of all plants except redges and fern which confirm palynological evidence of high rainfall. The same climatic picture emerges in the northern portion of Kosal confirmed by pollen zone I (10600-9250 BP); pollen zone II (9250 - 6400 BP) and pollen zone III (6400-4060 BP) of Lahuradeva lake. The monsoon rainfall at Lahuradeva constantly increases from 10600 - 4060 BP. It was confirmed by the increased frequency of aquatic plants and emergence of *Trapa* (*Singhara*) in its last phase. During this phase we find a frequent number of Mesolithic settlement in the south portion of Kosal as well as development of Early Farming Cultures in the northern portion. Thus, Kosal during this time span i.e. mid-phase

of the Holocene period was the center of attraction for early settlers. The available evidence of Mesolithic phase of Kosal region confirms a semi-sedantary settlement pattern, as defined by Binford, rather than a fully sedentary one. In that case the archaeological evidence of the Kosal region does not contradict the global prediction. How the unexpected pattern of semi-sedentism, rather than the nomadic pattern which local environmental conditions should theoretically have favoured developed in the southern portion of Kosal? The faunal material of Damdama, Sarai-Nahar-Rai, Mahadaha etc. revealed that they fall into hunting-gathering group. The fauna of these sites have revealed the presence of large mammals such as *Bos sp.* (perhaps wild cattle), gaur, wild buffalo, elephant and rhinoceros. Hippopotamus has also been identified at Sarai-Nahar-Rai by K.R. Alur. The range of wild mammals at these sites of Kosal region indicate that the hunting-gathering groups of people exploited all possible natural resources. The data analysis from Mahadaha shows that both these animals were killed year round, through the peak seasons of their respective cullinos were different. The faunal evidence thus suggests residential stability, as opposed to residential mobility at Mahadaha. This is further supported by the occurrence of rodent remains (*Batidicota bengalensis*) from Mahadaha and Warikalan-Mahadaha. This is also suppored by the evidence of pit-hearths and hearths at Sarai-Nahar-Rai, Mahadaha and Warikalan-Mahadaha. The excavations exposed several pit-hearths divisible into two groups: simple, shallow pit-hearths and hearths with clay plaster on side walls or bottom or both. The available evidence from hearths clearly indicate that Mesolithic folk used to roast meat before eating i.e. evidence of semi-sedentary life.

4. From *Circa* 5000 – 3500 BP, the area of south Kosal have relatively dry climate, while its northern portion have moderate climate. The pollen zone III of Sanai Tal (5000 – 2000 BP) and zone III (6600-2000 BP) of Misa Tal clearly indicate in the sharp decline in acquatic plants confirm the shrinkage of lake water and increase in marginal marsh zone due to low rainfall. The pollen zone IV of Lahuradeva (4060-1350 BP) corroborate the moderate monsoon rainfall in the area. Hence the agricultural practices increased by its domestication process which is marked by the increase in *Cerealia* and other cultural pollen taxa. Groves or forests turned more dense and diversified as demonstrated by the increased number of trees particularly *Madhuca indica, Syzygium, Holoptelea* and *Barringtonia.* Transformation of lake into swamp commenced with the influx of sediments in the lake basin as indicated by the expansion of grasses and simultaneously reduction in aquatic plants.

(5) From *Circa* 3500 to present time shows a fluctuation in rainfall in entire area of Kosal. The pollen analysis of Basaha Lake, Misa Tal and Lahuradeva confirm the humid spells are during 3500-3000 BP and 2000 – 1700BP; moderate rainfall between 3000 – 2000 BP and low rainfall around 2700 BP, 2000 - 700 BP and 1300 BP. Such type of climatic fluctuation is also corroborated by isotopes 0^{18} analysis from the teeth enamel of Charda (district Baharaich), Dadupur and Kali Pachchhim (district Lucknow). In recent years, the study of stable oxygen and carbon isotopes in teeth enamel developed as an important tool to determine rainfall pattern

and palaeovegetation in a region. The 0^{18} composition of mammalian tooth enamel is directly related to the oxygen isotope composition of the body water. The main source of body water is drinking water. It is usually assumed that the 0^{18} of local natural water would be the primary source of variations reflected in the 0^{18} teeth enamel for animals of a given species with similar feeding habits. In the area of Kosal, the main source of water is monsoon rainfall. The monsoon rainfall lower the value of 0^{18} but in dry season when it evaporates, the 0^{18} value of ground water increases. Thus higher value of 0^{18} in enamel confirm low rainfall and its lower value confirm higher rainfall. Thus, at Dadupur and Kalli Pachchhim 0^{18} result is as below:

At 3600 B.P. = 0^{18} is more = humid climate

At 2800 B.P. = 0^{18} is less = Dry climate.

This enamel tooth analysis also confirm the climatic amelioration of the Kosal region as it was propounded by floral and fauna remains.

The pollen analysis of Khoalan Jhil near to Lahuradeva and Basha lake which is located in the periphery of Kosal region provide valuable environmental fluctuations. The pollen zone I (1300 – 1200 BC) and zone II (1200 – 800 BC) at Basaha lake confirm a high rainfall in the area which was indicated by the increased number of aquatic plants along with higher frequency of *cerealia* and other cultural pollen taxa. These palaeobotanical remains confirm the development of agricultural practices in the area. The same picture emerges in the pollen zone II (3480 – 1960 B.C.) at Khoalan Jhil which confirm the growth of forest in the area of Kosal due to humid climatic condition.. Thus on the basis of the pollen analysis we can postulate that when the Chalcolithic settlers were resided in the area of Kosal, the climatic condition was humid with increased rainfall. Because at this time the pollen taxa seems to be dominated by aquatic plants and grasses having very low frequency. The appearance of ceralia and other cultural pollen taxa in the Khoalan Jhil during chalcolithic period confirm the large scale agricultural practice in the heartland of Kosal. Thus it is wrong to say that the area was not densely forested. In the Kosal region the forest were in the form of patches which provided shelter to the wild life.

But during early historical period, the area was not received higher rainfall, as it was seen during chalcolithic period. The pollen zone III (1960 BC – 540 AD) of Khoalan Jhil and pollen zone III (4600 BC – 100 A.D.) of Misa Tal confirm the decreasing tendency of aquatic plants and increasing tendency of grasses. But there is a sudden increase in *ceralia* and cultural pollen taxa confirm the agricultural practices in the area. It is pertinent to point out here that the palynological revealed that during the time of Buddha, the rainfall was not less which can affect the growth of forest in the area. The tendency of high humidity from 500 BC – 500 AD is also confirmed in the area of Kosal by 0^{18} teeth enamel study at Dadupur and Kali-Pachchhim in Lucknow district. Albeit around 1000 BC alkaline soil developed in its southern area which was a result of low rainfall, especially in the district of Pratapgarh, southern portion of Sultanpur district and neighbouring district of Rai Bareilly. The high pH of the soil retarded the development of Chalcolithic and early historical cultures in the area, although the area was earlier dominated by Mesolithic people.

The ancient literary source confirm that the ancient Kosal was densely forested in the past. The literary text referred the different names of *Vanai* and the great mountain Himalaya in its north formed the source of its life in the form of various rivers, and monsoon rainfall. Right from the foot of Himalaya *Tarai*, Kosal was interspersed with big and small forests. These forests must have also been instrumental in causing sufficient rains by maintaining low pressure area with high humidity. This has already been proved by the recent pollen studies of the area. The Buddhist texts refer some of the most important forests like *Mahavana, Anjanavana, Andhavana, Lumbinivana, Jetvana* which were related with the different events of Buddha. Beside these famous forests, there were many small and less note ones like *Ketakavana, Jalinavana, Tikantakivana, Kantakivana* etc. in the area of ancient Kosala. Lastly, there was the *Naimisaranya* i.e. the *Naimisa* forest, famous for its holy and hallowed character in the ancient Sanskrit literature which is identified with modern *Nimsar* in Sitapur district.

The ancient Kosal, which was in medieval and British records was a part of Avadh, now comprises in the commissionary of Faizabad, Devipatan and Lucknow was forested since past. Presently, the forests constitute about 13.8% of the total geographical area of the aforesaid three commissionaires. The *Tarai* and bhabhar area grow the *sal* and gigantic *haldu*, while along river courses the *Shisham* grows in abundance. The Calcutta Review, June 1856 under the heading "Physical Capabilities of Oude" mentioned the important forests of the area. In the same heading it was critically reviewed as "The Oude government had established customs posts at several stations on the rivers or on the outskirts of the forest for the purpose of levying a tax on timber, fuel and charcoal. The contracts for cutting down trees were also given to the influential person of the State. If one would travel through the length and breadth of the Oude territory, the richness of forest could well be seen." Again the Chief Commissioner of Awadh erroneously stated in his letter dated May 26, 1856, to the Secretary of States to the Government of India that forests in Avadh have never been considered government property but formed part of large *Taluqdaries* and *Zamindars.* In his concluding remark to the Government, he remarked that forest area of Awadh is a rich source of revenue especially Kheragarh and Kanchanpur forests were most valuable finest quality of sal is present. It could, therefore, be noted that though the administration of forest in Awadh during the period of reference may not have been very elaborate and effective, but confirm high richness of forest in the area.

Bibliography

Acharya, Prasanna Kumar (1981), *A Dictionary of Hindu Architecture*, Mansara Series, Vol. I, Second Edition, New Delhi.

Allen, John (1936), "Catalogue of the Coins of Ancient India,"*A Catalogue of the Indian Coins in the British Museum,* London.

Alur, K.R. (1980), "Faunal Remains from the Vindhyas and the Ganga Valley" in G.R. Sharma, V.D. Mishra, D. Mandal, B.B. Mishra and J.N. Pal (1980), *Beginnings of Agriculture*, Allahabad.

Bajpai, V. (1989), "Surface and Subsurface Evidences of Neotectonic and Aquifer Deposition in Central Alluvial Terrain of Kanpur-Unnao Region in Uttar Pradesh, India," *Photonirvachak, Journal of the Indian Society of Remote Sensing*, 17.

Bakker, Hans (1986), *Ayodhya*, Groningen, Netherland.

Bareau Andre (1979), "Ayodhyaet Mithila dans les textes canoniques du Bouddhisme ancient, in *Indologica Taurinensia*, EDIZIONI A.T.T.. TORINO, Italy.Vol. VII.

Beal, Samuel (1884), *Si-Yu-ki. Buddhist records of the Western World. Translation From the Chinese of Hiuen Tsiang (AD 629),* London.

Alexander, Cunningham, Simla (1871), Calcutta 1987, 23 Vols. (reprint Delhi, 1966-73, 21 Vols.) *Archaeological Survey of India,* Delhi.

Cunningham, Alexander (1871), *Ancient Geography of India,* London.

Dasgupta, Ch. Ch (1932), *Ancient Coins found in Panchala, Ayodhya, Kausambi and Mathura—A Study in Indian Historical Quarterly*, Vol. VIII, Calcutta.

Dey, N.L. (1927 rpt. 1971), *The Geographical Dictionary of Ancient and Medieval India*, 2nd ed., Luzac & Co., New Delhi

Fleet, J.F. (1886), "Sanskrit and Old Kanarese Inscription" in *Journal Asiatique*, XV, CNRS, PARIS, p. 105-110.

Frauwallner, E., (1951) "On the date of the Buddhist Master of the Law Vasubandhu, Roma, *Series Orientale*, Roma III.

Fuhrer, A. *Archaeological Survey of India* (New Series), Vol. I.XII, North-Western Provinces and Oudh , Monumental Antiquities and Inscriptions, Allahabad.

Ghosh, A. (1989), *An Encyclopaedia of Indian Archaeology*, New Delhi.

Gupta, H.P. (1976), "Holocene Palynology from Meander Lake in the Ganga Valley, District Pratapgarh, U.P.," *The Palaeobotanist*, Vol. 25, Lucknow.

Gupta, P.L. (1968), "The Coinage of the Local Kings of Northern India and the Date of Kanishka" in Basham, A.L. (ed.), *Date of Kanishka,* Leiden.

J. Legge (1971), *Trvels of Fa-Hien*, Delhi.

Joshi, M.C. (1978), "Archaeology and Indian Tradition: Some Observations" in *Puratattva,* Vol. 8 and 9(1975-76), Delhi.

Kajale, M.D. (1996), "Plant Resources and Diet among the Mesolithic Hunters and Foragers," in *The Pre-history of Asia and Oceania: Colloquium XXXIII*, Bioarchaeology of Mesolithic India: An Integrated Approach.

Kajale, M.D. and B.C. Deotare, 1988. "Pollen Analysis and Chemical Examinations of a Prehistoric Lake Site at Damdama," *Puratattva* No. 19, Delhi.

Kane, P.V. (1930-62), *History of Dharmasastra(Ancient and Medieval), Religious And Civil Law in India*, Poona, 5 Vols, Government Oriental Series, Clan B, No. 6; Vol. IV, Poona

Kanungo, A.K. and V.N. Mishra, (2003-2004), "Excavation at Kopia: A Preliminary Report," *Puratattva*, No. 36, Delhi.

Kennedy, K.A.R. (2000), *Gods Apes and Fossil Men: Palaeoanthropology in South Asia*. Ann Arbor: University of Michigan Press, Michigan.

Kennedy, K.A.R., J.R. Lukacs, R.F. Pastor, T.L. Johnston, N.C. Lorell, J.N. Pal, B.E. Hemphill and C.B. Burrow, (1992),

Human Skeletal Remains from Mahadaha: A Gangetic Mesolithic Site, South Asia Occasional Papers and Thesis No. 11. Cornell University, New York.

Kumar, G., P.C. Khanna and S. Prasad (1996), "Sequence Stratigraphy of the Foredeep and the Evolution of Indo-Gangetic Plain, Uttar Pradesh." Proceedings of *Symposium NW Himalaya and Foredeep*, Feb. 1995, Geological Survey of India, Special Publication No. 21 (2).

Law, B.C., (1943), "Ayodhya in Ancient India," in *The Journal of Ganganath Jha Research Institute*, Vol. I, Allahabad.

Law, B.C. (1954), *Historical Geography of Ancient India*, Societe Asiatique De Paris, Paris.

Lukacs, J.R. and J.N. Pal (1993), "Mesolithic Subsistence in North India: Inferences from Dental Attributes," *Current Anthropolog*, 34 (5).

Lukacs, J.R., J.N. Pal, and V.D. Mishra (1996), "Chronology and Diet in Mesolithic North India: A Preliminary Report of New AMS C-14 dates, Delta C-13 Isotope Values, and their significance", in *The Prehistory of Asia and Oceania: Colloquium XXXIII, Bioarchaeology of Mesolithic India: An Integrated Approach*, Allahabad.

Majumdar, R.C. (ed.) (1951-71) *The History and Culture of Indian People* (11 Vols.), Bharatiya Vidya Bhavan, Bombay.

Mani, B.R. (2003-04), "Excavations at Siswania (District Basti, U.P.) 1995-1997," *Puratattva*, No. 34, Delhi.

Mishra, A.K. (1989), *The Indian Black Wares (First Milleunium B.C.)* Delhi.

Mishra, V.D. (1977), *Some Aspects of Indian Archaeology*, Allahabad.

Mitra, Debala, (1971) *Buddhist Monuments*, Calcutta.

Narain, A.K., (1957) *The Indo-Greeks*, Oxford.

Oldham, R.D. (1917), "The Structure of Himalayas and the Gangetic Plain as Elucidated by Geodetic Observations in India," *Memoirs, Geological Survey of India*, 42, Calcutta.

Pal, J.N. (1985-86), "Microlithic Industry of Damdama," *Puratattva*, No. 16, Delhi.

Pal, J.N. (1996), "Lithic Use Wear Analysis and Subsistence Activities Among the Mesolithic. People of North India in he Pre-History of Asia and Oceania: Colloquium, XXXIII, *Bioarchaeology of Mesolithic India: An Integrated Approach*, Allahabad.

Pal, J.N. (1992), "Burial Practices and Archaeological Recovery," in Kennedy, K.A.R., *Human Skeletal Remains from Mahadaha: A Gangetic Mesolithic Site,* South Asia Occasional Papers and thesis No. 11, Cornell University, New York.

Pal, J.N. (1988), "Mesolithic Double Burials from, Damdama," *Man and Environment*, Vol. 13, Pune.

Pandey, J.N. (1996), "Burial Practices and Funerary Practices of Mesolithic India," in *The Prehistory of Asia and Ocenia : Colloquium XXXIII* Bioarchaeology of Mesolithic India: An Integrated Approach, Allahabad.

Pargiter, F.E. (1913), *The Purana Text of the Dynasties of Kali Age*, London.

Pargiter, F.E. (1922), *Ancient Indian Historical Tradition*, Oxford University Press, London.

Pascoe, E.H. (1973), *Manual of Geology of India and Burma* (Vol. I-III). Delhi: Government of India Publications, Delhi.

Pathak, Vishuddhanand (1963), *History of Kosala Upto The Rise of the Mauryas*, Delhi.

Petech Luciano (1976), *Indiens bis zur Mitte des 6. Jahrkunderts*, Berlin.

Pilgrim, G.E. (1919), "Suggestions Concerning the History of the Drainage of Northern India Arising Out of a Study of the Siwalik Boulder Conglomerate," *Journal of Asiatic Society of Bengal*, 15, Calcutta.

Ptolemy (1843-45), *Claudii Ptolemaei Geographia*. Edidit C.F. A. Nobbe cum introductione a Aubery Diller. Leipzig.

Rhys Davids, F.W. (1903), *Buddhist India—The Story of the Nation*, Vol. 61, London.

Robbins, Giwen, V.D. Mishra, J.N. Pal and M.C. Gupta (2003), *Mesolithic Damdama: Dental Histology and Age Estimation*, Allahabad.

Raychaudhuri, H.C. (1977), *Political History of Ancient India*, with a commentary by B.N. Mukherjee, Delhi.

Sircar, D.C. (1963) "The Account of the Yavanas in the Yuga-Puranas" in *Journal of Royal Asiatic Society*, London.

Sharma, R.S. (1973), "Decay of the Gangetic Town in Gupta and Post-Gupta Times" in *journal of Indian History (Golden Jubilee Volume)*, Delhi.

Sharma, G.R. (1973), "Mesolithic Lake Cultures in the Ganga Valley," Proceedings of the Prehistory Society XXXIX, Pune.

Sharma, G.R., V.D. Mishra, D. Mandal, B.B. Mishra and J.N. Pal (1980), "From Hunting and Food Gatherings to Demestication of Plants and Animals," *Beginning of Agriculture* (Epi-Palaeolithic to Neolithic Excavations at Chopani-Mando, Mahadaha and Mahagara), Allahabad.

Sharma, M., H.J. Tobschall and I.B. Singh (2003), "Environmental Impact Assessment in Moradabad Industrial Area (River-Ramganga-Ganga Interfluve), Ganga Plain, India," *Environmental Geology* 43, Berlin.

Shukla, U.K., I.B. Singh, M. Sharma and S. Sharma (2001), "A Model of Alluvial Megafan Sedimentation: Ganga Megafan Sedimentary." *Geology*, 144, University of Chicago Press (USA).

Shukla, K.S. (1986), *Archaeology of Unnao District*, Delhi.

Singh, I.B. (1999), "Tectonic Control of Sedimentation in Ganga Plain Foreland Basin: Constraints on Siwalik Sedimentation Models in Geodynamism of the NW Himalaya," *Gondwana Research Group Memoir* (A.K. Jain and R.M. Manickavasagam, eds.), 6.

Singh, I.B. (1996), "Late Quaternary Sedimentation of Ganga Plain Foreland Basin," Proceeding. *Symposium NW Himalaya and Foredeep*, Feb. 1995. Geological Survey of India, Special Publication No. 21(1).

Singh, I.B. (2005), "Land Form Development and Palaeoenvironment Vegetation in Late Quaternary of

Ganga Plain: Implications for Anthropogenic Activity," *Pragdhara* 15, Lucknow.

Singh, R.L. (1973), (ed.). *India: A Regional Geography.* Varanasi: National Geographical Society of India, Varanasi.

Singh, I.B. and D.K. Ghosh (1992), "Interpretation of Late Quaternary Geomorphic and Tectonic Features of Gangetic Plain using Remote Sensing Techniques." Proceedings National Symposium on Remote Sensing and Sustainable Development, Lucknow.

Singh, I.B. (1996), "Geological Evolution of Ganga Plain—An Overview," *Journal of Paleoontological Society, India*, 41, Lucknow.

Singh, I.B. (1987), "Sedimentological History of Quaternary Deposits in Gangetic Plain." *Indian Journal of Earth Sciences*, 14, Calcutta.

Singh, I.B. (2001), "Proxy Records of Neotectonics, Climate Changes and Anthropogenic Activity in the Late Quaternary of Ganga Plain." *National Symposium Role of Earth Sciences Integrated Development and Related Societal Issue,* Geological Survey of India, Special Publication, No. 65 (I) 2001: xxxiii-1.

Singh, I.B. (2004), "Late Quaternary History of the Ganga Plain," *Journal of Geological Society of India*, 64.

Singh, I.B. (2002), "Late Quaternary Evolution of Ganga Plain and Proxy Records of Climate Change and Anthropogenic Activity," *Pragdhara* 12 (2001-2002).

Singh, I.B. (2005), "Quaternary Paleoenvironments of the Ganga Plain and Anthropogenic Activity," *Man and Environment*, XXX (1).

Singh, P. (1994), *Excavations at Narhan (1984-89)*. Varanasi.

Singh, P., A.K. Singh, Indrajeet Singh (1991-92), "Excavations at Imlidih Khurd," *Puratattva*, No. 22, Delhi.

Singh, P., Ashok Singh, Indrajeet Singh (1991-92), "Trial Digging at Dhuriapar," *Pragdhara*, No. 02, Lucknow.

Singh, P.N., R.N. Singh & Ashok Kumar Singh (2008-09), "Archaeology of Gomati Basin with Special Reference to Excavations at Saripur, District Jaunpur,: *Bharti*, Vol. 33, Varanasi.

Sinha, K.K. (1967), *Excavations at Srvasti—1959*, Varanasi.

Singh, S.D. and S.B. Singh, 1970, *The Archaeology of Lucknow Region*.

Srivastava, P., I.B. Singh, M. Sharma and A.K. Singhvi (2003a), "Luminescence Chronometry and Late Quaternary Geomorphic History of the Ganga Plain, India, " *Palaeogeography, Palaeoclimatology, Palaeoecology*, 197.

Srivastava, P. (1998), "Sedimentology and Geomorphology of Interfluve Areas of Central Ganga Plain," Ph.D. Thesis, Lucknow University, Lucknow.

Srivastava, P., I.B. Singh, S. Sharma, U.K. Shukla and A.K. Singhvi (2003b), "Late Pleistocene-Holocene Hydrologic Changes in the Interfluve Areas of Central Ganga Plain, India," *Geomorphology*, 54.

Takakusu, J. (1904), *The Life of Vasu-Bandhu by Paramartha (AD 499-500)*, Paris.

Tewari, Rakesh, R.K. Srivastav, K.K. Singh, K.S. Saraswat and I.B. Singh (2002-2003), "Preliminary Report of Excavation at Lahuradeva, District Sant Kabir Nagar, U.P., 2001-2002: Wider Archaeological Implications," *Pragdhara*, No. 13, Lucknow.

Tewari, Rakesh, R.K. Srivastava, K.K. Singh, K.S. Saraswat (2005-06), "Further Excavations at Lahuradeva, District Sant Kabir Nagar (U.P.): Preliminary Observations," *Puratattva* No. 36, Delhi.

Tiwari, Rakesh (2004), "The Myth of Dense Forests and Human Occupation in the Ganga Plain." *Man and Environment*, XXIX (2), Delhi.

Tewari, Rakesh, Hemraj, Rakesh Kumar Srivastav (1995-96), "Excavations at Hulaskhera," *Pragdhara*, No. 6, Lucknow.

Tewari, Rakesh, R.K. Srivastava, K.K. Singh (2001-02), "Dadupur Excavations 1999-2000-2001, District Lucknow, Uttar Pradesh: A Preliminary Report," *Pragdhara*, No. 12, Lucknow.

Tewari, D.P. (2002), *Excavations at Charda*, Lucknow.

Tewari, D.P. (2006), *Excavations at Pirvitanisarif-Trilokpur*, Lucknow.

Tewari, D.P. (1999), *Antiquarian Remains from Kalli Pachchhim Excavations*, Lucknow.

Thaplyal, Kiran Kumar, (1972), *Studies in Ancient Indian Seals*, Lucknow.

Thomas, Edward J. (1949), *The Life of Buddha as Legend and History*, London.

Thomas, P.K., P.P. Joglekar, V.D. Mishra, J.N. Pandey and J.N. Pal (1995), A Preliminary Report on the Faunal Remains from Damdama," *Man and Environment*, XX(1), Delhi.

Thomas, P.K., P.R., Jogelkar, V.D. Mishra, J.N. Pandey and J.N. Pal, (1996), "Faunal Evidence for the Mesolithic Food Economy of the Gangetic Plain with Special Reference to Damdama", in *Bioarchaeology of Mesolithic India: An Integrated Approach*, Colloquium XXXIII of the International Union of Prehistoric and Protohistoric Sciences (G.E. Ajanaser, S. Cleuziou, J.R. Lukacs and M. Tosi, eds.), Forli: ABA Co, Edizioni.

Thomas, P.K., P.P. Joglekar, V.D. Mishra, J.N. Pandey and J.N. Pal (2002), "Faunal Remains from Damdama: Evidence for the Mesolithic Food Economy of the Gangetic Plain," in *Mesolithic India* (V.D. Mishra and J.N. Pal, eds.), pp. 366-380. Allahabad, Department of Ancient History, Culture & Archaeology, University of Allahabad, Allahabad.

Tripathi, Vibha (2007-08), "Excavations at Hariharpur, District Jaunpur," *Purarattva*, No. 38, Delhi.

Tripathi, Ram Shankar (1937), *History of Kannauj to the Muslim Conquest*, Benaras.

Vaidya, C.V. (1979), *History of Medieval Hindu India,* 3 Vols, Delhi.

Verma, R.K., V.D. Mishra, J.N. Pandey and J.N. Pal (1985),"A Preliminary Report on the Excavations at Damdama (1982-84)," *Man and Environment*, IX, Delhi.

Verma, R.K. (1985), "The Mesolithic Culture of India," *Puratattva*, No. 13 & 14, Delhi.

Index

H

I

T